A Painting For A Family Dinner
Alina and Jeff Bliumis

FOREWORD / VORWORT   REGINA SELTER

(EN)   In February 2025, the artists Alina and Jeff Bliumis staged their project *A Painting For A Family Dinner* in Dortmund—the first iteration in Germany and the sixth one in total, following stops in Bat Yam (Israel), the Bronx (New York City, USA), Lecce (Italy), Beijing (China), and Tokyo (Japan).

Why was *A Painting For A Family Dinner* such a good fit for Dortmund? That is a question with many possible answers. One of them that was especially central to Museum Ostwall at the Dortmunder U was how the project reflected our museum's way of working. Everyday experiences often serve as the starting point for our exhibitions. We want to have an effect on society—be it through the presentation of our collection, special exhibitions, or our wide spectrum of art education offerings. *A Painting For A Family Dinner* achieves all of them at once: Alina and Jeff Bliumis approached people, shared their everyday lives for a brief moment over dinner, and gave something back in return through their visit and a specially created painting. The exhibition presents the photographic portraits taken during these dinners, blurring the boundaries between the private sphere and the museum, between everyday life and art.

Another possible answer lies in the openness and enthusiasm of the people in the Ruhr region. The number of people who got in touch to express their interest testifies to an open-mindedness that decisively contributed to the project's success. The registrations ranged from individuals with their own friends as guests to whole flatshares and associations, reflecting the diversity of households, lifestyles, and food cultures in Dortmund. For the curators Christina Danick and Michael Griff, *A Painting For A Family Dinner* was the starting point for the exhibition *At the Table. Eating and Drinking in Contemporary Art*, which focuses on the cultural and social aspects of shared meals.

With this exhibition and the invitation of various artists, the curators show how connections and communities can be created through art in a diverse world. In the course of *A Painting For A Family Dinner*, Alina and Jeff Bliumis have participated in sixty-two dinners around the world. Their experiences, compiled in this book for the first time, are as different as they are connecting: they bear witness to the small differences and the many similarities when eating together.

I would like to thank Alina and Jeff Bliumis, as well as all the participants of *A Painting For A Family Dinner*, without whom the project would not have been possible.

(DE) In Dortmund haben die Künstler*innen Alina und Jeff Bliumis ihr Projekt *A Painting For A Family Dinner* im Februar 2025 nach Stationen in Bat Yam (Israel), der Bronx (New York City, USA), Lecce (Italien), Beijing (China) und Tokyo (Japan) zum ersten Mal in Deutschland und insgesamt zum sechsten Mal durchgeführt.

Warum passt *A Painting For A Family Dinner* so gut zu Dortmund? Auf diese Frage gibt es viele mögliche Antworten. Eine für das Museum Ostwall im Dortmunder U besonders zentrale ist, dass das Projekt wunderbar die Arbeitsweise unseres Hauses spiegelt. Alltagserfahrungen dienen uns häufig als Ausgangspunkt für unsere Ausstellungen. Wir möchten in die Gesellschaft hineinwirken — sei es durch Sammlungspräsentation, Sonderausstellungen oder vielfältige Angebote der Kunstvermittlung. *A Painting For A Family Dinner* schafft beides zugleich: Alina und Jeff Bliumis gingen auf die Menschen zu, teilten beim gemeinsamen Abendessen für einen kurzen Moment ihren Alltag und gaben im Gegenzug durch ihren Besuch und ein eigens angefertigtes Gemälde etwas zurück. Die Ausstellung präsentiert die bei den Abendessen entstandenen fotografischen Porträts und lässt so die Grenzen zwischen dem Privaten und dem Museum, zwischen Alltag und Kunst verschwimmen.

Eine weitere mögliche Antwort liegt in der Offenheit und Begeisterungsfähigkeit der Menschen im Ruhrgebiet. Die vielen Interessent*innen, die uns geschrieben haben, zeugen von einer Aufgeschlossenheit, die maßgeblich zum Gelingen des Projekts beigetragen hat. Die Anmeldungen reichten von Einzelpersonen, die Freund*innen einluden, und Wohngemeinschaften bis hin zu Vereinen und spiegelten so die Vielfalt der Haushalte, Lebensentwürfe und Esskulturen der Dortmunder*innen wider. Für die Kurator*innen Christina Danick und Michael Griff war *A Painting For A Family Dinner* das Ausgangswerk für die Ausstellung *Am Tisch. Essen und Trinken in der zeitgenössischen Kunst*. Sie nimmt kulturelle und gesellschaftliche Aspekte rund um gemeinsame Mahlzeiten in den Blick.

Die Kurator*innen zeigen mit dieser Ausstellung und der Einladung an verschiedene Künstler*innen, wie in einer vielfältigen Welt durch Kunst Verbindungen und Gemeinschaften entstehen können. Im Rahmen von *A Painting For A Family Dinner* haben Alina und Jeff Bliumis weltweit mittlerweile an 62 Abendessen teilgenommen. Ihre Erlebnisse, die in diesem Buch erstmals zusammengefasst sind, sind ebenso verschieden wie verbindend: Die Erfahrungen von Alina und Jeff Bliumis zeugen von den kleinen Unterschieden und den vielen Gemeinsamkeiten beim gemeinschaftlichen Essen.

Ich möchte mich herzlich bei Alina und Jeff Bliumis bedanken, sowie bei allen Teilnehmenden von *A Painting For A Family Dinner*, ohne die es das Projekt nicht gegeben hätte.

WHO REPRESENTS A CITY?   CHRISTINA DANICK AND MICHAEL GRIFF

(EN) Can artists capture the impression of a city through their work? How are their experiences of cities reflected? And who or what actually represents a city?

The artistic project *A Painting For A Family Dinner* by the artist couple Alina and Jeff Bliumis offers rather unusual answers to these questions. It started in 2008 as a collaboration with the Museums of Bat Yam (MoBY) in Israel and it is as simple as the title seems. The MoBY initially circulated a call for participation in a local newspaper. The ad, whose text remained the same in subsequent editions or was only minimally adjusted, read as follows: "Husband and wife artist team is offering a painting in exchange for an invitation to a family dinner. Please email or call for more info." The people interested then got in touch and registered, and the artists visited as many homes as possible. Anyone could take part, and they did not necessarily have to be families in the strict sense—i.e., the participants did not have to be related. Nor did Alina and Jeff Bliumis make any selection: it was first come, first served.

A painting was prepared in advance for each visit. These were always still lifes with fruit and the inscription "Thank you for your dinner!" At the end of each dinner, a photo was shot with the help of local photographers. The arrangement was always the same: all the dinner guests gathered on a couch, with the painting hung in the middle behind them. The painting remained with the families after the evening.

The procedure stayed the same in every subsequent city. A simple advertisement was always placed in advance; the hosts always received a similar painting with the same inscription; and a medium-format portrait of the hosts with the artists was always shot afterwards.

After being launched in 2008, Alina and Jeff Bliumis toured the project to other cities: In 2012 it traveled to the Bronx (New York City, USA) as part of an exhibition at The Bronx Museum of the Arts; in September 2013, to Beijing as part of the Inside-Out Art Museum's residency program; in October 2013, to Lecce as part of a residency program by Ammirato Culture House; and in 2021, to Tokyo as part of the 2020/2021 Tokyo Biennale. Due to the Covid-19 pandemic, the dinners at the latter edition had to take place via video calls. The sixth and latest edition so far took place in Dortmund in 2025 as part of the exhibition *At the Table. Eating and Drinking in Contemporary Art* at Museum Ostwall at the Dortmunder U. The photographs were shown in public presentations in Bat Yam, the Bronx, Tokyo, and Dortmund.

According to Alina and Jeff Bliumis, the project has two main sources of inspiration. On the one hand, they draw on the myth of "starving artists" who offer their works in return for food and accommodation. The myth that artists are fundamentally poor, and that this is what ensures the "purity" of their work, goes back to the beginning of the nineteenth century—despite the fact that, at least in Europe and the US, this era can also be seen as a period of increasing professionalization of artists and commodification of artworks, a process that has reached its peak today. Nevertheless, the myth persists. There are countless anecdotes about artists who would regularly exchange their works for meals and in some cases subsequently helped their hosts acquire unexpected wealth. Though in most cases, it is impossible to determine whether they are true for sure. But what we do know is that bartering has been completely replaced by money exchange in many places around the world. Alina and Jeff Bliumis return to bartering in *A Painting For A Family Dinner* and thus also explore the social interactions that result from this form of transaction.

Both the shared meal and the art stimulate exchange. But who is actually the artist and who is the audience in this project? On closer inspection, the boundaries between the creators of the works, Alina and Jeff Bliumis, and the households they visit become blurred—the artists may have created the paintings, but without the invitation of the respective households and the involvement of local photographers, the dinners could never be made into an overarching *Gesamtkunstwerk*. In some sense, it is a collaborative work. The encounters and dialogues play a central part within it and form the basis of *A Painting For A Family Dinner*. For Alina and Jeff Bliumis, the second foundational element for their approach is the work of the Russian literary theorist Mikhail Bakhtin. As early as the 1920s, Bakhtin argued that authors and recipients of literary works should be considered as equals.[1] For Bakhtin, recipients have an active role and are directly involved in the events of the work: by reading a book and comprehending it in their own words, readers complete the work. The act of reading thus becomes an act of "creative participation" and "interaction."[2] Applied to the visual arts, this implies that art only opens up to its recipients through an interactive and co-creative process. In the case of *A Painting For A Family Dinner*, this is exactly what happens during the respective dinners and the encounters within them. Following Bakhtin's train of thought, such encounters dissolve clearly defined categories of artist, recipient, and audience. Instead, art itself becomes a motive for communication.

Alina and Jeff Bliumis came up with the specific idea for the project while on a stroll during one of their city trips: many people are familiar with the curiosity that comes with looking into the windows of strangers' apartments. Sometimes in your own town, but even more so when visiting a still unfamiliar city. After all, only walking through the streets hardly gives you any idea of how people actually live in a city or what their everyday lives are like.

---

1   In the fragments of his writings that remain, Bakhtin describes this process as a dialogue between the authors of novels and their readers. For Bakhtin, the process of "responsive under-standing" is central to this. See Mikhail M. Bakhtin, *Die Ästhetik des Wortes* (Frankfurt am Main, 1979), p. 173.

2   Mikhail M. Bakhtin, *Die Ästhetik des Wortes* (Frankfurt am Main, 1979), pp. 170–175.

The window frames a snippet of a world that we would not usually get to see in its entirety. One might vaguely recognize the rudiments of furniture, decorations, or perhaps even people. They provide a basis for conjectures about the lives of the people living there—but these often remain speculative and can rarely be verified. So why not simply invite yourself and visit other people's homes?

Alina and Jeff Bliumis visited sixty-two households in the six cities where *A Painting For A Family Dinner* was held. According to the artists, each visit was different. The variety of dishes ranged from simple cold dinners to multi-course menus. More importantly, the type and preparation of the dishes varied depending on where the hosts lived and where they came from, as did the way it was eaten. At what time do they meet? Has the food already been cooked or is it still being cooked while the guests are there? And do the guests help out with the cooking? Where does the group sit or stand? What is the setting and sequence of the meal? What do they drink? Are there any family rituals or specific customs that are performed? What do people talk about? How long do they stay together? The illustrated diary in the second half of this book reproduces the entries Alina Bliumis made after each dinner and offers some insights into these aspects. The artists do not make any evaluations in their accounts. Every situation, every meal seems to be of equal value. According to them, it was not really about the food itself, its quality, or preparation to begin with. Rather, it is about the occasion for exchange, which is initiated by handing over the painting at the very latest.

We can assume that the project allowed Alina and Jeff Bliumis to learn about the cities in a different way than the usual casual visit—they ultimately got a look behind the scenes, so to speak. They often "warmed up" to their hosts over the course of an evening, got to know each other, and had long conversations. According to the artists, being introduced to a social environment creates a feeling of familiarity. Alina and Jeff Bliumis use the terms *familiar* and *familial* to describe what happens during the evening: over time, the boundaries between what is *familiar* and what is *familial* become blurred. The process of dissolution or overlapping can be understood in both directions. The fact that Alina and Jeff Bliumis were explicitly searching for *family dinners* in their advertisements, but allowed for any kind of social gathering, demonstrates their broad understanding of family, which is to be understood more in the sense of a *familiarity* between the participants than an actual blood relation.

However, the social experience of the respective evening is hardly conveyed in the subsequent medium-format portrait photographs that document it. Since they are always arranged in the same way, they only provide nuanced information about the people portrayed and the meal they shared. Only the painting in the background, already received in exchange and installed in the room, indicates that the dinner and thus the main act of the evening has been completed. In fact, the photographs have a rather distinguished character. The arrangement of the people lined up next to each other or, in the case of large groups, placed in rows front of each other reflects the structure of classic family portraits. The setting is not usually the kitchen, but rather the living room—which has historically been the primary site of social distinction in the private household. Much like the passing view through the window, the highly staged photographs only give a suggestion of the kind of social interactions that have taken place.

As historian Sandra Starke has shown, this pictorial composition has its origins in the nineteenth century. The popularization of *Cartes De Visite* also made distinguished portraits more popular for individuals as well as groups. A clear arrangement of the subjects was crucial here. On the one hand, the photographs were taken in studios and were expensive to produce. On the other hand, Starke shows that these photographs also became constitutive of a bourgeois identity, and there were already how-to guides from the era with advice on the best pose for a good photo.[3] *A Painting For A Family Dinner* not only interrogates this multilayered history of the classic family portrait through the composition of the images, but also through the choice of medium-format photography, whose square proportions recall nineteenth-century photographs.

Just like the photographs themselves, the hanging of the pictures in the Dortmund exhibition was also intended to take the aspect of social distinction as a starting point. From the outset, the aim was to present all sixty-two family portraits taken to date in one room. The portraits were supplemented by documentary photographs of the visits, which can also be found in this book. Small gifts and mementos that the artists received during the projects were also presented in display cases, much like historical artifacts.

But what form of presentation is suitable for the numerous photographs? In previous exhibitions of *A Painting For A Family Dinner*, a grid hanging was often used since it went well with the images' squarish format. In Dortmund, we opted for a different type of presentation. Inspired by Baroque hangings, which are largely geared towards social distinction, we created a grouping of photographs that emphasizes fullness and symmetry. The works are hung very close together and on top of each other. This creates an impression of abundance and opulence that is intended to overwhelm the viewer. In the classic salon hanging, important works like ancestral portraits served as the central focal points, while landscapes or still lifes would be grouped around them. Prominent works were placed along the central axes and "filler pieces" were specifically acquired to fill the gaps. This was intended to emphasize the artistic sensibility as well as the wealth of the respective owners. In the context of *A Painting For A Family Dinner*, the baroque hanging opens up a further level of reflection on questions of representation: Who or what actually represents a city?

---

3   See Sandra Starke, "Fenster und Spiegel: Private Fotografie zwischen Norm und Individualität," in *Historische Anthropologie* 19 (2011), pp. 477–474, here pp. 451–453.

Questions of social status and appearance, of the embodiment of a social class, are not necessarily relevant for the photographs in *A Painting For A Family Dinner*. Rather, they represent the cities in which they were taken and the diversity of the respective realities of life. In terms of the questions posed at the beginning, they offer insights into people's daily lives in their private environments—as individual microcosms. They embody the city as well as its architecture, infrastructure, and institutions of public life.

Like the exhibition display, this book provides an overview of all the project's stations to date. In addition to the portraits, the documentary material, and the diary, it also contains recipes from the different hosts. We should not forget that eating together was the reason for all these visits. Perhaps these recipes will inspire you to invite your own guests and cook for them, too.

WER REPRÄSENTIERT EINE STADT?　　　　　　　　CHRISTINA DANICK UND MICHAEL GRIFF

(DE) Können Künstler*innen in ihrer Arbeit den Eindruck einer Stadt einfangen? Wie werden die Erfahrungen wiedergegeben, die Künstler*innen in Städten machen? Und wer oder was repräsentiert eigentlich eine Stadt?

Das künstlerische Projekt *A Painting For A Family Dinner* (deutsch: *Ein Gemälde für ein Familienessen*) des Künstler*innen-Ehepaares Alina und Jeff Bliumis gibt eher ungewöhnliche Antworten auf diese Fragen. Es begann 2008 als Kooperation mit den Museums of Bat Yam (MoBY) in Israel und ist auf den ersten Blick so simpel wie sein Titel. Das MoBY verbreitete zunächst einen Aufruf zur Teilnahme in lokalen Zeitungen und in den sozialen Medien. Die Anzeige, die auch in den folgenden Ausgaben den gleichen oder einen minimal abgewandelten Text hatte, lautete wie folgt: „Künstler*innen-Ehepaar bietet ein Gemälde gegen Einladung zum Familienessen. Für weitere Informationen bitte telefonisch oder per E-Mail melden." Interessierte Personen meldeten sich daraufhin für eine Anmeldung und die Künstler*innen besuchten so viele Haushalte wie möglich. Teilnehmen durfte jede*r, es musste sich nicht zwangsläufig um Familien im engeren Sinne handeln, d. h. die Teilnehmenden mussten nicht verwandt sein. Alina und Jeff Bliumis trafen zudem keine Auswahl: Wer sich zuerst meldete, bekam einen Platz.

Für jeden Besuch wurde im Vorfeld ein Gemälde vorbereitet. Dabei handelte es sich immer um ein Stillleben mit Früchten mit der Aufschrift „Thank you for your dinner!" *(Danke für Ihr/Dein Abendessen!)*. Am Ende eines jeden Abendessens entstand in Zusammenarbeit mit lokalen Fotograf*innen ein immer gleich arrangiertes Foto: Alle Teilnehmer*innen des Abendessens versammelten sich auf einer Couch, das Gemälde hing mittig hinter ihnen. Es verblieb nach dem Abend bei den Familien.

Der Ablauf des Projekts war in allen Städten, in denen es durchgeführt wurde, gleich. Immer wurde eine einfache Anzeige geschaltet, immer erhielten die Gastgeber*innen ein ähnliches Gemälde mit der gleichen Aufschrift, immer wurde im Anschluss ein Porträt der Gastgeber*innen mit dem Künstler*innen-Ehepaar im Mittelformat angefertigt.

Nach dem Auftakt 2008 führten Alina und Jeff Bliumis das Projekt in verschiedenen anderen Städten durch: 2012 im Stadtteil Bronx (New York City, USA) als Teil einer Ausstellung des The Bronx Museum of the Arts; im September 2013 in Beijing, als Teil des Residenzprogramms des Inside-Out Art Museum; im Oktober 2013 in Lecce als Teil eines Residenzprogramms des Ammirato Culture House; und im Jahr 2021 in Tokyo, als Teil der Tokyo Biennale 2020/2021. Aufgrund der Coronapandemie fanden die Dinner bei der letztgenannten Ausgabe per Videokonferenz statt. Die sechste und bisher letzte Ausgabe fand 2025 in Dortmund im Rahmen der Ausstellung *Am Tisch. Essen und Trinken in der zeitgenössischen Kunst* im Museum Ostwall im Dortmunder U statt. In Bat Yam, im New Yorker Stadtteil Bronx, in Tokyo und in Dortmund wurden die Fotografien im Anschluss im Rahmen öffentlicher Präsentationen gezeigt.

Für Alina und Jeff Bliumis gibt es ihrer eigenen Aussage nach zwei zentrale Inspirationsquellen für das Projekt. Zum einen greifen sie den Mythos der „hungrigen Künstler*innen" auf, die ihre Werke als Gegenleistung für Essen und Unterkunft anbieten. Der Mythos, demnach Künstler*innen prinzipiell arm seien und ihre Kunst erst dadurch „rein" sei, geht auf den Anfang des 19. Jahrhunderts zurück — trotz der Tatsache, dass diese Epoche zumindest in Europa und den USA als eine Phase zunehmender Professionalisierung von Künstler*innen und der Kommodifizierung von Kunstwerken gesehen werden kann, die heute ihren bisherigen Höhepunkt erreicht hat. Trotzdem hält sich der Mythos hartnäckig. Anekdoten zu Künstler*innen, die ihre Werke regelmäßig gegen Mahlzeiten eingetauscht und den Bewirtenden in so manchem Fall später zu unvorhergesehenem Reichtum verholfen haben sollen, sind zahlreich. Ob sie wahr sind, lässt sich meist nicht abschließend feststellen. Dass der Tauschhandel im Gegensatz zum Geldhandel an vielen Orten auf der Welt beinahe gänzlich verschwunden ist, allerdings schon. Alina und Jeff Bliumis praktizieren ihn in *A Painting For A Family Dinner* und erproben damit auch, welche sozialen Interaktionen sich aus diesem Tauschgeschäft ergeben.

Sowohl die gemeinsame Mahlzeit als auch die Kunst regen zum Austausch an. Doch wer ist bei diesem Projekt eigentlich Künstler*in und wer Publikum? Bei genauerer Betrachtung verschwimmen die Grenzen zwischen den Urheber*innen der Werke, Alina und Jeff Bliumis, und den Personen, bei denen sie zu Besuch sind — zwar haben die Künstler*innen das jeweilige Gemälde angefertigt, doch ohne die Einladung der Haushalte und die Einbeziehung lokaler Fotograf*innen wären die Abendessen als Gesamtkunstwerke nie entstanden. Es handelt sich in gewisser Weise um ein gemeinschaftlich entstandenes Werk. Einen zentralen Stellenwert nehmen darin die Begegnungen und Dialoge ein, welche die Basis für *A Painting For A Family Dinner* schaffen. Grundlegend für diese Arbeitsweise ist laut Alina und Jeff Bliumis das Werk des russischen Literaturtheoretikers Michail Bachtin, dessen Schriften eine weitere Inspirationsquelle für die Künstler*innen sind. Bachtin argumentierte bereits in den 1920er Jahren dafür, Autor*innen und Rezipient*innen literarischer Werke als gleichwertig zu betrachten.[1] Für Bachtin haben Rezipient*innen eine aktive Rolle und sind am Werkgeschehen unmittelbar beteiligt: Indem die Leser*innen einen Text in ihre eigenen Worte übersetzen, um ihn zu verstehen, würden sie das Werk erst vervollständigen. Der Akt des Lesens werde somit zu einem Akt „kreativer Mitwirkung" und „Interaktion".[2] Bezogen auf die bildende Kunst bedeutet das, dass Kunst sich Rezipient*innen erst durch einen interaktiven und co-kreativen Prozess eröffnet. Im Fall von *A Painting For A Family Dinner* sind diese Prozesse die jeweiligen Abendessen

1   In seinen fragmentarisch erhaltenen Schriften beschreibt Bachtin diesen Prozess als einen Dialog zwischen Autor*innen von Romanen und deren Leser*innen. Zentral ist für Bachtin hierbei der Prozess des „antwortenden Verstehens". Siehe Bachtin, Michail M.: Die Ästhetik des Wortes, Frankfurt a. M., 1979, S. 173.

2   Bachtin, Michail M.: Die Ästhetik des Wortes, Frankfurt a. M., 1979, S. 170–175.

und die Begegnungen dabei. Folgt man den Überlegungen von Bachtin, lösen sich in diesen Begegnungen klar abgrenzbare Kategorien von Künstler*in, Rezipient*in und Publikum auf. Vielmehr wird die Kunst selbst zu einem Motiv für Kommunikation.

Die konkrete Idee zum Projekt kam Alina und Jeff Bliumis beim Spazierengehen auf ihren Städtereisen: Die Neugier, die der Blick in die Fenster von Wohnungen erzeugt, kennen viele. Sei es am eigenen Wohnort, mehr noch allerdings beim Besuch einer Stadt, die noch nicht bekannt ist. Schließlich lässt ein Rundgang durch die Straßen längst nicht erahnen, wie die Menschen in einer Stadt tatsächlich leben und wie ihr Alltag aussieht. Das Fenster bildet den Rahmen um einen Ausschnitt einer Welt, die wir für gewöhnlich nicht in Gänze zu Gesicht bekommen. Möbel, Einrichtungsgegenstände und vielleicht Personen lassen sich in Ansätzen erkennen. Sie bieten eine Grundlage für Vermutungen über die Lebensrealität der dort wohnenden Menschen — doch diese bleiben oft spekulativ und lassen sich selten verifizieren. Warum sich also nicht einfach einladen lassen und fremde Wohnungen besuchen?

62 Haushalte haben Alina und Jeff Bliumis in den sechs Städten besucht, in denen *A Painting For A Family Dinner* durchgeführt wurde. Jeder Besuch war, folgt man den Erzählungen der Künstler*innen, anders. Die Vielfalt der Speisen reichte von simplen kalten Abendessen bis hin zu mehrgängigen Menüs. Wichtiger noch, die Art und Zubereitung der Speisen variierte je nach Wohnort und Herkunft der Gastgeber*innen, ebenso wie die Art des Verzehrs. Wann wird sich getroffen? Ist gekocht worden oder wird noch gekocht, während die Gäste da sind? Wird eventuell mit den Gästen gemeinsam gekocht? Wo sitzt oder steht die Gruppe? Wie sind Setting und Ablauf des Essens? Was wird getrunken? Gibt es familiäre Rituale, die begangen werden, oder bestimmte Bräuche? Worüber wird gesprochen? Wie lange bleibt man zusammen? Einen Einblick in diese Aspekte gibt das bebilderte Tagebuch in der zweiten Hälfte dieses Buchs, dessen Einträge Alina Bliumis nach jedem Abendessen angefertigt hat. Bewertungen gibt es in den Erzählungen der Künstler*innen nicht. Jede Situation, jedes Essen scheint gleichwertig. Ohnehin, so sagen sie, gehe es gar nicht so sehr um das Essen selbst, dessen Qualität oder Zubereitung. Vielmehr sei es Anlass zum Austausch, der spätestens durch die Übergabe des Gemäldes initiiert wird.

Wir können davon ausgehen, dass Alina und Jeff Bliumis die Städte, die sie im Rahmen des Projekts besuchten, anders kennengelernt haben als es bei den meisten Stadtbesuchen der Fall ist — schließlich haben sie gewissermaßen hinter deren Kulissen geschaut. Oft sind sie mit den Gastgeber*innen im Laufe eines Abends „warm geworden", haben sich kennengelernt und lange Gespräche geführt. Eingeführt in das soziale Umfeld entstehe, so die Künstler*innen, ein Gefühl von Vertrautheit. So ziehen Alina und Jeff Bliumis die englischsprachigen Begriffe *familiar* und *familial* heran, um zu beschreiben, was während des Abends passiert: Im Laufe der Zeit verschwimmen die Grenzen zwischen dem, was vertraut (*familiar*) ist und dem, was familiär (*familial*) im Sinne von die Familie betreffend ist. Die Unterscheidung, die sich in diesem Fall auflöst, gibt es im Deutschen nicht, da *familiär* beide Bedeutungen inhärent sind. Der Prozess der Auflösung oder Überlappung lässt sich in beide Richtungen verstehen. Dass Alina und Jeff Bliumis in ihren Annoncen wörtlich nach *Family Dinners* suchen, allerdings jegliche Art der sozialen Zusammenkunft zulassen, belegt ihr weites Familienverständnis, das eher im Sinne einer *Familiarität* zwischen den Teilnehmenden als einer tatsächlichen Verwandtschaft zu verstehen ist.

Die soziale Erfahrung des jeweiligen Abends wird jedoch in dem verbleibenden Dokument, dem entstandenen fotografischen Mittelformat-Porträt, kaum transportiert. Immer gleich angeordnet, gibt es nur in Nuancen Aufschluss über die dargestellten Personen und das abgeschlossene gemeinsame Essen. Lediglich das im Tausch erhaltene Gemälde im Hintergrund, bereits im Raum installiert, gibt Aufschluss darüber, dass das Abendessen und damit der Hauptakt des Abends vollzogen ist. Vielmehr haben die Fotografien einen stark repräsentativen Charakter. Die Anordnung der Personen nebeneinander aufgereiht oder, bei großen Gruppen, voreinander platziert, spiegelt den Aufbau klassischer Familienporträts wider. Das Setting ist nicht etwa die Küche, sondern meist das Wohnzimmer — historisch der Ort der Repräsentation im Privathaushalt. Ähnlich wie der Blick durchs Fenster, wenn im Gegensatz dazu auch vollständig inszeniert, geben die Fotografien lediglich eine Idee dessen wieder, was an sozialer Interaktion stattgefunden hat.

Wie die Historikerin Sandra Starke zeigt, hat dieser Bildaufbau seine Ursprünge im 19. Jahrhundert. Durch die zunehmende Verbreitung der *Carte des Visites* wurden repräsentative Porträts, ob einzeln oder in der Gruppe, populär. Eine klare Anordnung der Personen war hierbei entscheidend: Zum einen wurden die Fotografien in Studios angefertigt und waren in der Herstellung teuer. Zum anderen wurden solche Aufnahmen, schreibt Starke, Teil einer bürgerlichen Identität — so gibt es bereits aus dieser Zeit Ratgeberliteratur für die beste Pose für ein gutes Foto.[3] Nicht nur mit dem Bildaufbau, sondern auch mit der Wahl des Mittelformats, das in seiner fast quadratischen Form an Fotografien des 19. Jahrhunderts erinnert, befragt *A Painting For A Family Dinner* diese vielschichtige Geschichte des klassischen Familienporträts.

Ebenso wie die Fotografien selbst sollte auch die Hängung der Bilder in der Dortmunder Ausstellung den Aspekt der Repräsentation als Ausgangspunkt nehmen. Von Anfang an war es das Ziel, alle bislang entstandenen 62 Familienportraits in einem Raum zu präsentieren. Ergänzt wurden die Portraits durch dokumentarische Fotografien der Besuche, die ebenfalls in diesem Buch zu finden sind. Kleine Geschenke und Erinnerungsstücke, welche die Künstler*innen während der Projekte erhielten, wurden zudem in Vitrinen präsentiert — ähnlich wie historische Artefakte.

3   Siehe Starke, Sandra: „Fenster und Spiegel. Private Fotografie zwischen Norm und Individualität". In: *Historische Anthropologie* 19 (2011), S. 447–474, hier S. 451–453.

Doch welche Form der Präsentation eignet sich für die zahlreichen Fotografien? In früheren Ausstellungen von *A Painting For A Family Dinner* wurde häufig eine Rasterhängung verwendet, da sie sich für die Mittelformat-Fotografien besonders anbietet. In Dortmund entschieden wir uns für eine andere Art der Präsentation: Inspiriert von der stark auf Repräsentation ausgerichteten barocken Hängung schufen wir eine Gruppierung der Fotografien, die auf Fülle und Symmetrie ausgerichtet ist. Die Werke werden hierbei sehr dicht nebeneinander und übereinander gehängt. Es entsteht ein Eindruck der Fülle und Opulenz, der die Betrachter*innen überwältigen soll. In der klassischen Salonhängung bildeten wichtige Werke wie Ahnenportraits die zentralen Blickpunkte, während Landschaftsmalereien oder Stillleben um sie herum gruppiert wurden. Prominente Werke wurden entlang der Mittelachsen platziert und für die entstandenen Lücken wurden gezielt „Füllstücke" gesammelt. Damit sollten der Kunstsinn und Reichtum der jeweiligen Besitzer*innen betont werden. Im Kontext von *A Painting For A Family Dinner* eröffnet die barocke Hängung eine weitere Reflexionsebene zu Fragen der Repräsentation: Wer oder was repräsentiert eigentlich eine Stadt?

Fragen nach einem standesgemäßen Auftreten und Erscheinungsbild, nach der Verkörperung eines gesellschaftlichen Standes, sind für die Fotografien von *A Painting For A Family Dinner* nicht relevant. Vielmehr repräsentieren sie die Städte, in denen sie jeweils entstanden sind, sowie die Vielfalt der jeweiligen Lebensrealitäten. Im Sinne der eingangs gestellten Fragen geben sie Einblicke in das tägliche Leben von Menschen in ihren privaten Umgebungen — als individuelle Mikrokosmen. Sie verkörpern die Stadt ebenso wie deren Architektur, Infrastruktur oder Institutionen des öffentlichen Lebens.

Ebenso wie die Ausstellungspräsentation bietet dieses Buch einen Überblick über alle bisherigen Stationen des künstlerischen Projekts. Zusätzlich zu den Portraits, dem dokumentarischen Material und dem Tagebuch enthält es Rezepte der Gastgeber*innen. Nicht zu vergessen ist schließlich, dass das gemeinsame Essen Anlass all dieser Besuche war. Vielleicht regen diese Rezepte dazu an, selbst einmal wieder Gäste einzuladen und für sie zu kochen.

Family Portraits

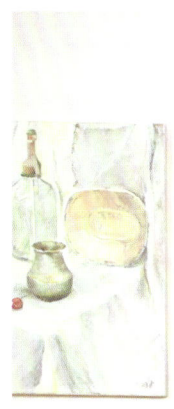
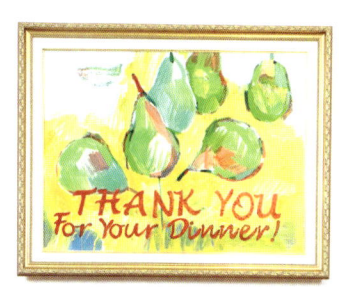
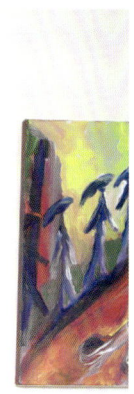

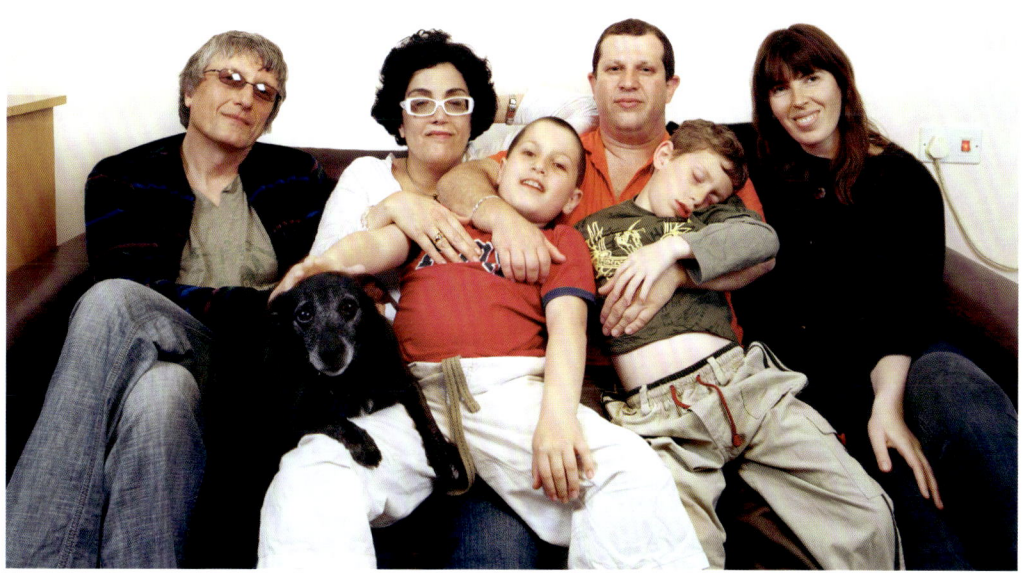

BAT YAM, ISRAEL / APRIL 7, 2008
Jeff Bliumis, Ada Weiszlovitz, Snir Weiszlovitz,
Tal Weiszlovitz, Roni Weiszlovitz, Alina Bliumis

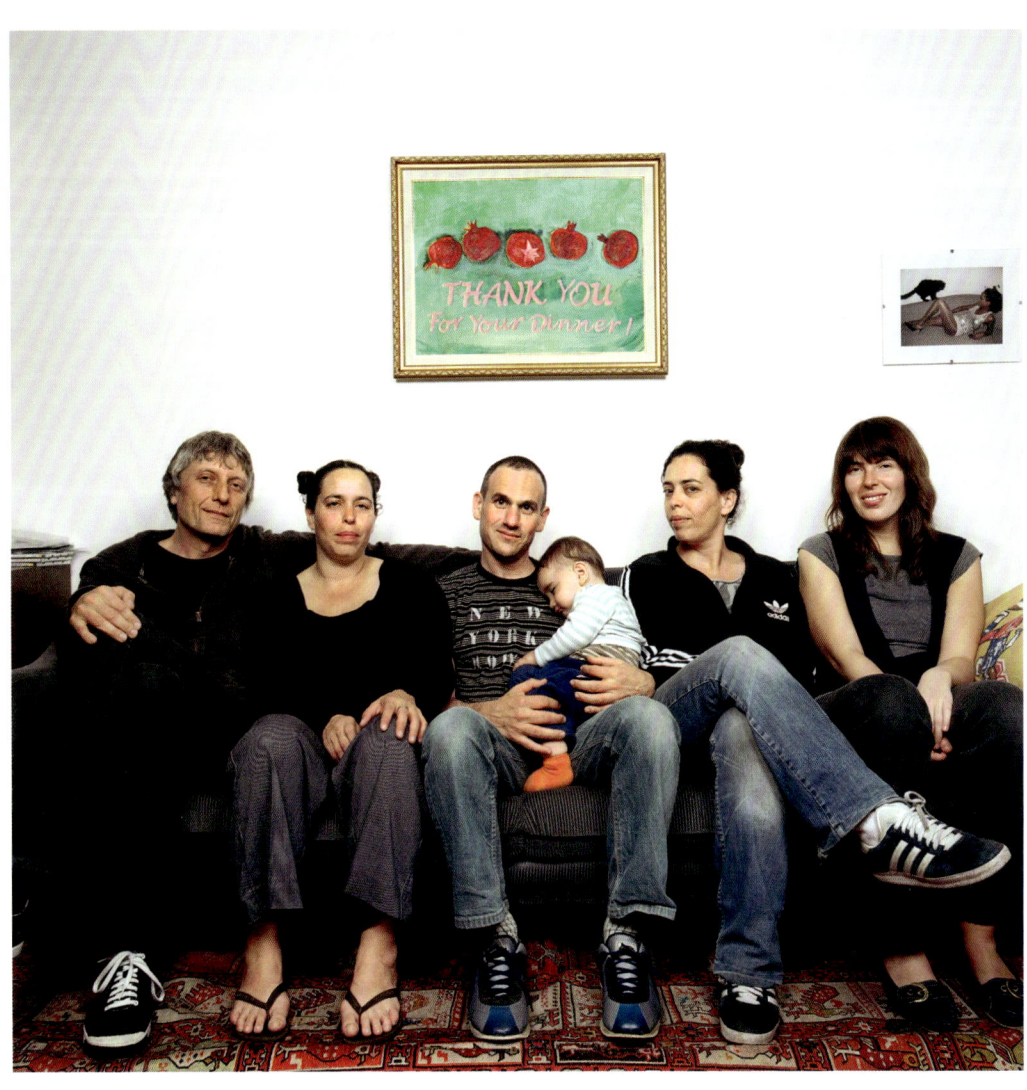

BAT YAM, ISRAEL / APRIL 8, 2008
Jeff Bliumis, Shiri Cnaani, Guri Nadler,
Nadav Cnaani Nadler, Roni Cnaani, Alina Bliumis

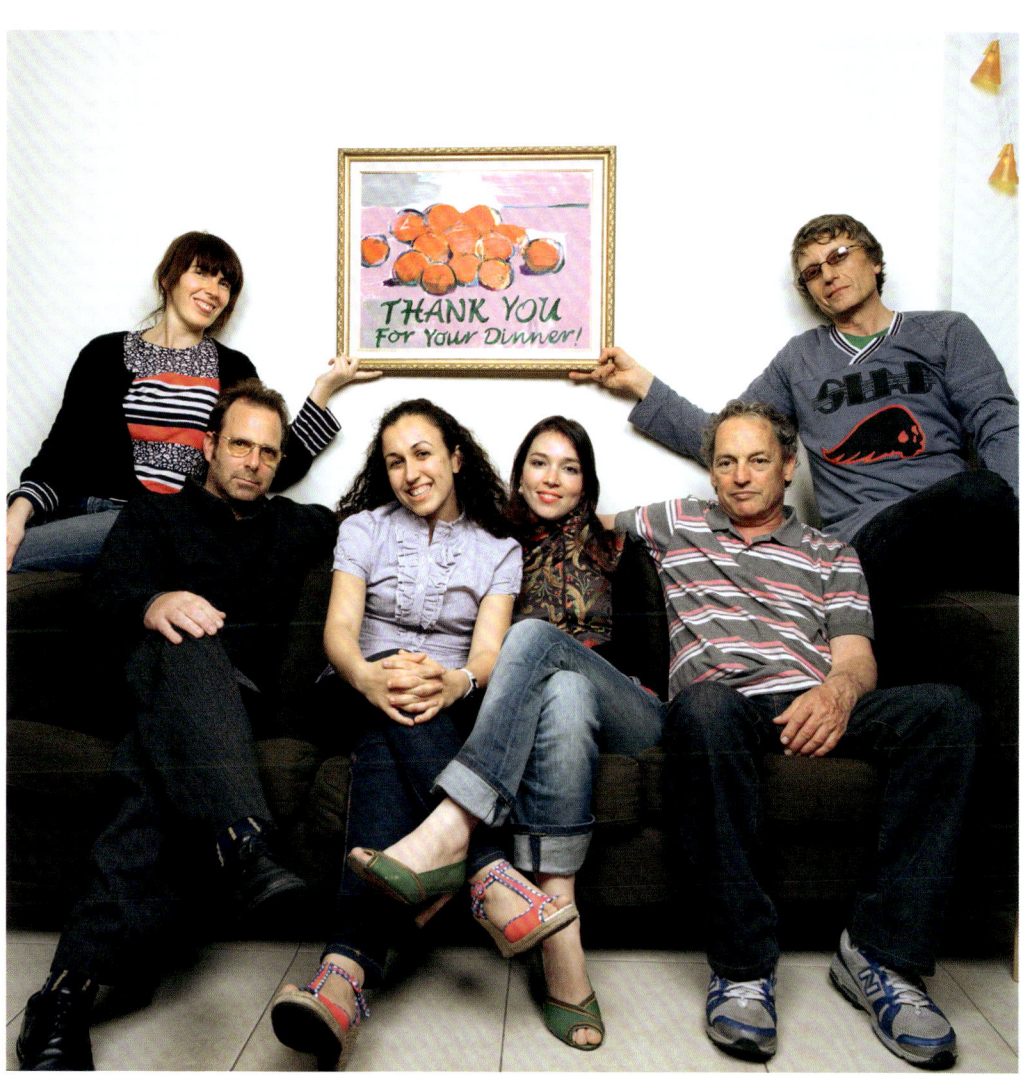

BAT YAM, ISRAEL / APRIL 9, 2008
Alina Bliumis, Matti Lohat, Michal Gitnik,
Sigalit Layderman, Liam Fraunfurt, Jeff Bliumis

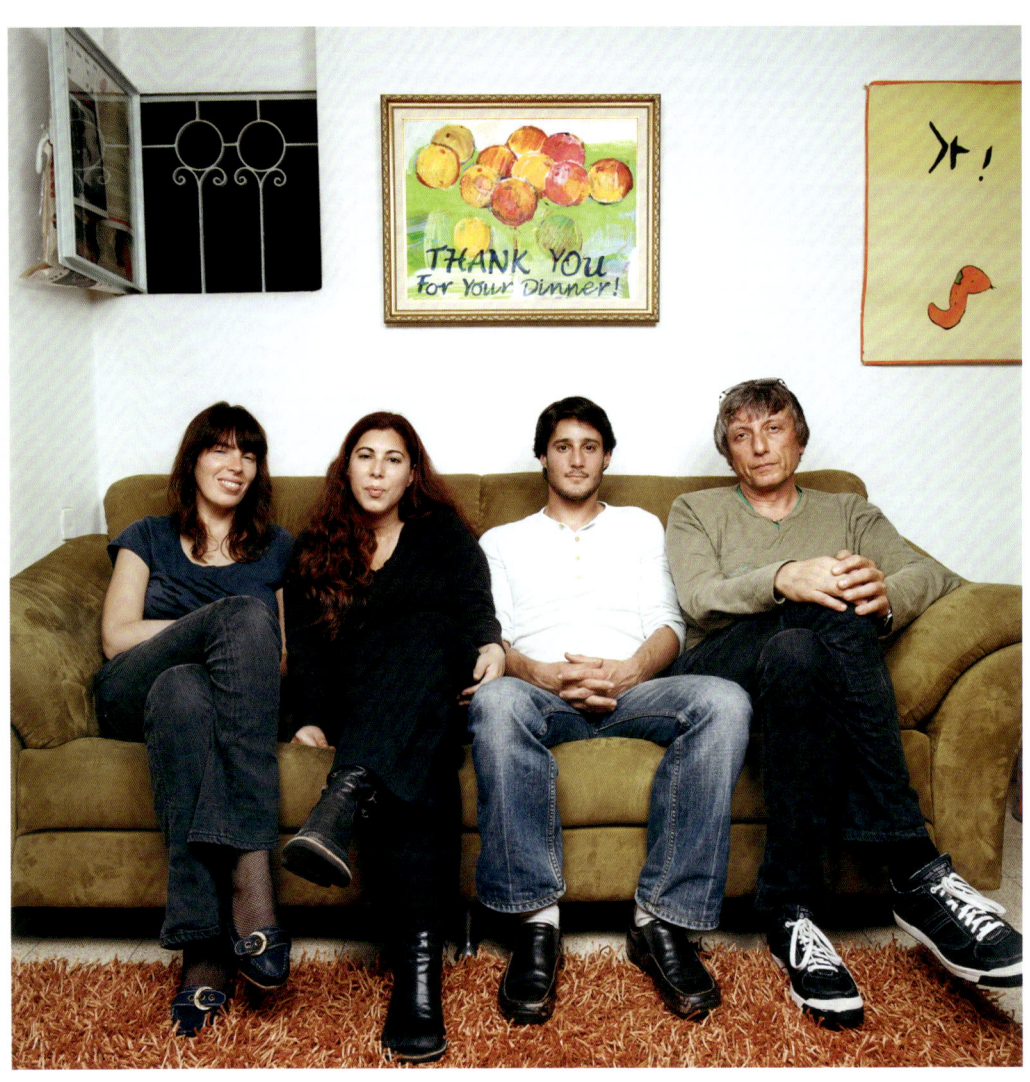

BAT YAM, ISRAEL / APRIL 10, 2008
Alina Bliumis, Miki Riess, Ron Konefka, Jeff Bliumis

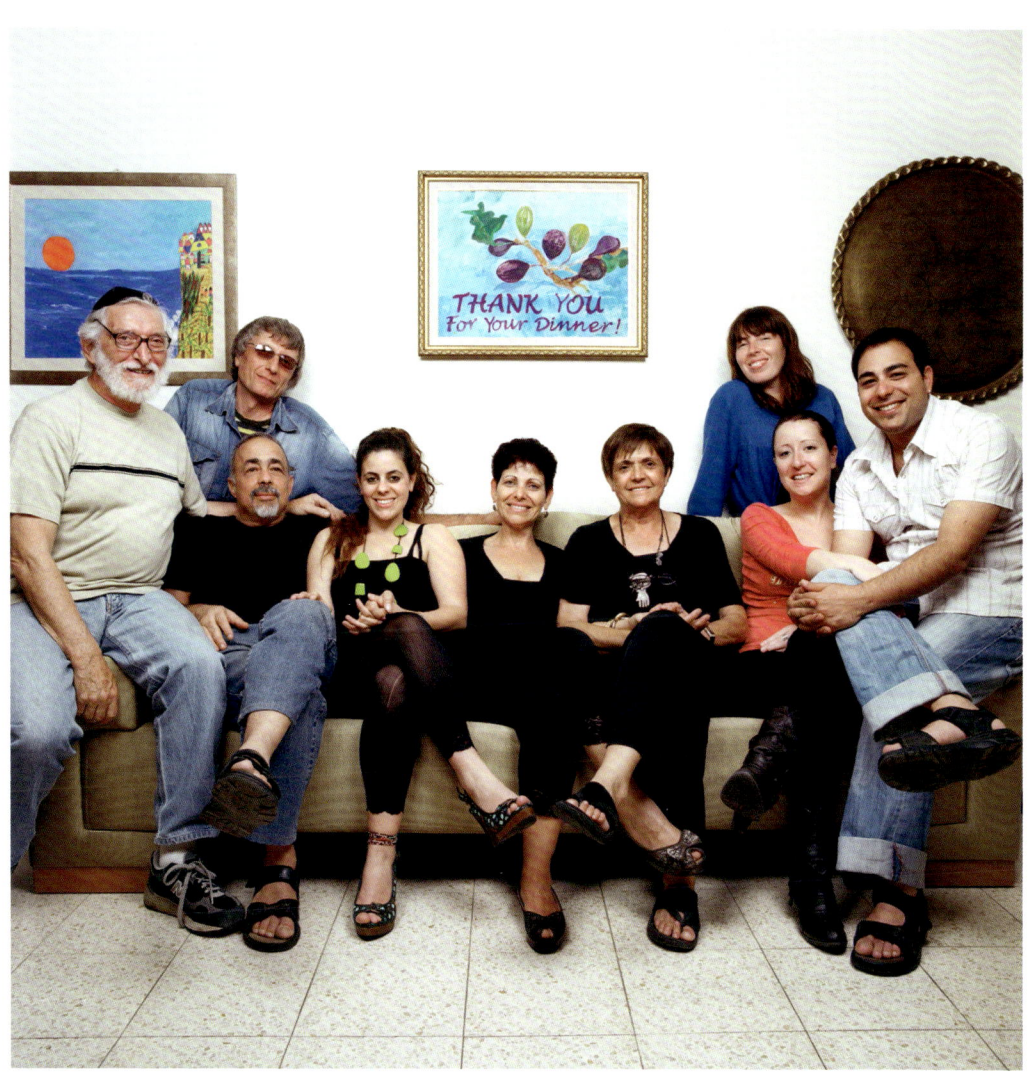

BAT YAM, ISRAEL / APRIL 11, 2008
Jeff Bliumis, Ya'ara, Rei, Arale, Avigial, Hagar,
Miriam, David, Alina Bliumis

23

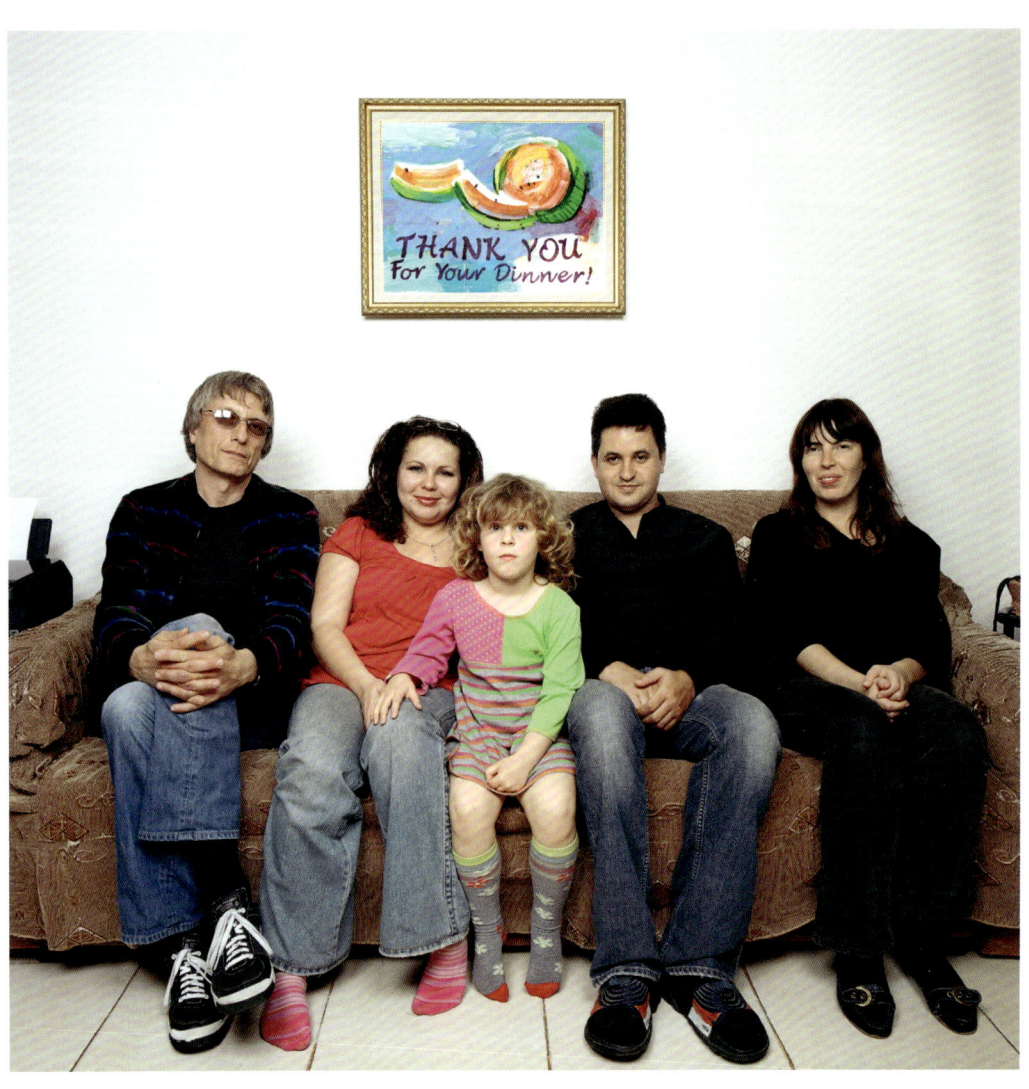

BAT YAM, ISRAEL / APRIL 12, 2008
Jeff Bliumis, Diana, Masha, Andrey, Alina Bliumis

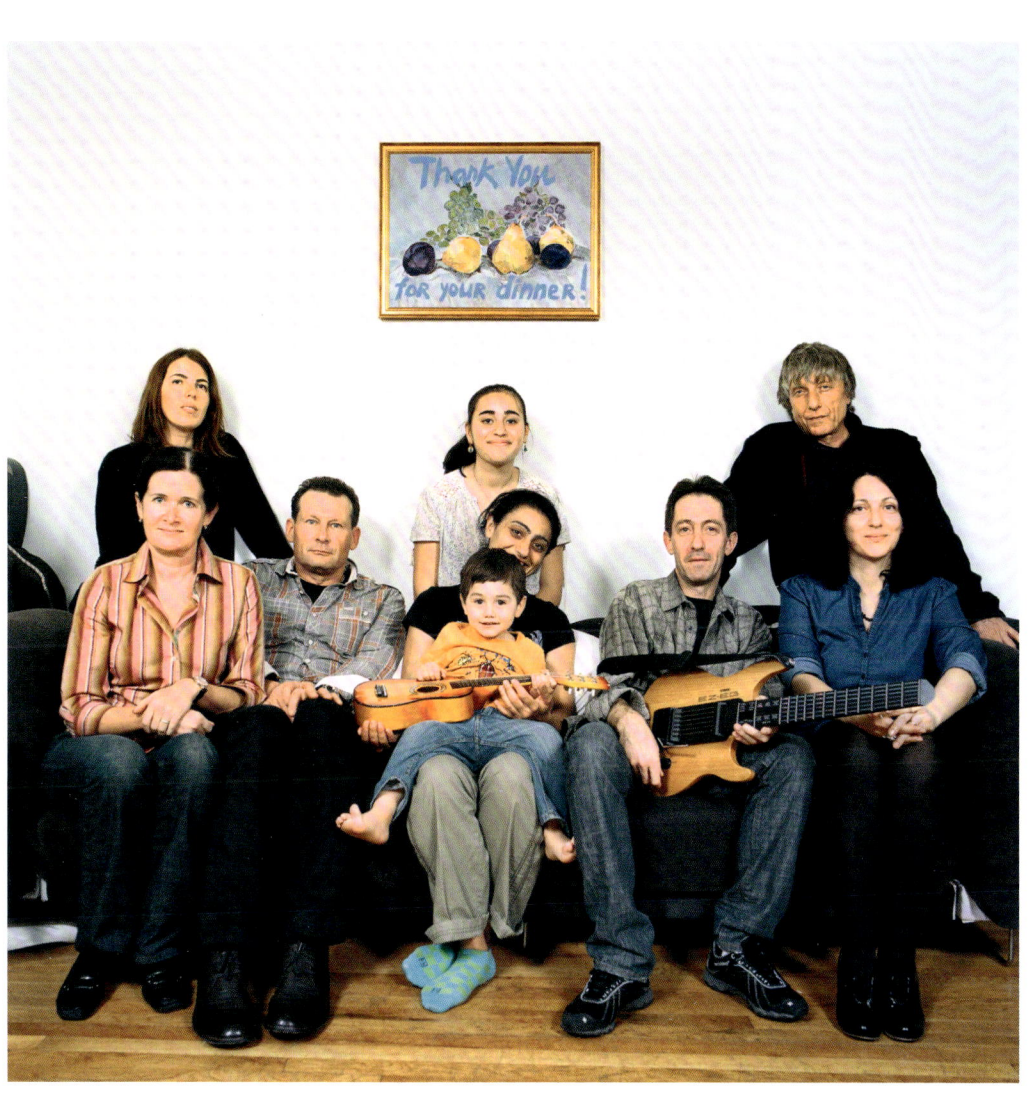

BRONX, NY, US / MARCH 24, 2012
Alina Bliumis, Natalia, Pavlo, Ani, Liliya, Pavlo,
Bohdan, Inga Koroleva, Jeff Bliumis

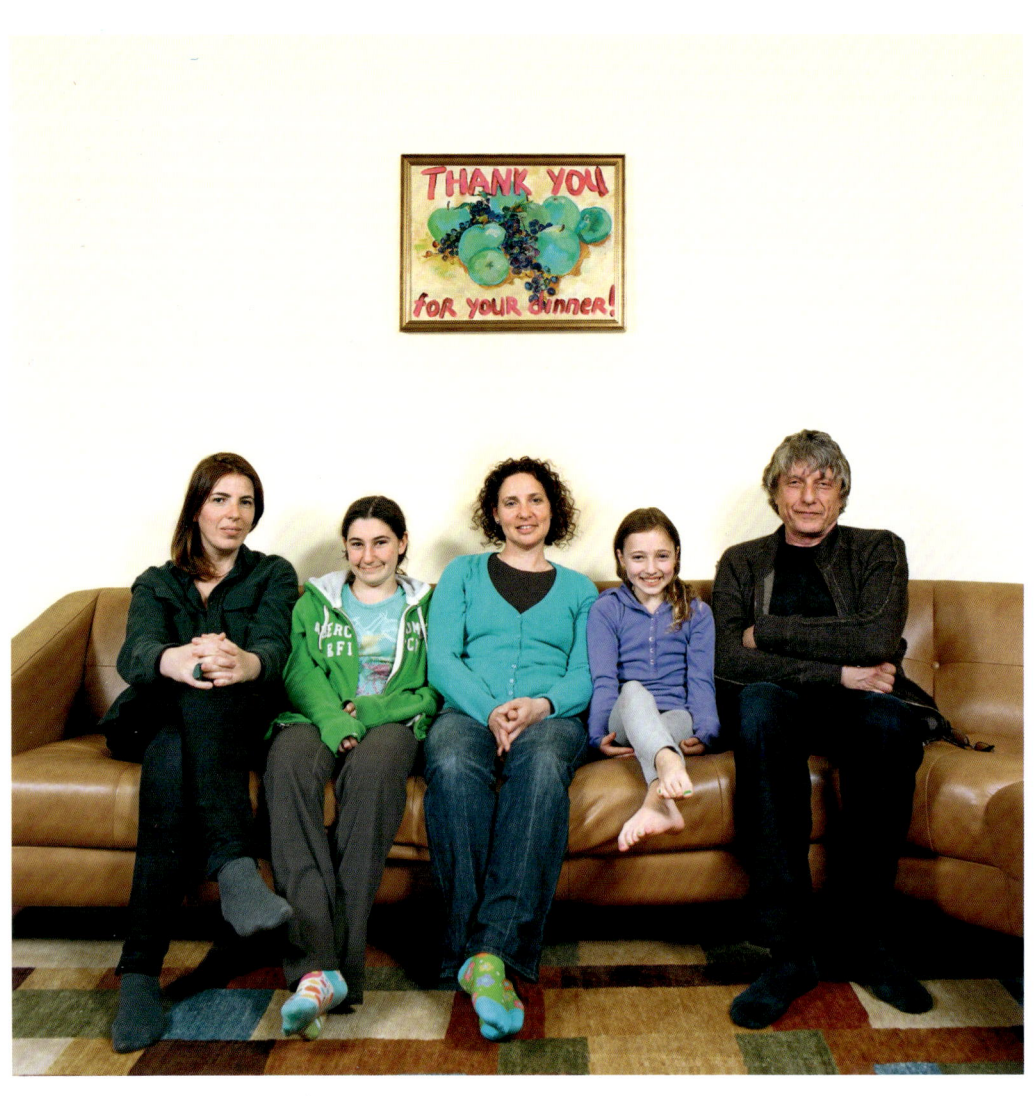

BRONX, NY, US / MARCH 29, 2012
Alina Bliumis, Emma Simon, Laura Kaufman Simon,
Josei Simon, Jeff Bliumis

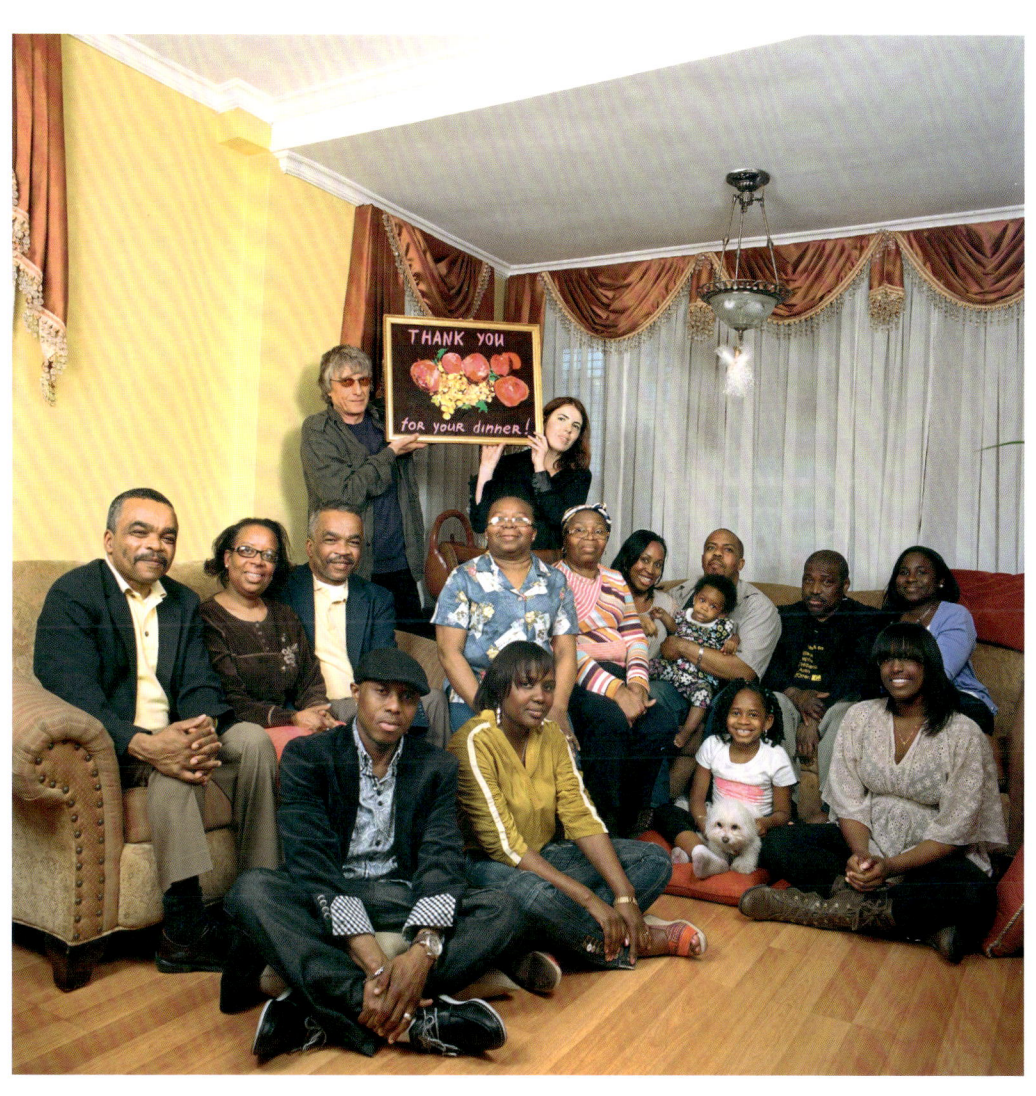

BRONX, NY, US / APRIL 8, 2012
Jeff Bliumis, Jose F. Avila, Ava Avila,
Thomas A. Avila, Teofilo Garcia, Diega Jaime,
Sulma Arzu-Brown, Bella Victoria Brown,
Maurice Brown, Escolastico Arzu, Isidra Sabio,
Dwight Dockery, Monica Bernardez, Suleni T. Sabio,
Arzu Brown, Sparkle, Perla Gonzales, Alina Bliumis

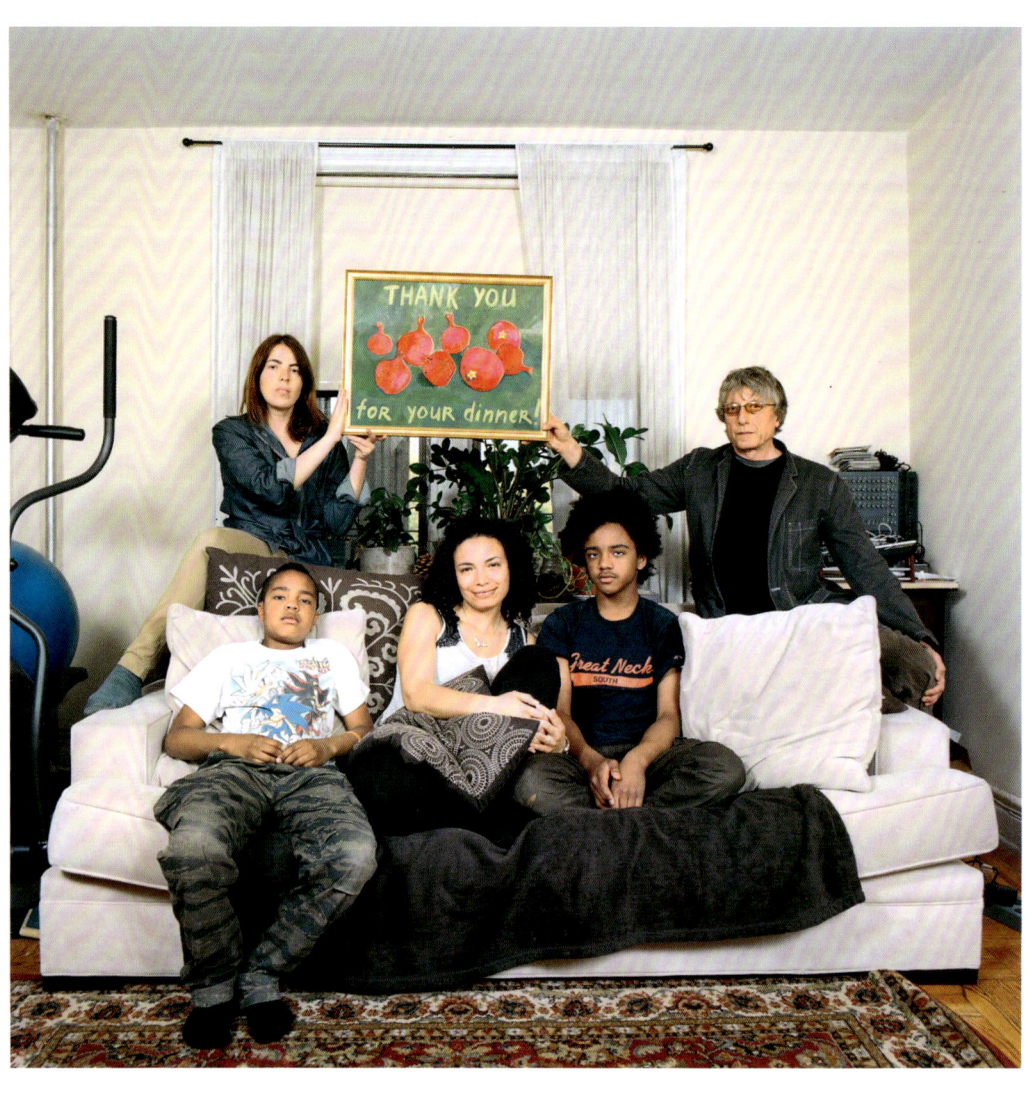

BRONX, NY, US / APRIL 10, 2012
Alina Bliumis, Jahsaia, Maiysha, Lohan, Jeff Bliumis

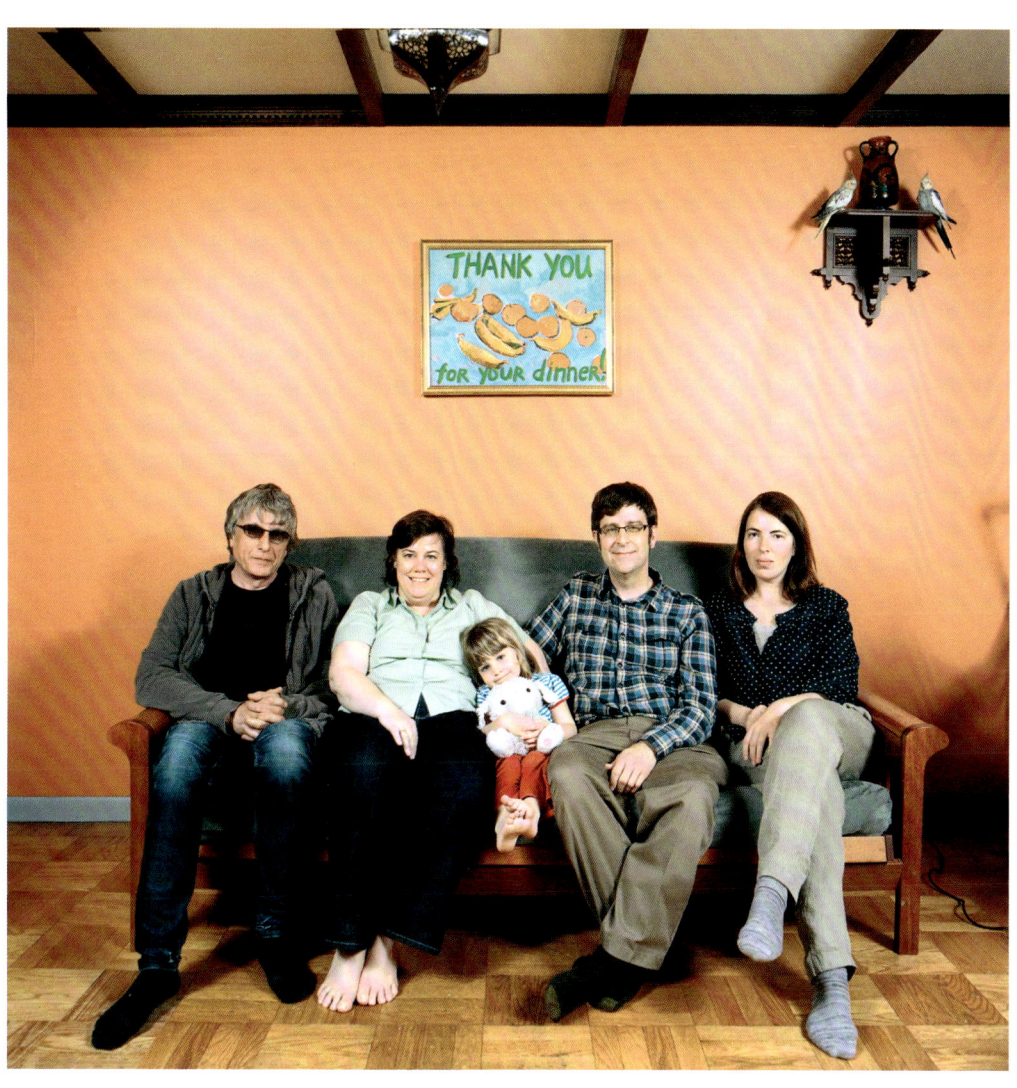

BRONX, NY, US / APRIL 15, 2012
Jeff Bliumis, Gayle Snible, Charlotte Snible, Lambie,
Ed Snible, Betty, Lothar, Alina Bliumis

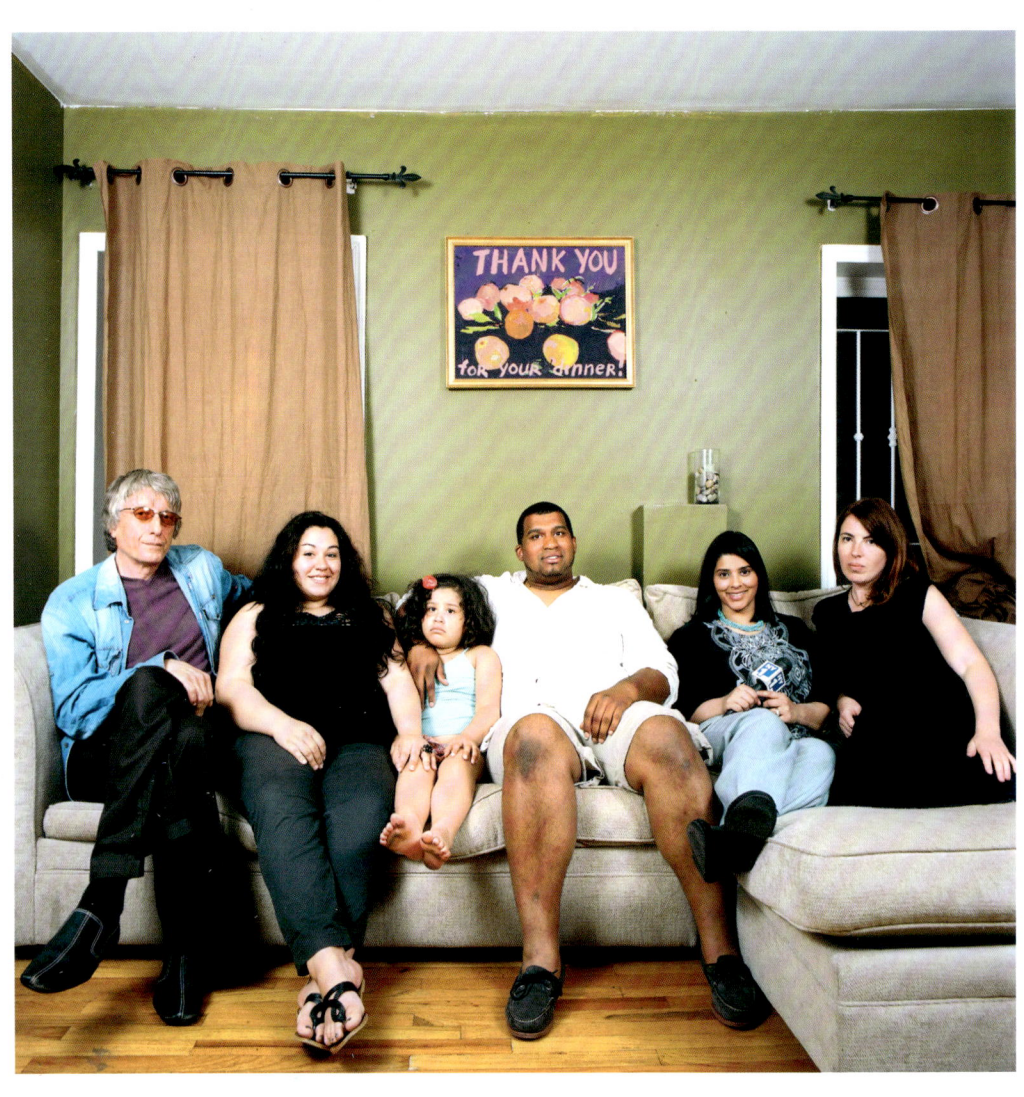

BRONX, NY, US / APRIL 16, 2012
Jeff Bliumis, Nicole Perrino, Briana Geronimo,
Luis Geronimo, Shazia T. Khan, Alina Bliumis

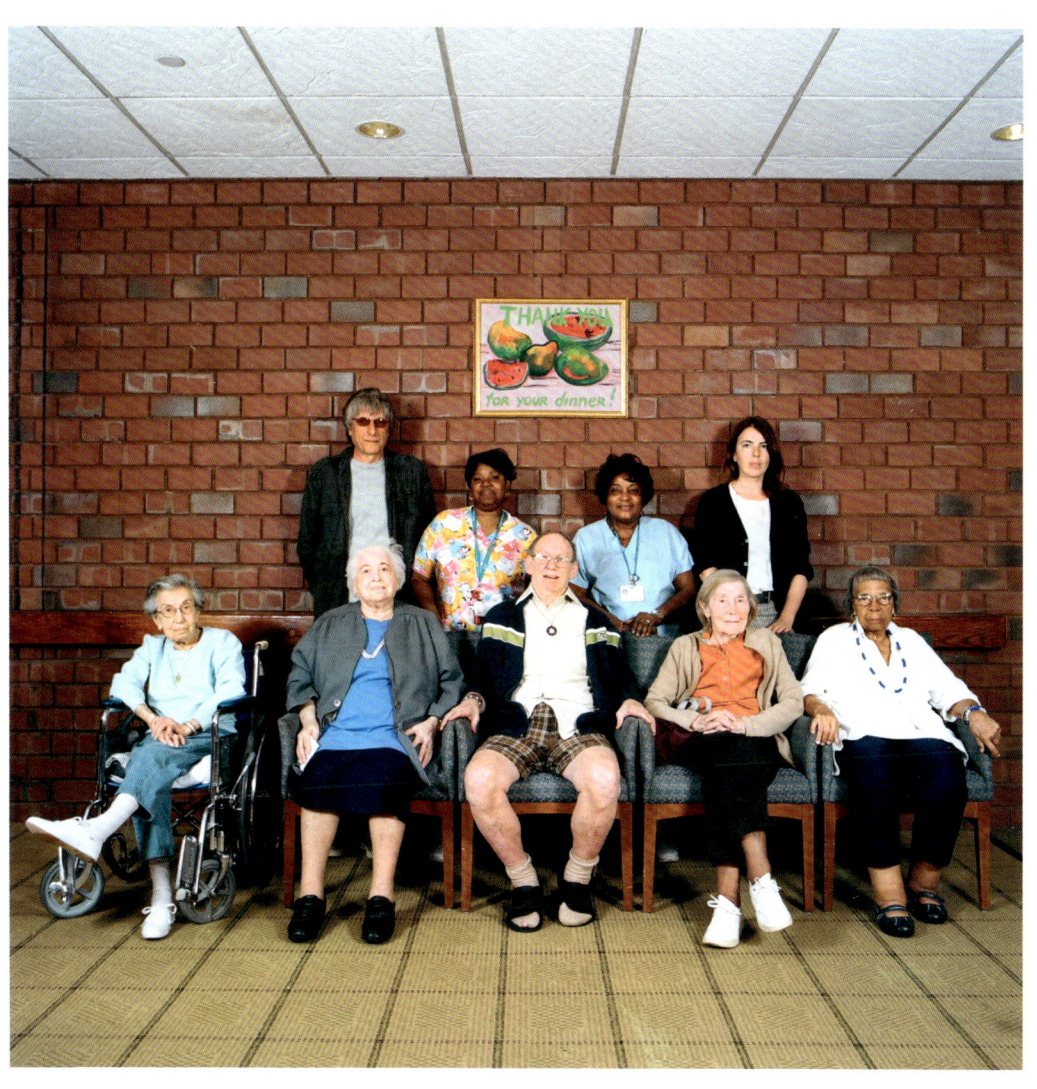

BRONX, NY, US / APRIL 17, 2012
Jeff Bliumis, Jeanette Gordon, Sherryl Minott,
Alina Bliumis, Beth Mintz, Fay Weingarten,
Howard A. Zeimer, Ruth Lasner, Alice Sebastian

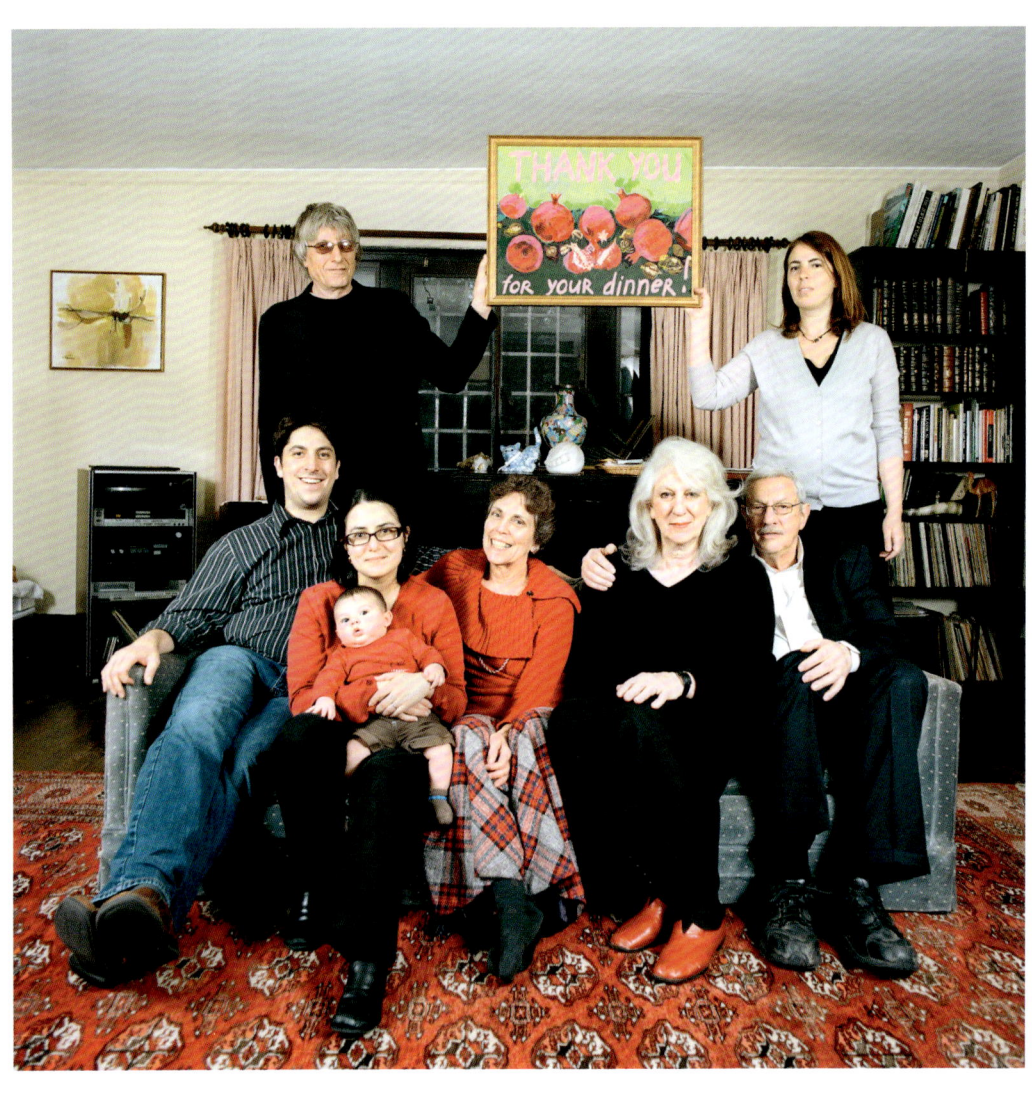

BRONX, NY, US / APRIL 27, 2012
Jeff Bliumis, Avi B., Erin M., Alex, Judy G.,
Mierle Laderman Ukeles, Jack Ukeles, Alina Bliumis

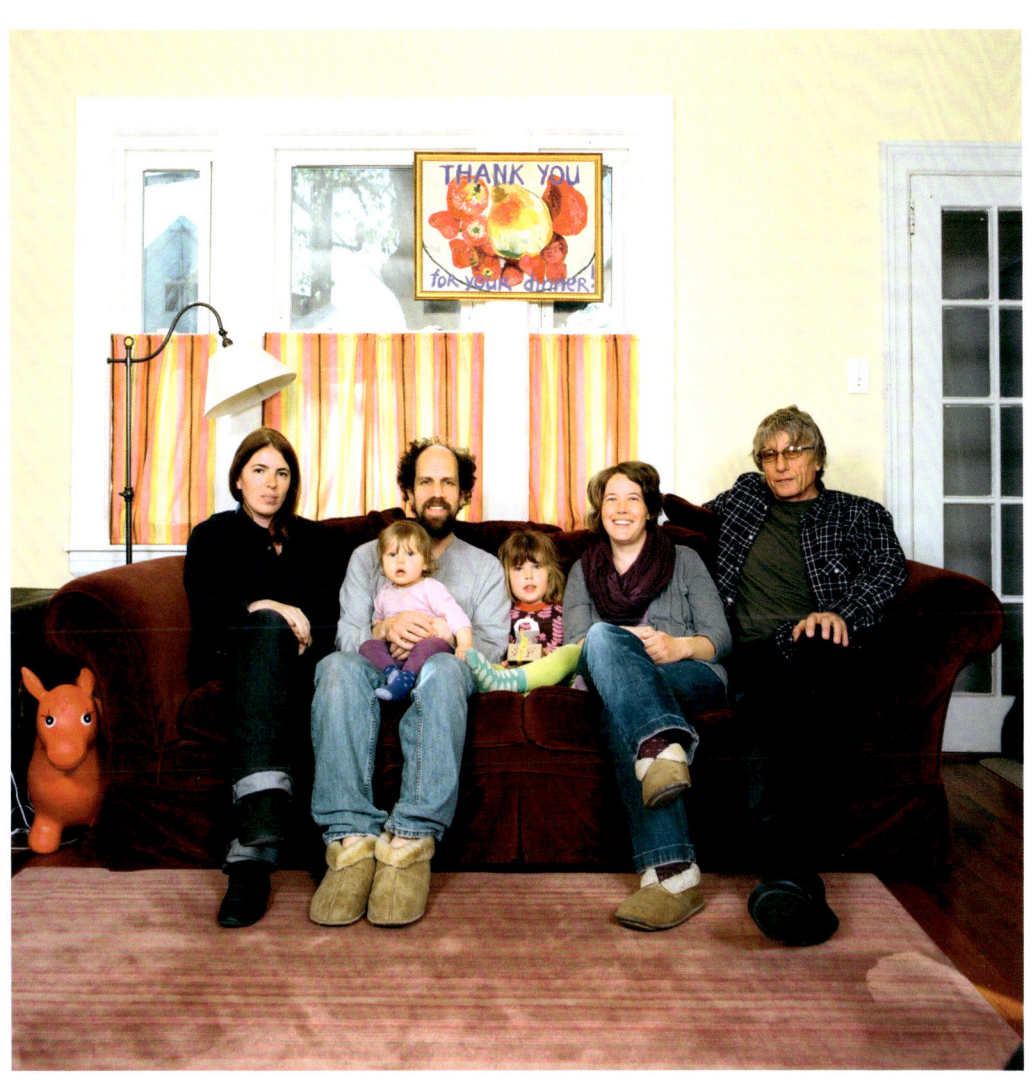

BRONX, NY, US / APRIL 27, 2012
Alina Bliumis, Sasha Wilson, Magnolia Sibley-Wilson,
Delphinium Sibley-Wilson, Kendra Sibley, Jeff Bliumis

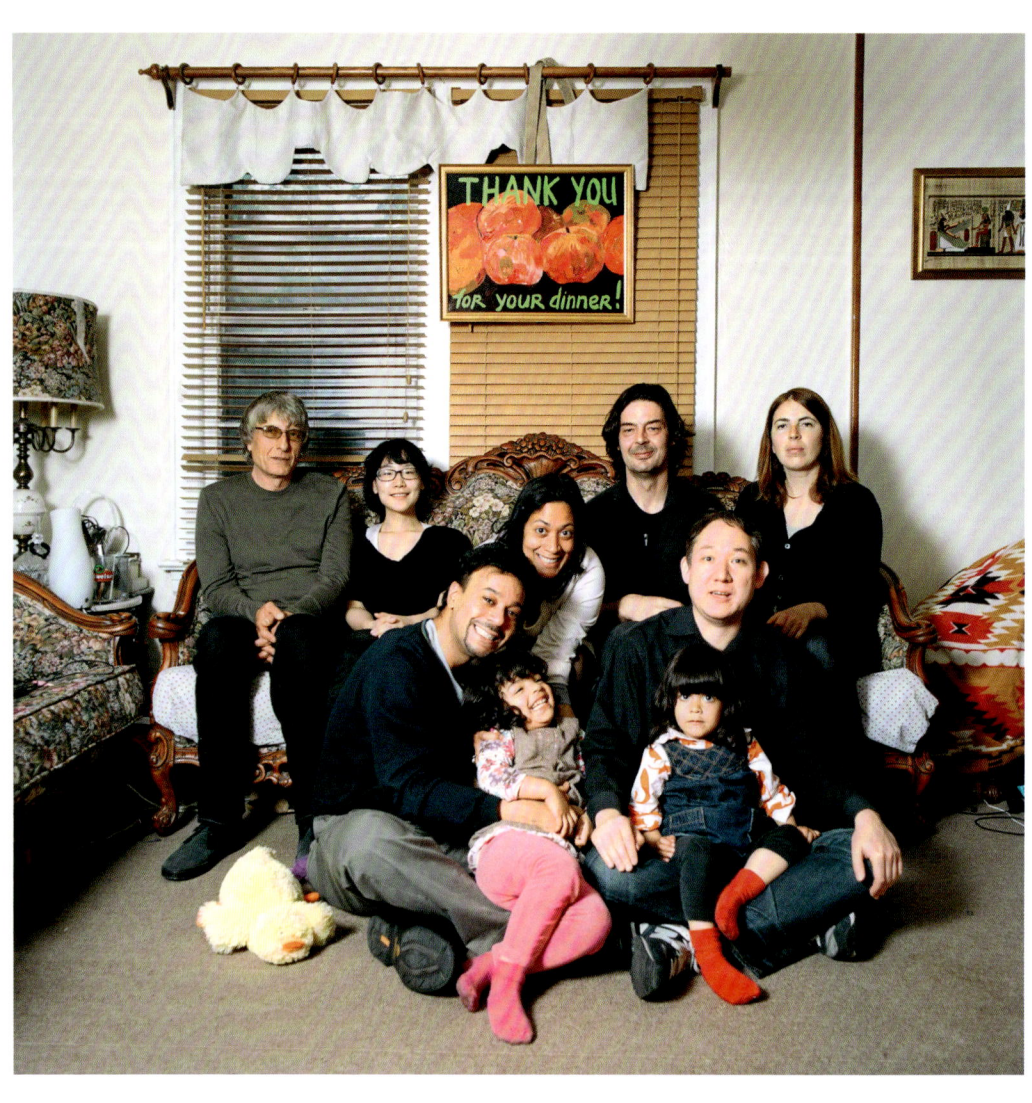

BRONX, NY, US / APRIL 29, 2012
Jeff Bliumis, Woorim Kim, Cesar A. Grullon,
Eija Barends, Alicia Grullon, Johan Barends,
Ignacio Cltoi, Elielle Barends, Alina Bliumis

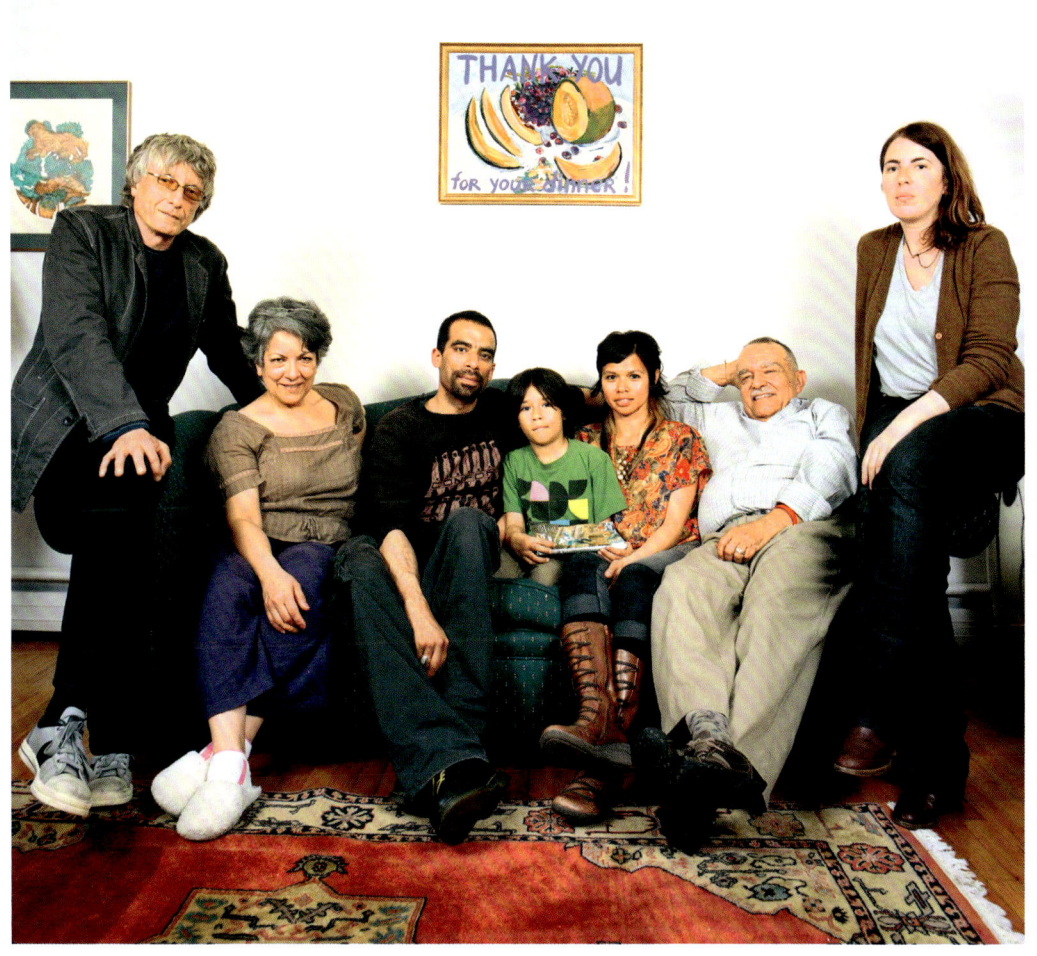

BRONX, NY, US / MAY 5, 2012
Jeff Bliumis, Noemi Santana, Manny "Megman"
Oquendo, Ezra Oquendo, Beatrice Tinio,
Francisco "Paco" Lugovina, Alina Bliumis

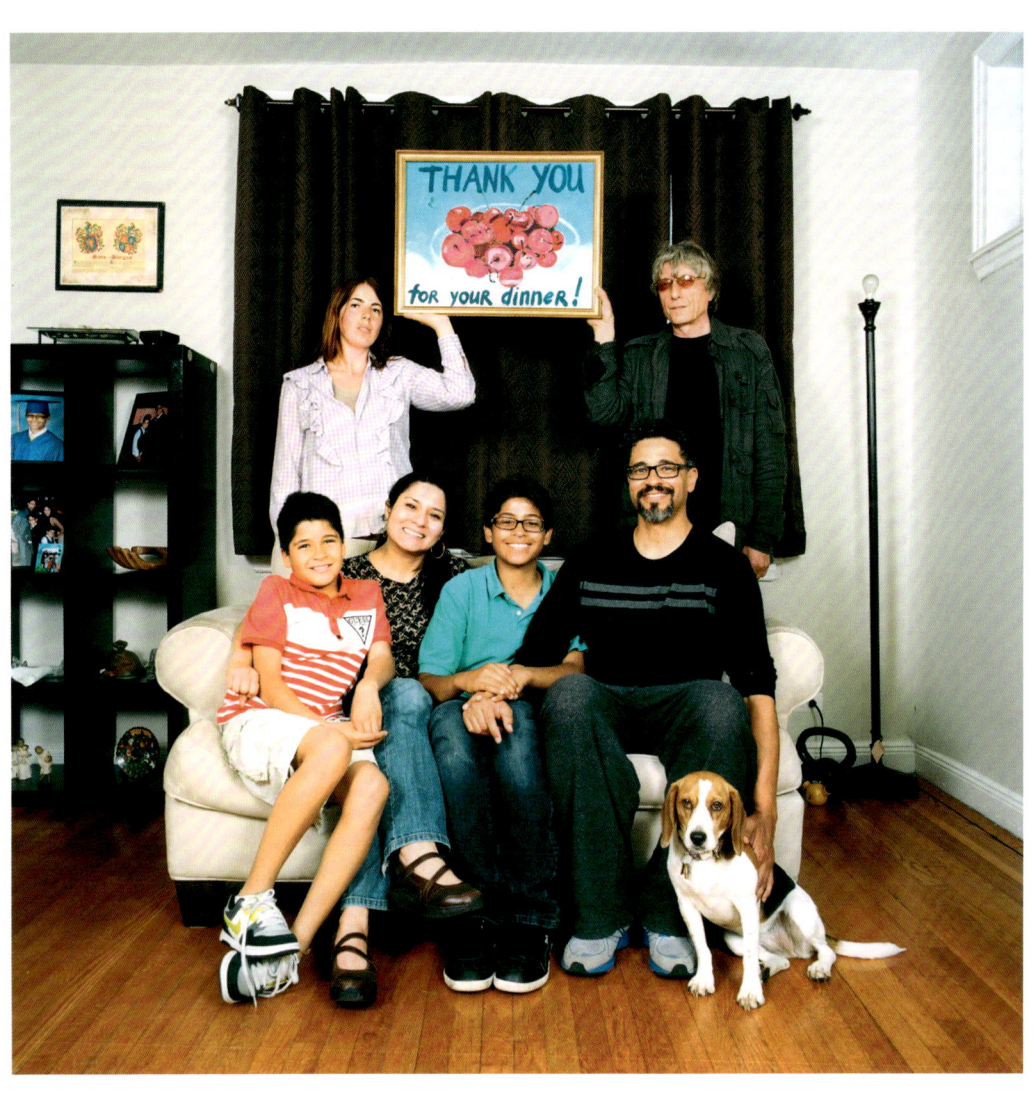

BRONX, NY, US / MAY 6, 2012
Alina Bliumis, Andres Soto Burgos,
Sandra Burgos Hidalgo, Xavier Soto Burgos,
Israel Soto Duprey, Nena, Jeff Bliumis

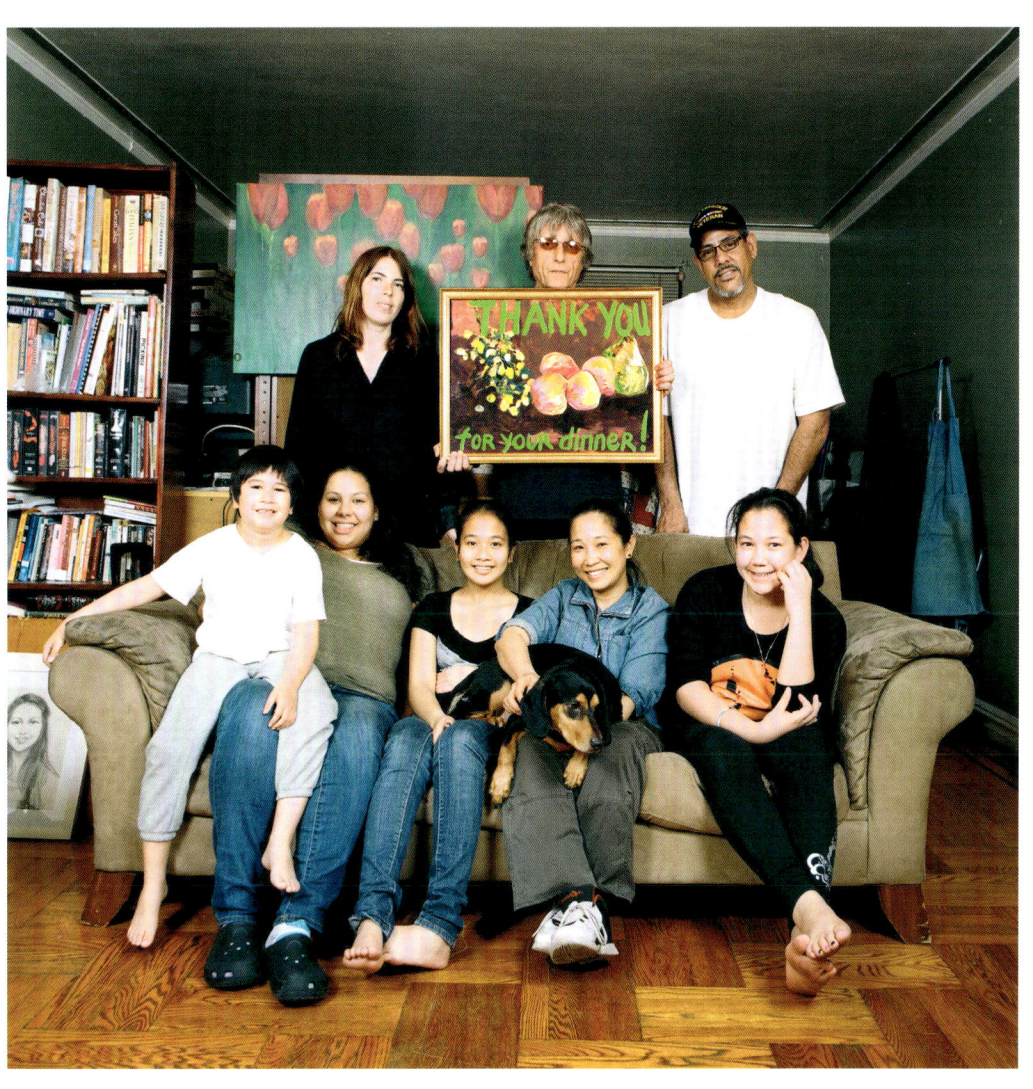

BRONX, NY, US / MAY 6, 2012
Alina Bliumis, Jeff Bliumis, Hector L. Lopez,
Nicolas R. Provenzano, Leana J. Lopez,
Narunee Meesawan, Manaswinee Meesawan,
Astro Boy, Tera Meesawan

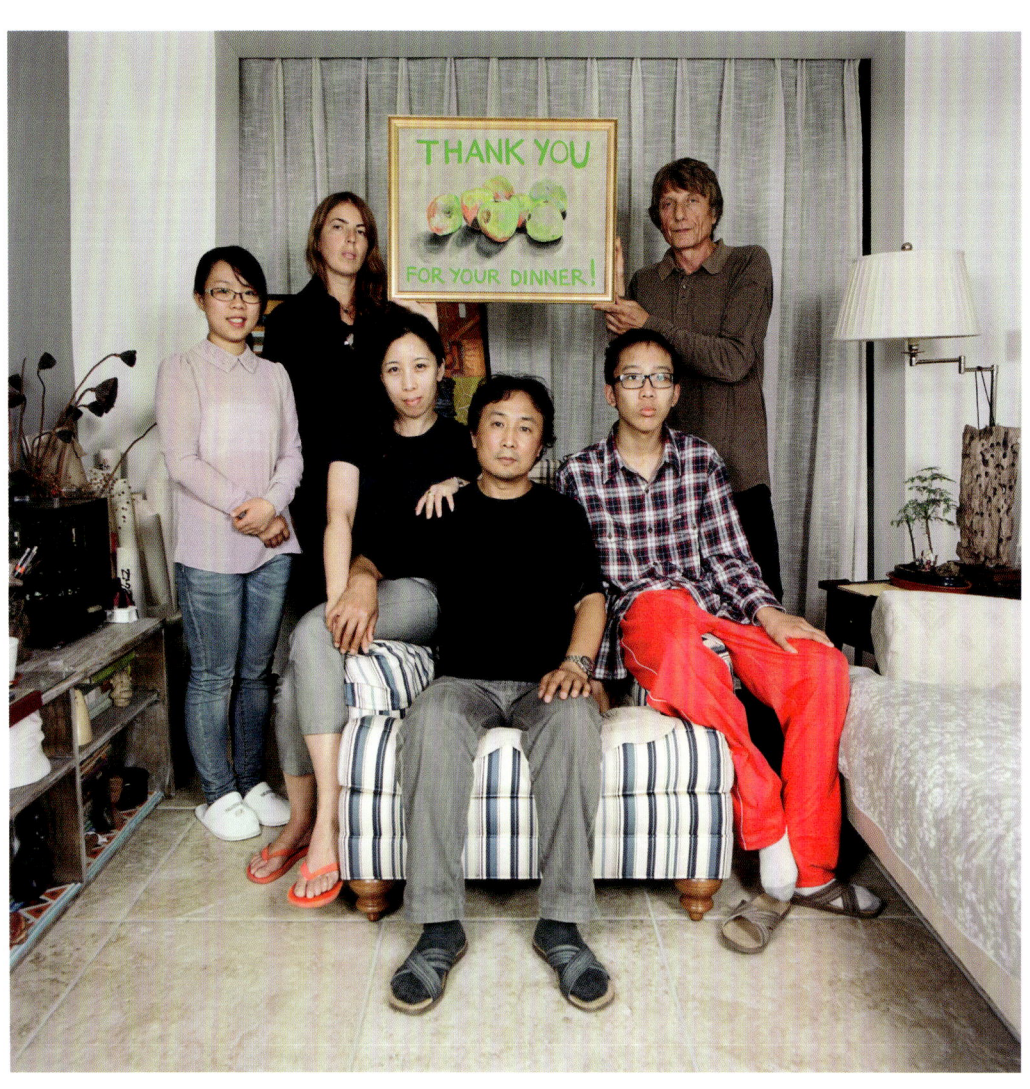

BEIJING, CHINA / SEPTEMBER 13, 2013
Alina Bliumis, Cici Zeng, Yang Xue Li, Cheng Le Yu,
Cheng Tao Ning, Jeff Bliumis

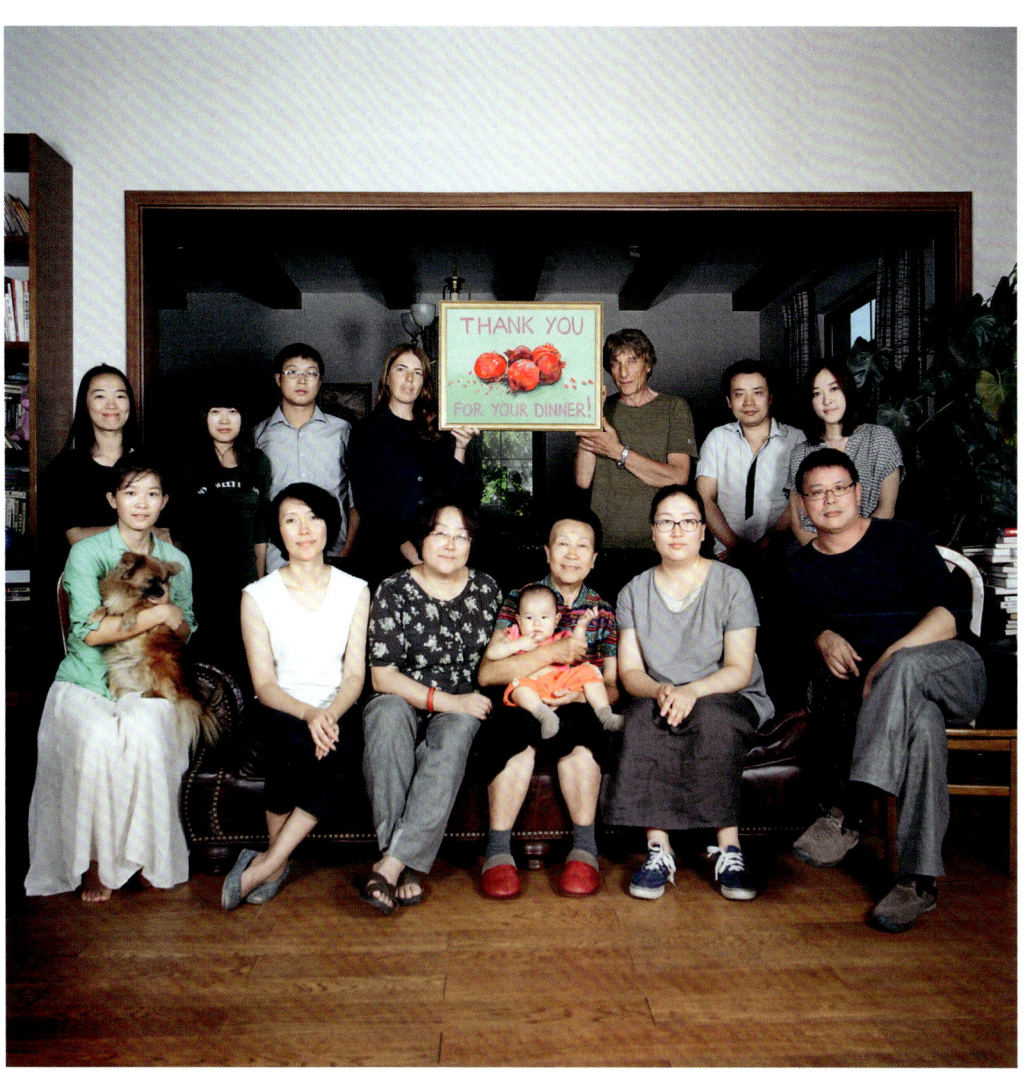

BEIJING, CHINA / SEPTEMBER 14, 2013
Alina Bliumis, Sanquo Cheng, Yanhong Kong,
JiQiong Yang, Yanjun Kong, Na Meng, Dan Cheng,
Yan Cheng, Chao Duan, ZiCheng Zhang, Cheng Jin
Zhang, Ling Qing Yang, QiuWei Zhuang,
Dian Dian, Jeff Bliumis

39

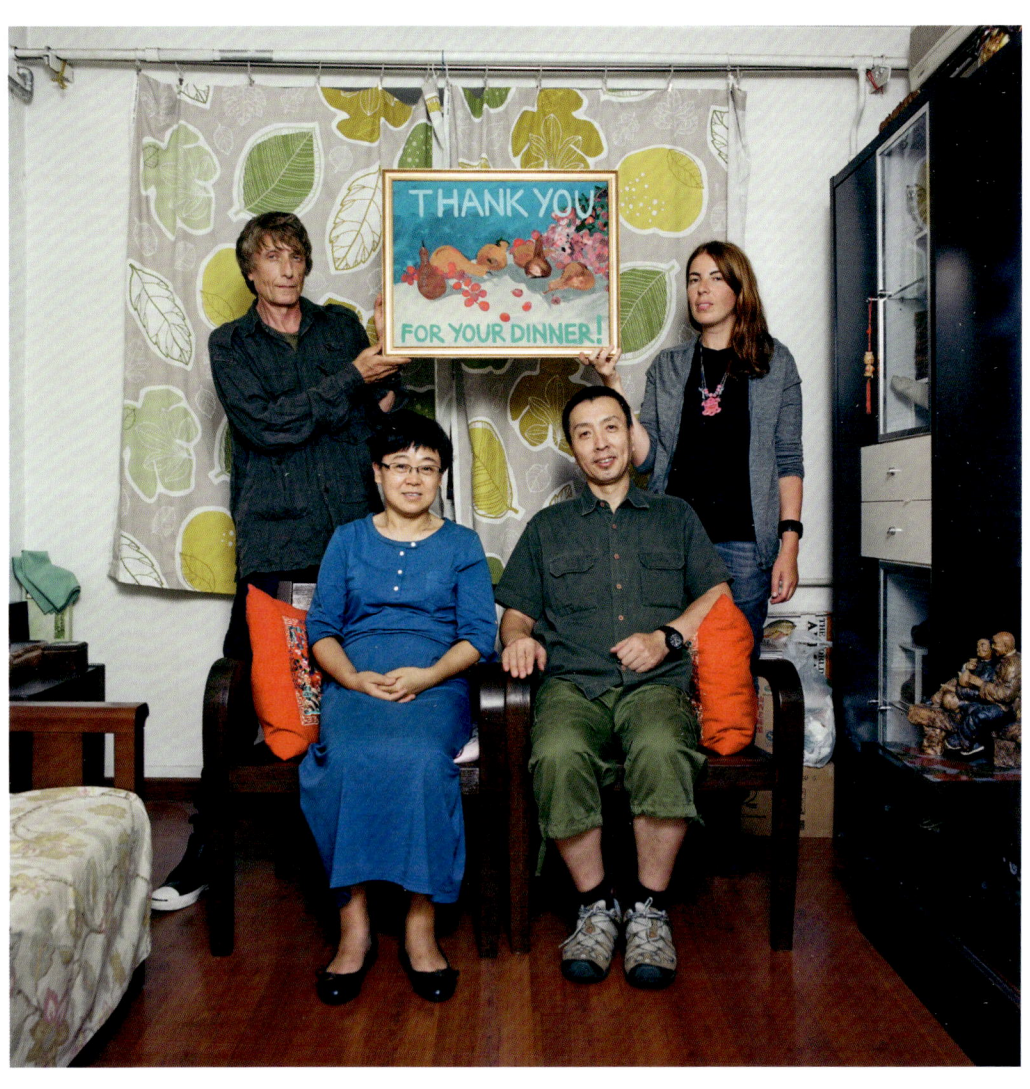

BEIJING, CHINA / SEPTEMBER 14, 2013
Jeff Bliumis, Li Zhiyan, Liu Wenbin, Alina Bliumis

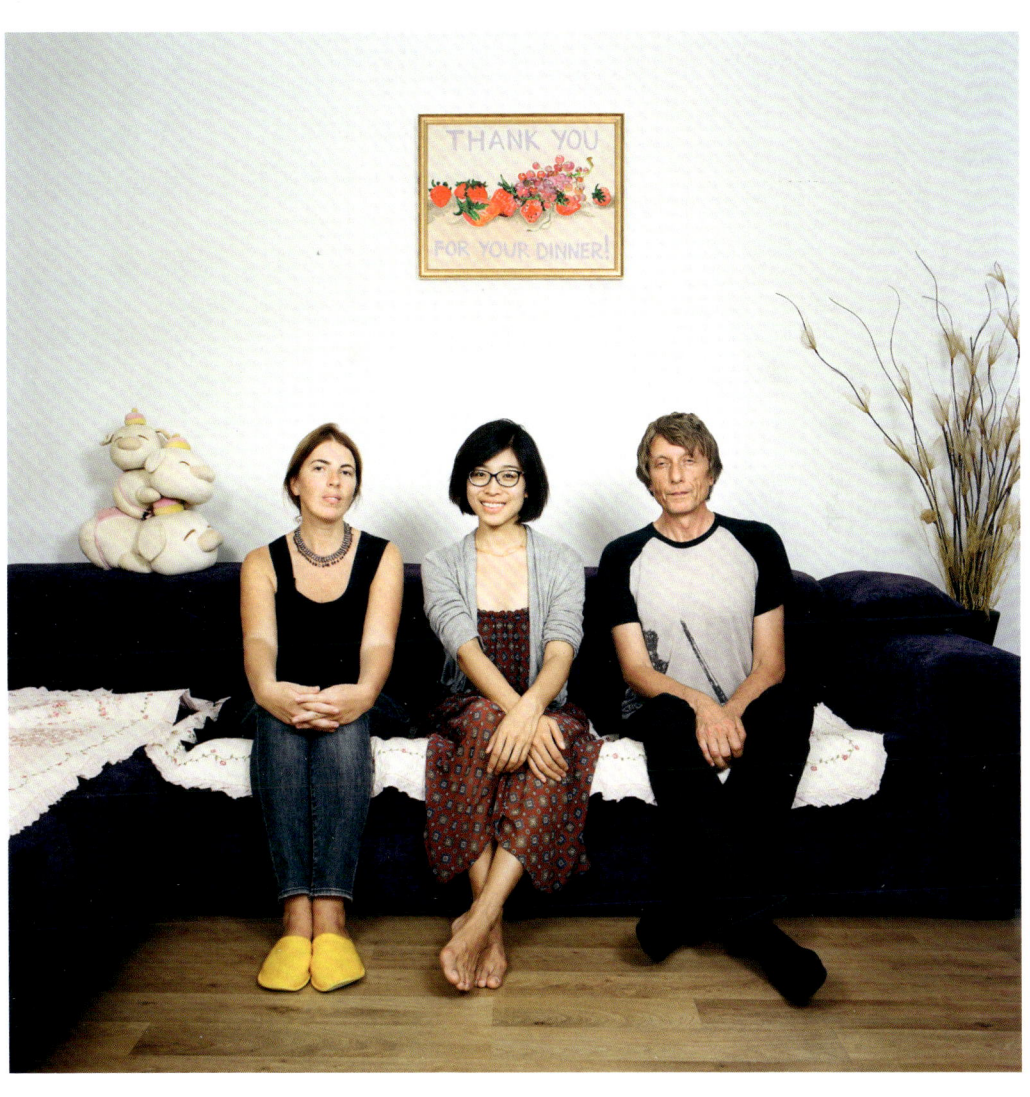

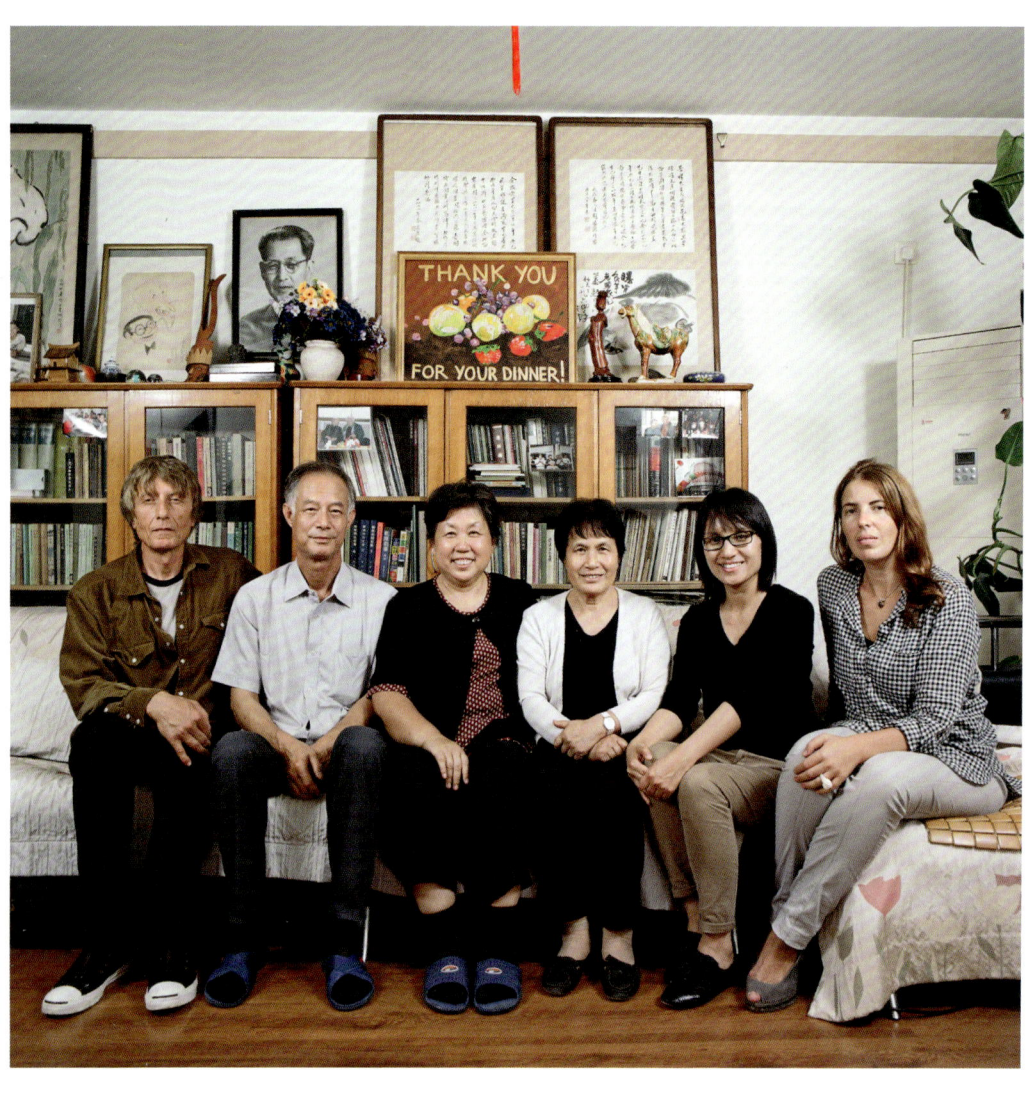

BEIJING, CHINA / SEPTEMBER 15, 2013
Jeff Bliumis, HaoXiang Chen, Hanjun Guo,
Shengli Liu, Wei Zhai, Alina Bliumis

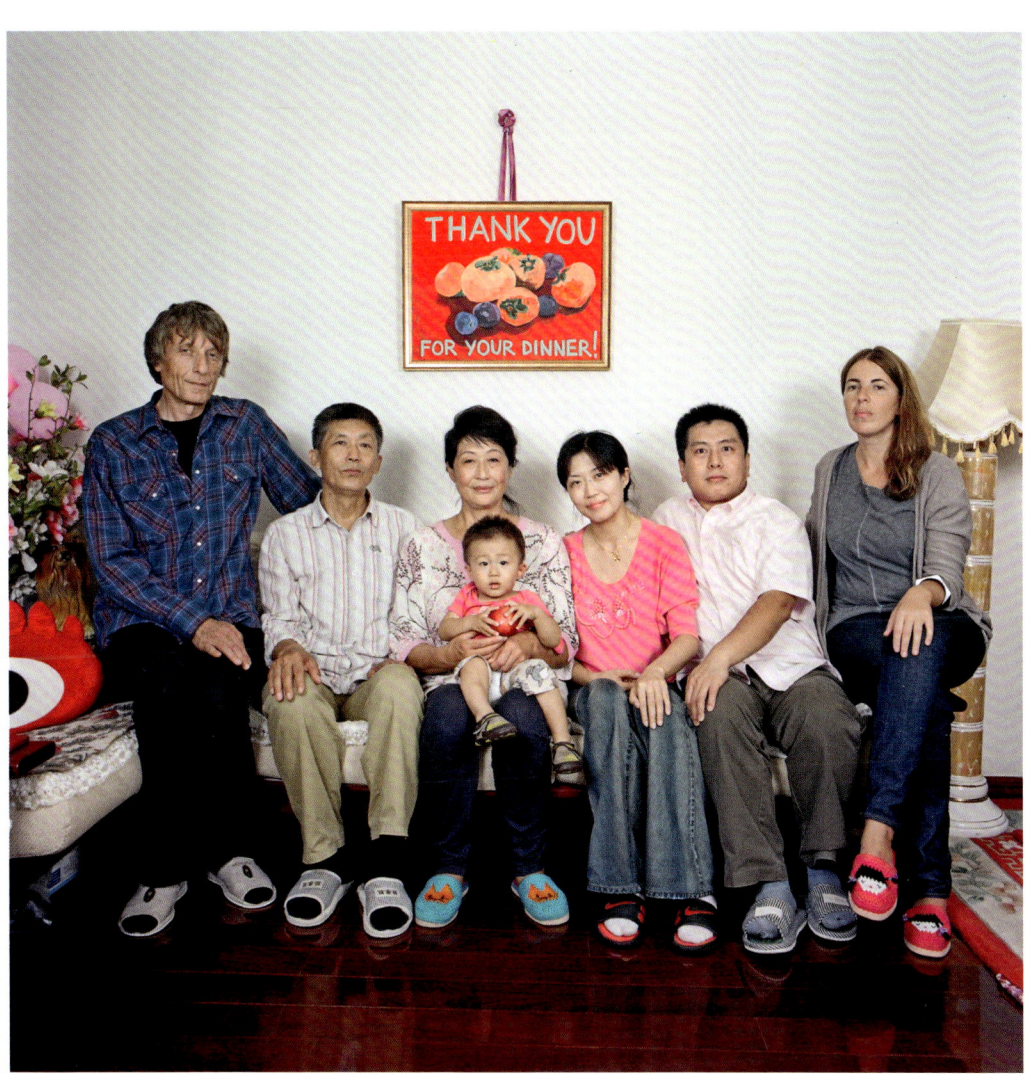

BEIJING, CHINA / SEPTEMBER 16, 2013
Jeff Bliumis, Shao Yingzhi, Du Shuhua, Dai Mingyang,
Shao Jun, Dai Jing, Alina Bliumis

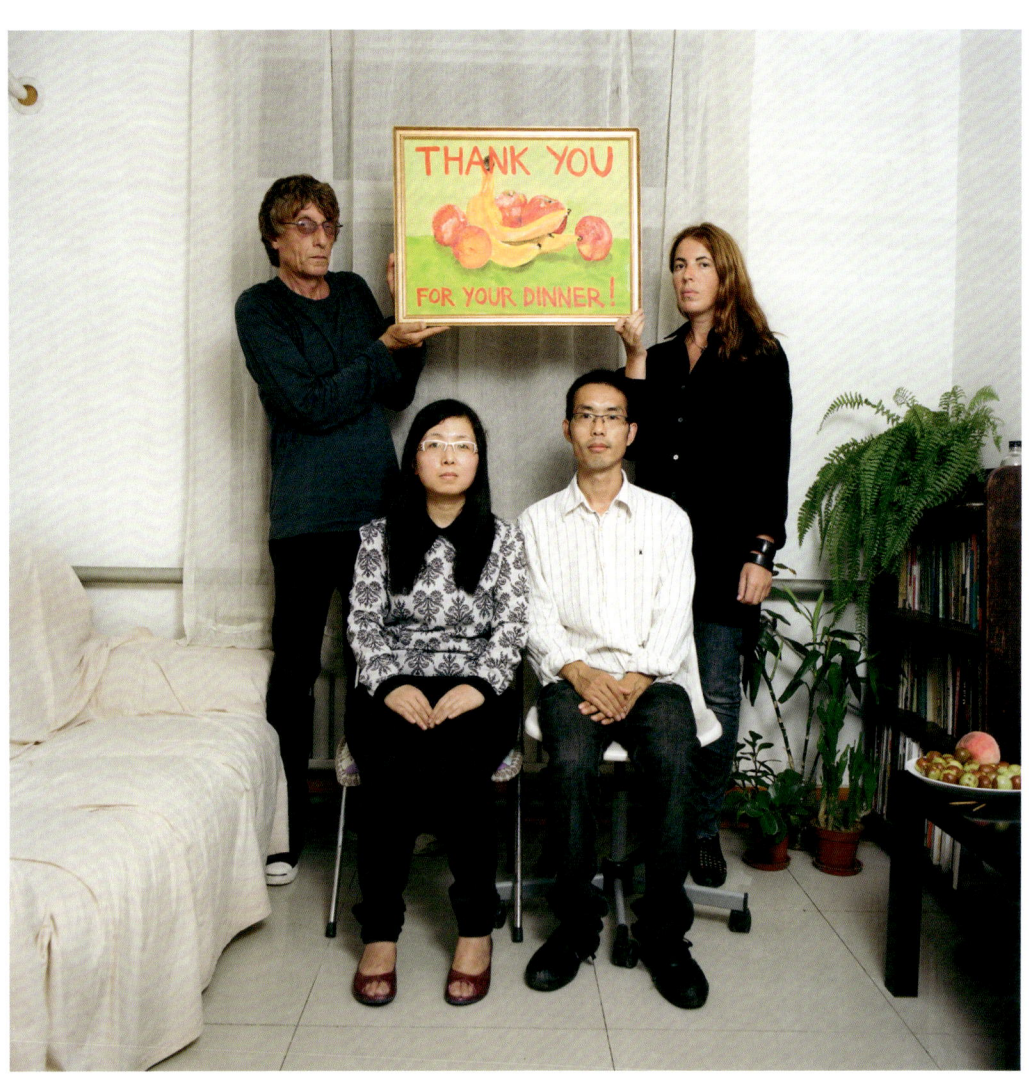

BEIJING, CHINA / SEPTEMBER 17, 2013
Jeff Bliumis, Xunbo Guo, Zongxi Zhang, Alina Bliumis

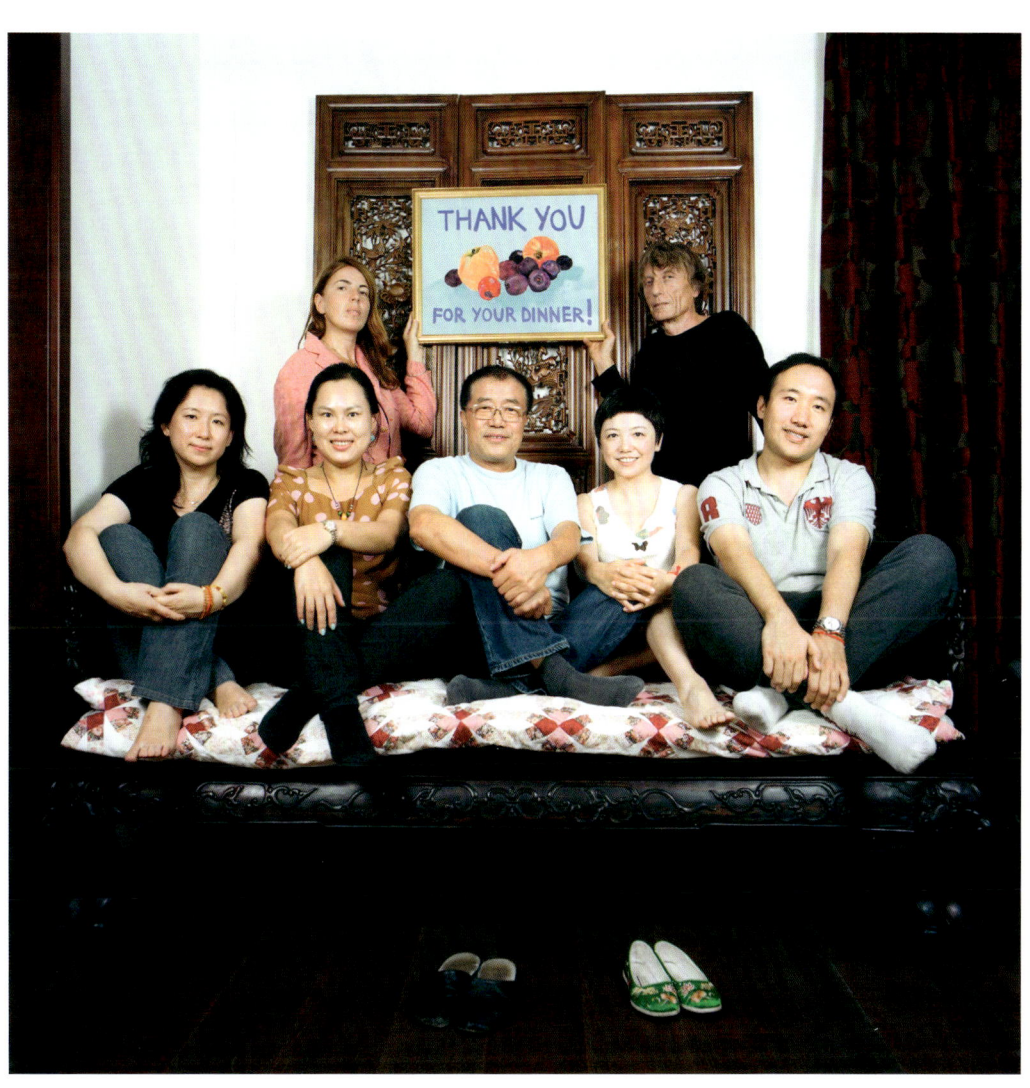

BEIJING, CHINA / SEPTEMBER 20, 2013
Alina Bliumis, May Ren, Abby Wang, Liangjun Xu,
Mini Li, Eric Sun, Jeff Bliumis

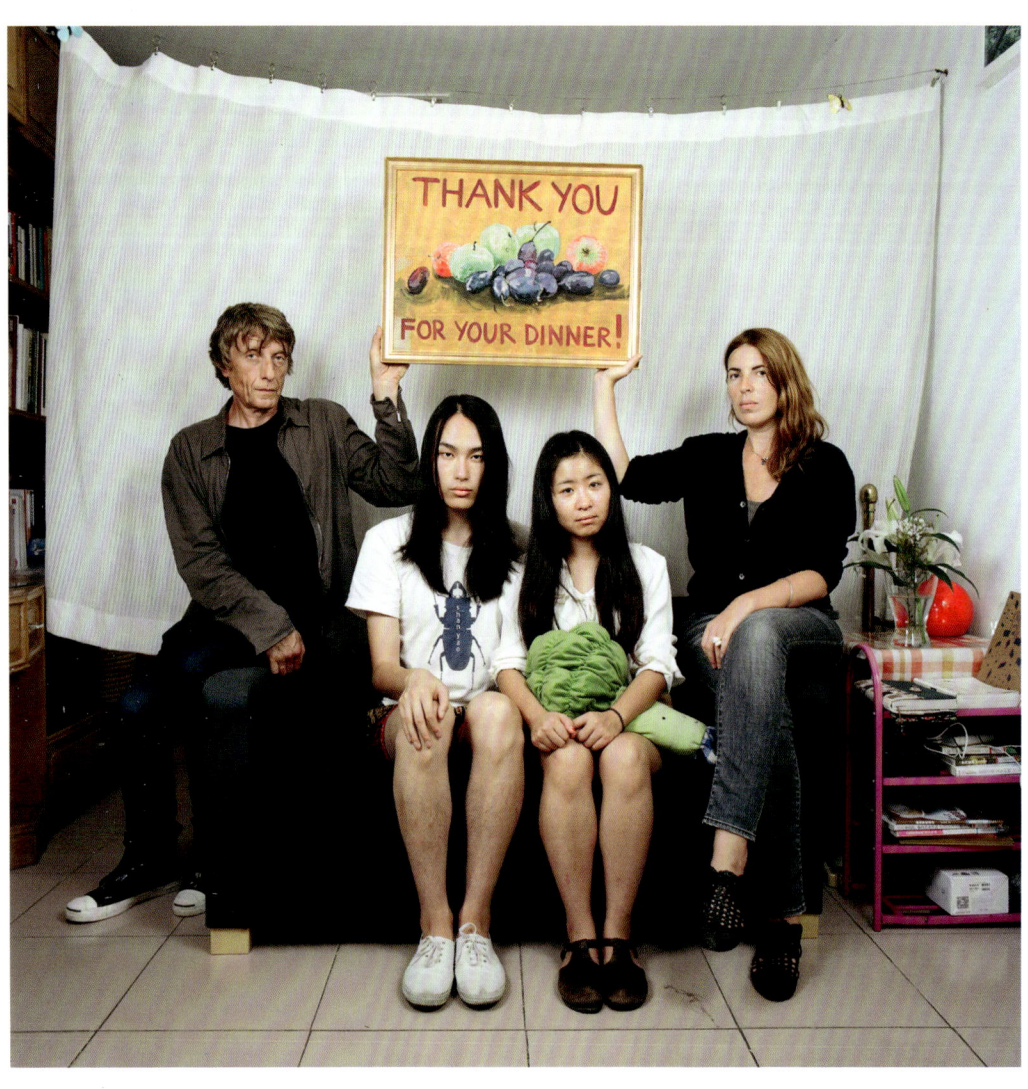

BEIJING, CHINA / SEPTEMBER 20, 2013
Jeff Bliumis, Cao Chao, Wu Xuan, Alina Bliumis

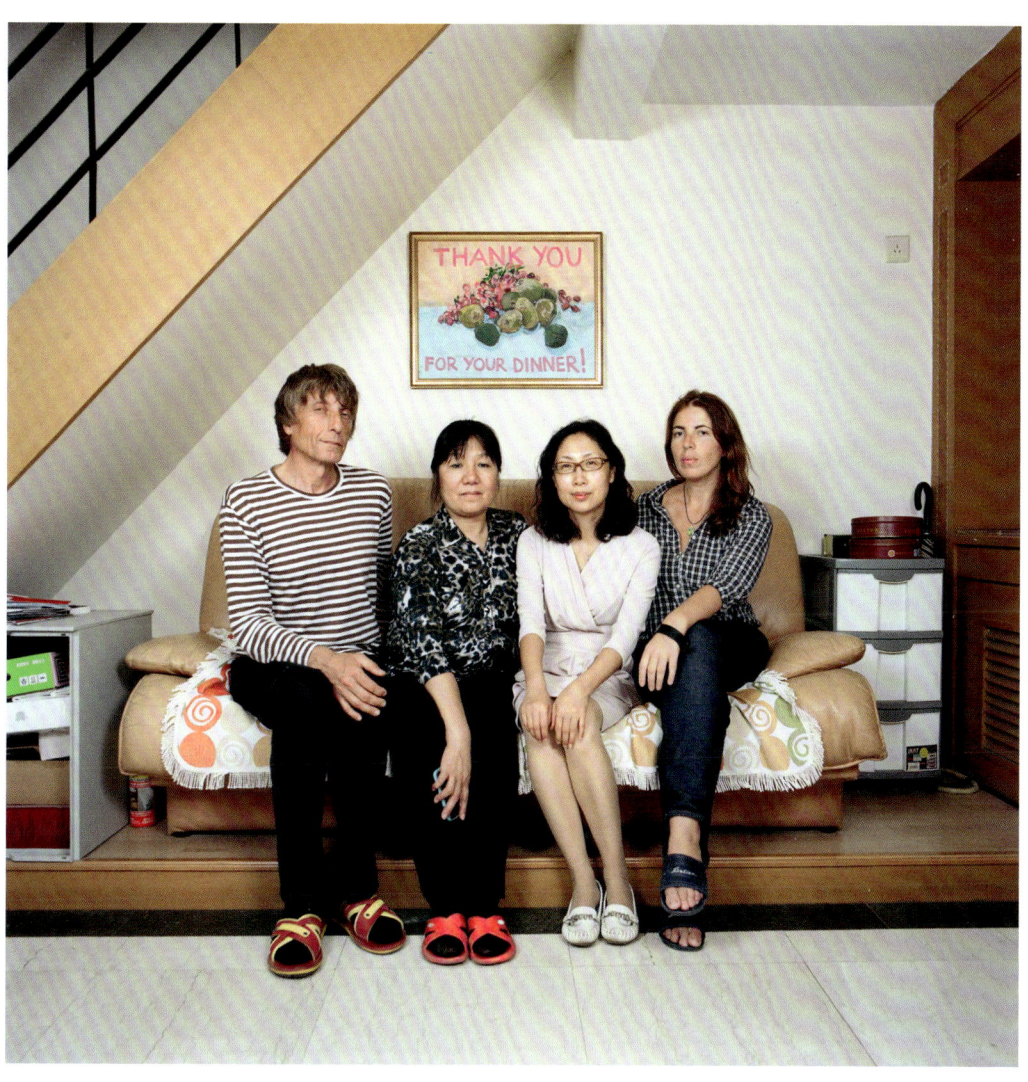

BEIJING, CHINA / SEPTEMBER 21, 2013
Jeff Bliumis, Zhang Hong Ya, XiaoMei Qiu,
Alina Bliumis

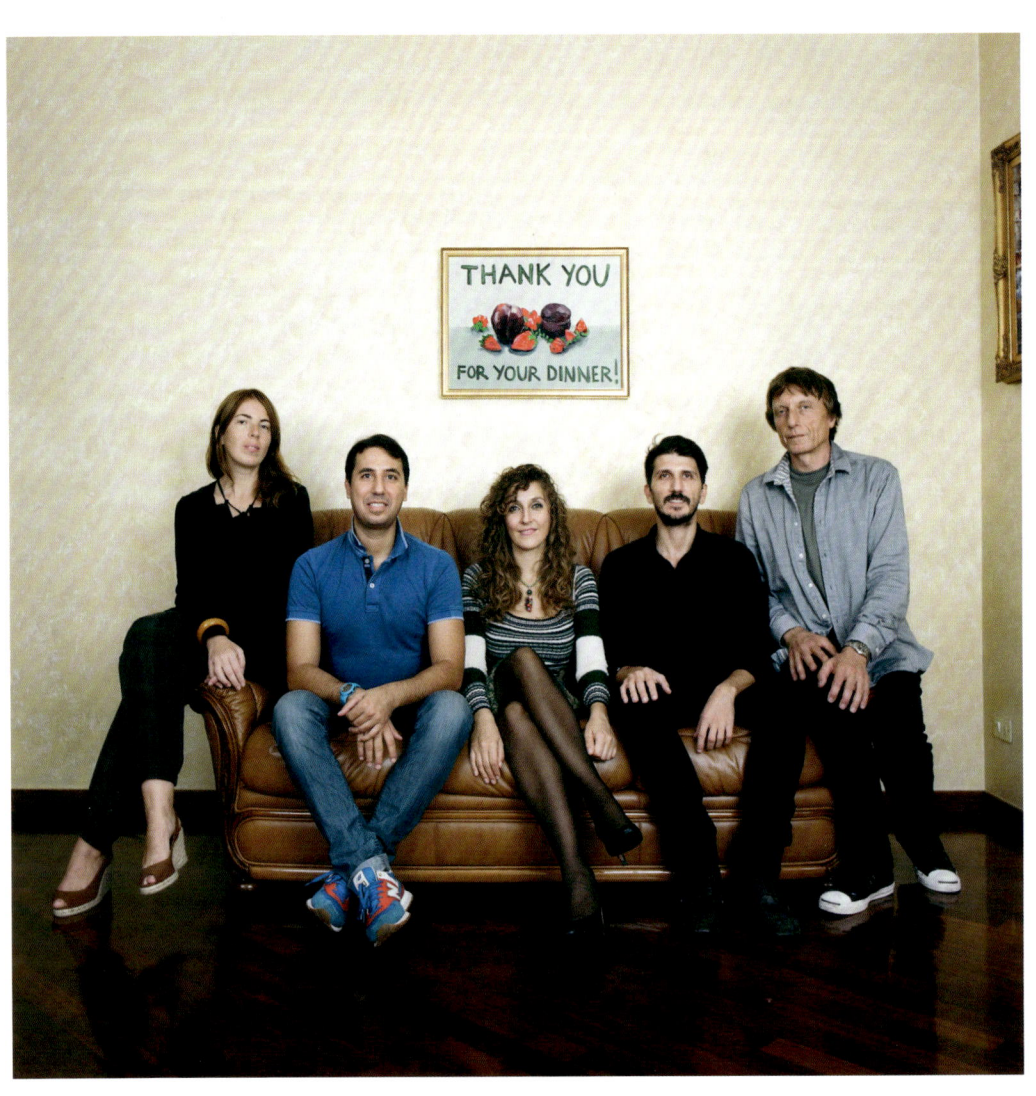

LECCE, ITALY / OCTOBER 11, 2013
Alina Bliumis, Antonio Giulio Baglivi,
Annarita Candeca, Nicola Baglivi, Jeff Bliumis

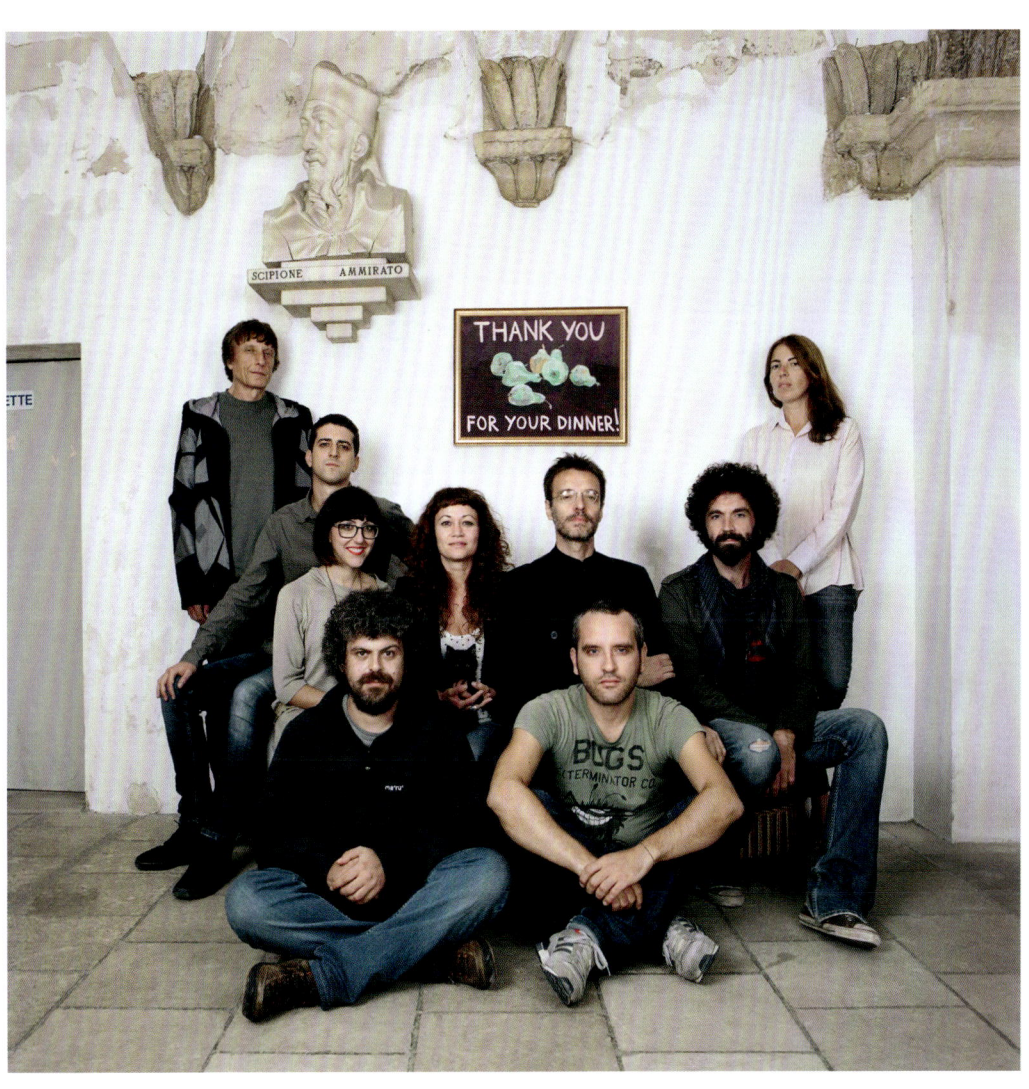

LECCE, ITALY / OCTOBER 12, 2013
Jeff Bliumis, Mattia Epifani, Viviana Bello,
Marcella Buttazzo, Luigi Negro, Federico Bollino,
Mattia Soranzo, Francesco Lefons, Alina Bliumis

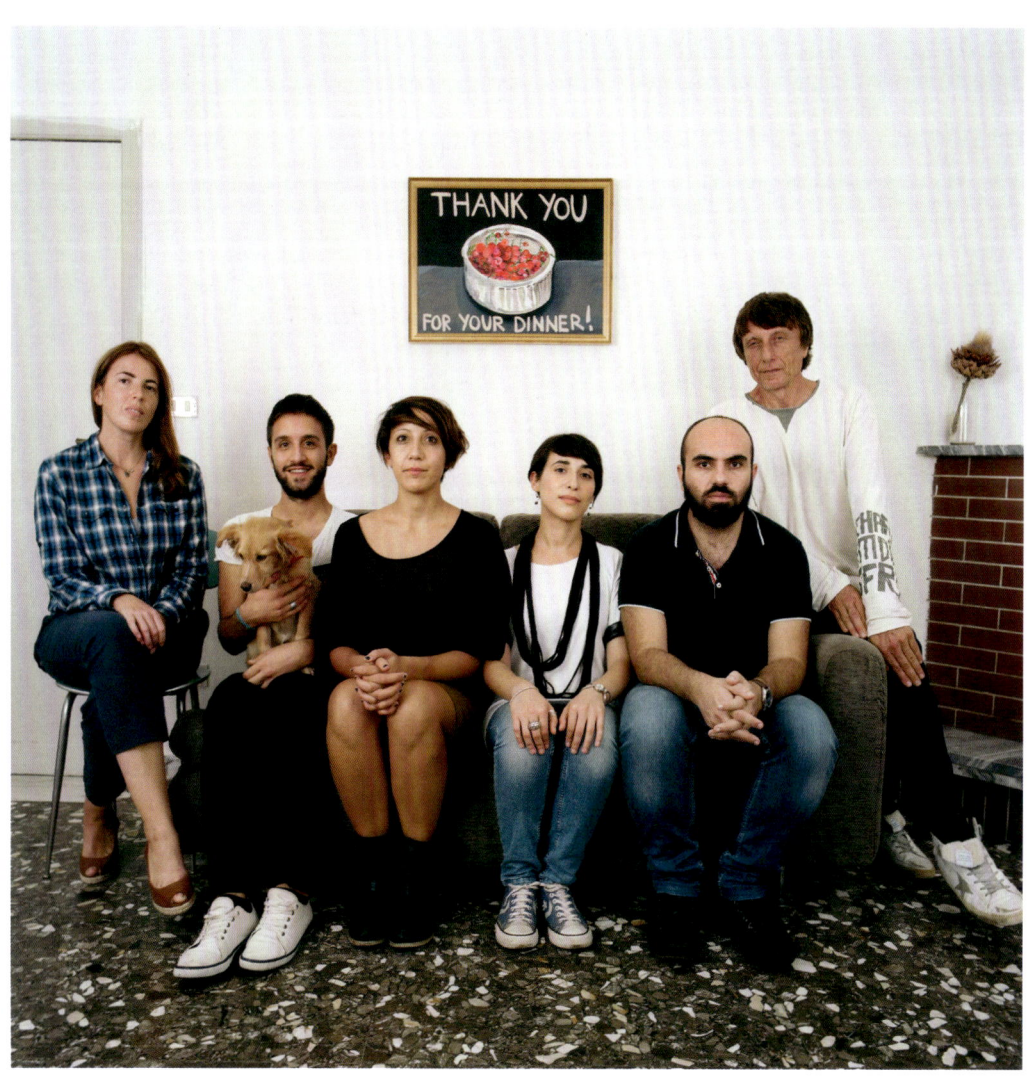

SAN PIETRO IN LAMA, ITALY / OCTOBER 12, 2013
Alina Bliumis, Marco Rollo, Dean, Alessia Rollo,
Valeria Raho, Antonio Peciccia, Jeff Bliumis

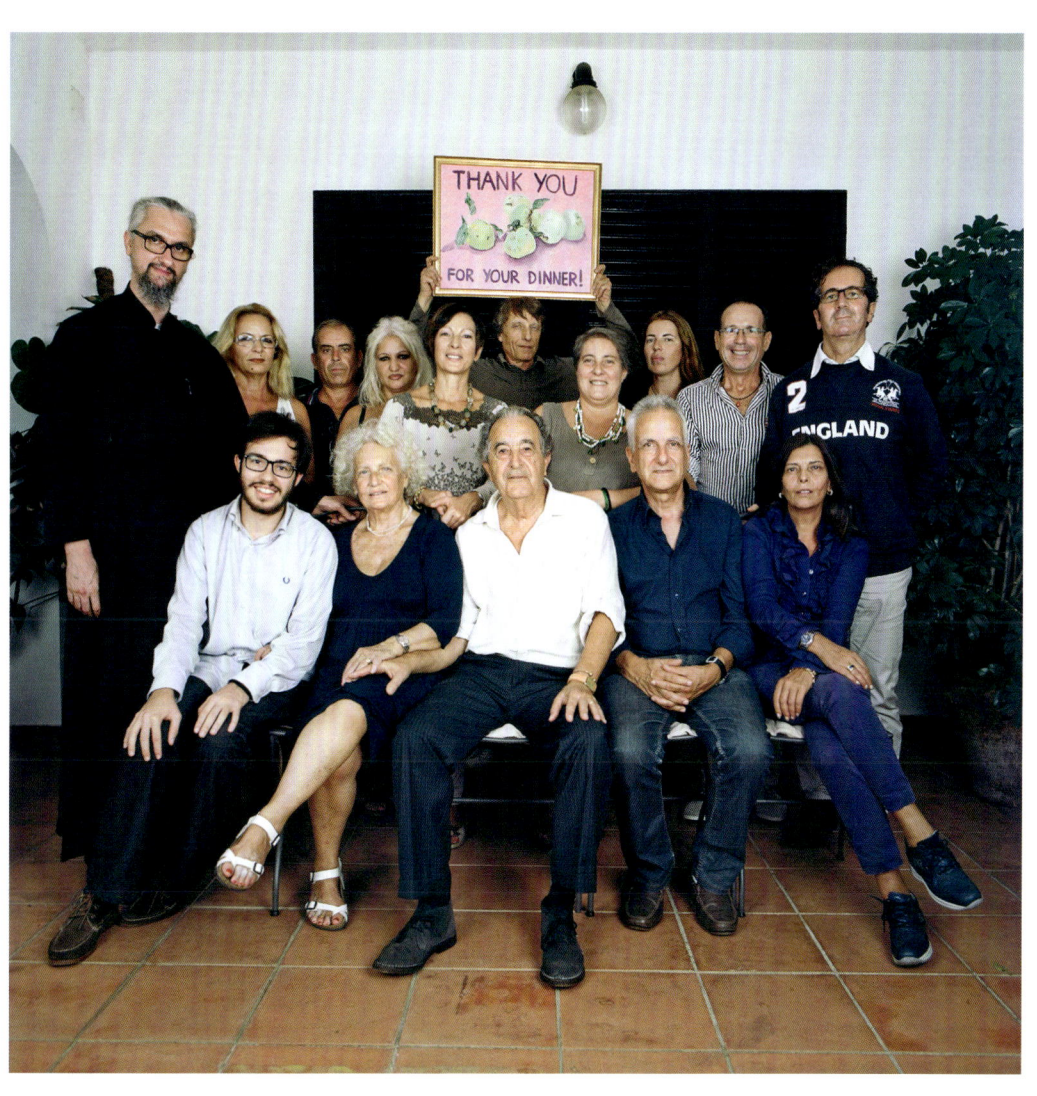

LECCE, ITALY / OCTOBER 13, 2013
Father Arsenios, Loredana Mangia, Luciana
Pomarico, Gaetano Pomarico, Francesco Giordano,
Anna Rita Della Bona, Gianni Colucci, Lory Della
Bona, Giulio Colucci, Francesco Russo, Kaci Eduard,
Brunga Vittoria, Brunga Luisa, Alina Bliumis,
Jeff Bliumis

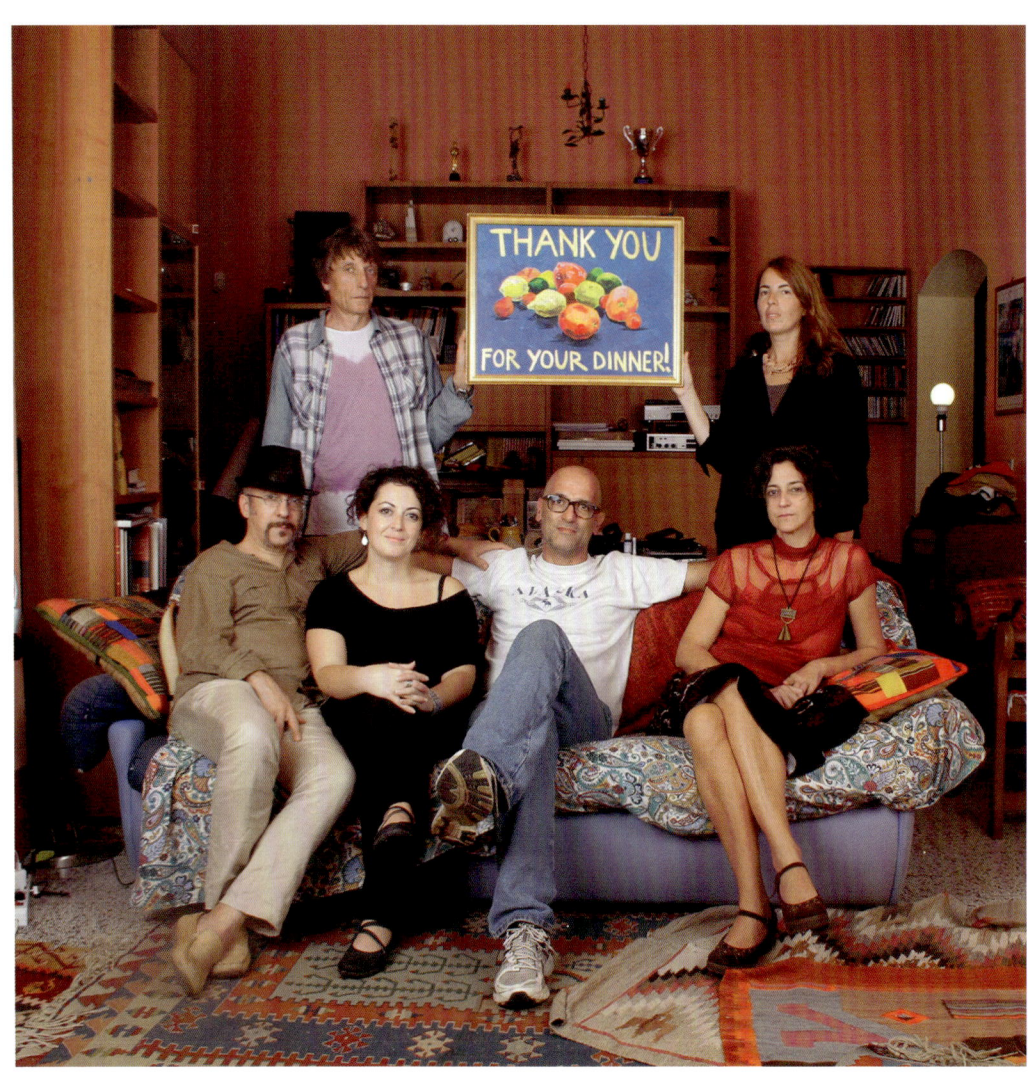

LECCE, ITALY / OCTOBER 13, 2013
Jeff Bliumis, Massimiliano Manieri, Simona Schirinzi,
Gabriele Molendini, Anna Lopalco, Alina Bliumis

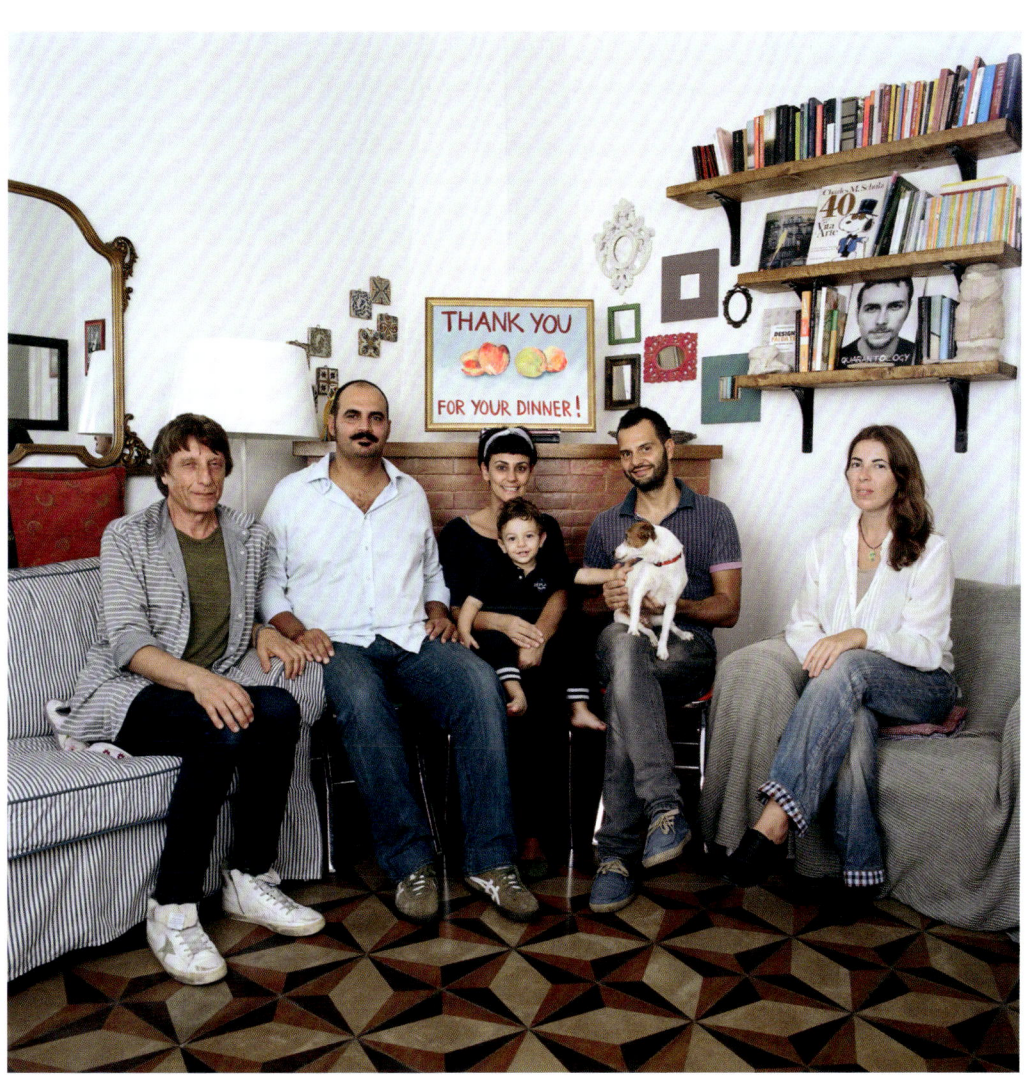

LECCE, ITALY / OCTOBER 14, 2013
Jeff Bliumis, Paolo La Peruta, Marica La Peruta,
Marco Petrelli, Michele Ferdinando Petrelli,
Matilde, Alina Bliumis

53

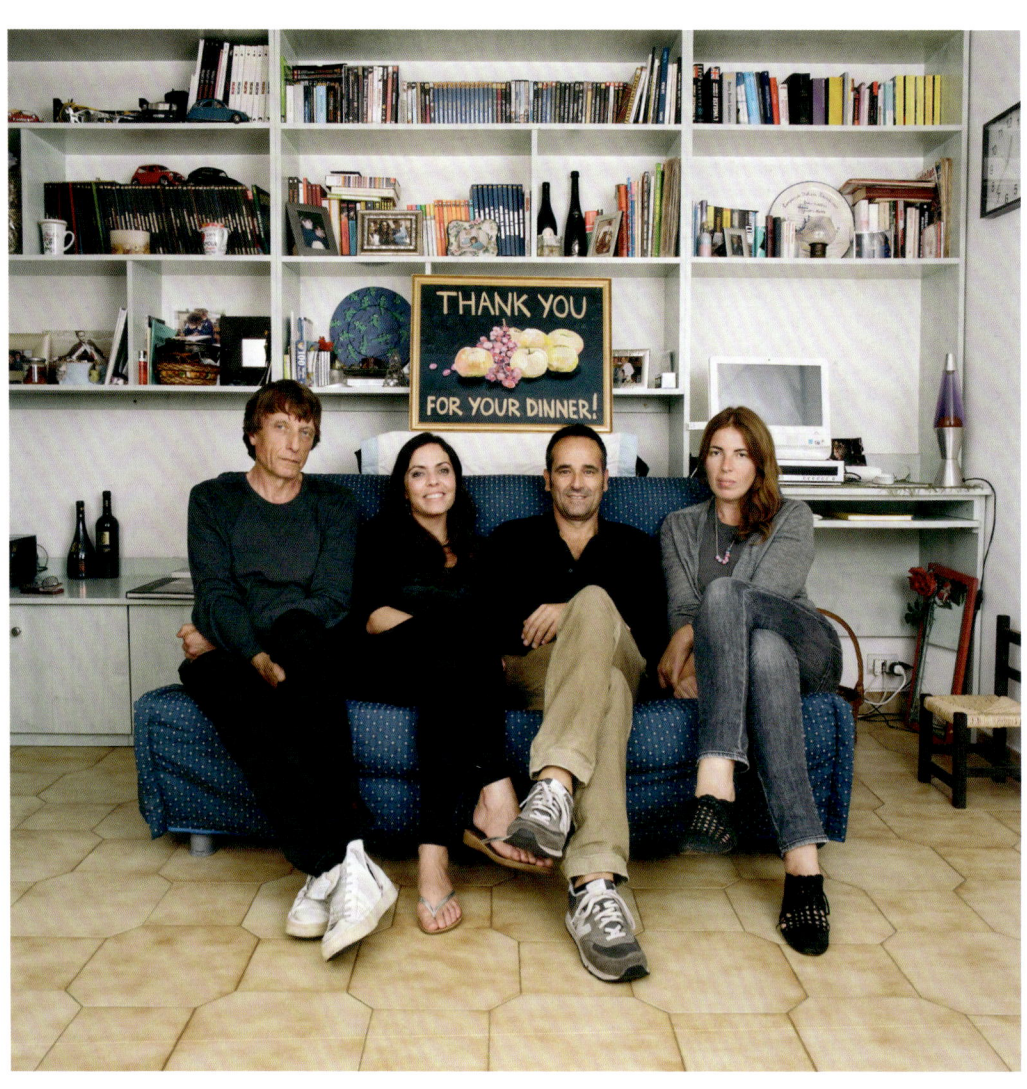

LECCE, ITALY / OCTOBER 14, 2013
Jeff Bliumis, Francesca Nannini, Alessandro Gravili,
Alina Bliumis

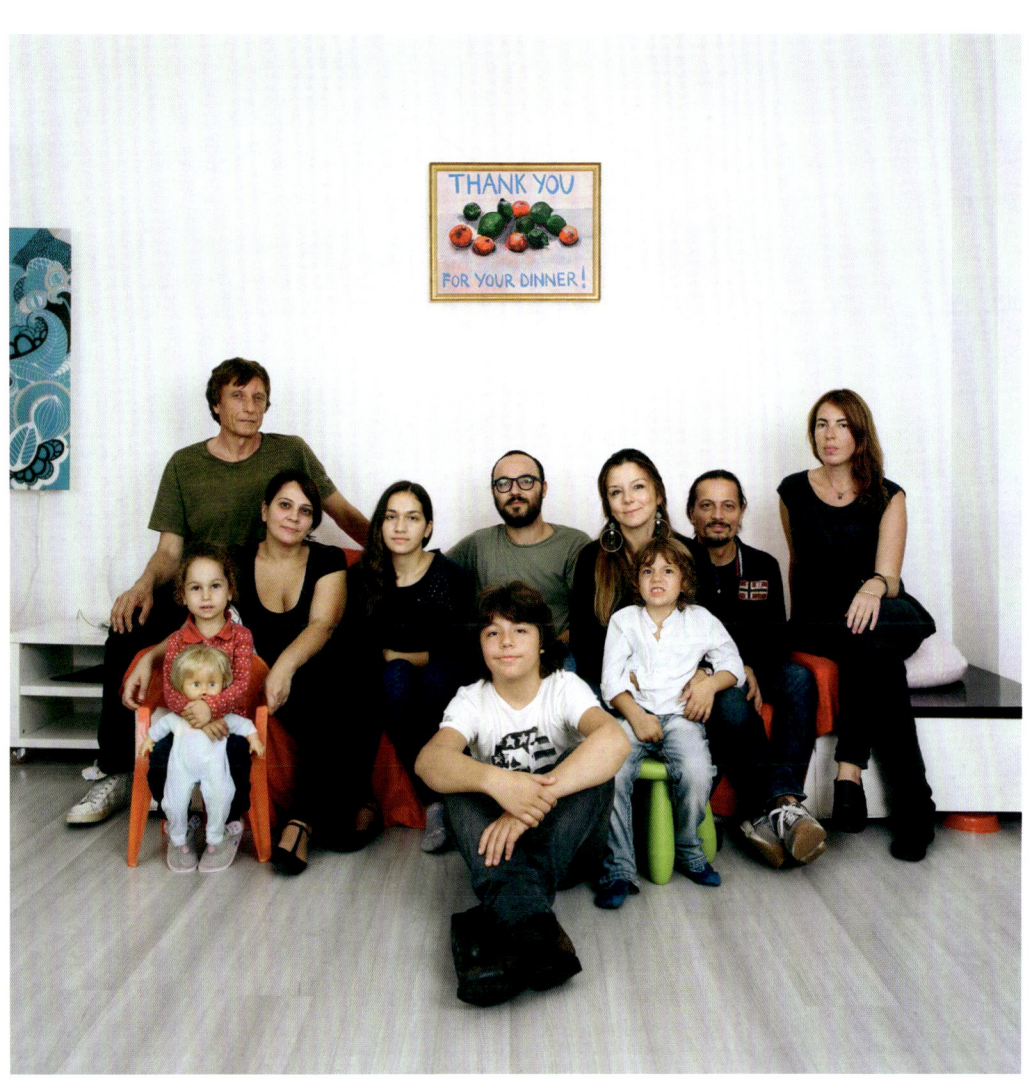

LECCE, ITALY / OCTOBER 14, 2013
Jeff Bliumis, Caterina Scaiera, Simona Cleopazzo,
Micol Grasso, Danilo Scaiera, Melissa Perrone,
Giuseppe Guerrieri, Ernesto Guerrieri,
Edoardo Guerrieri, Alina Bliumis

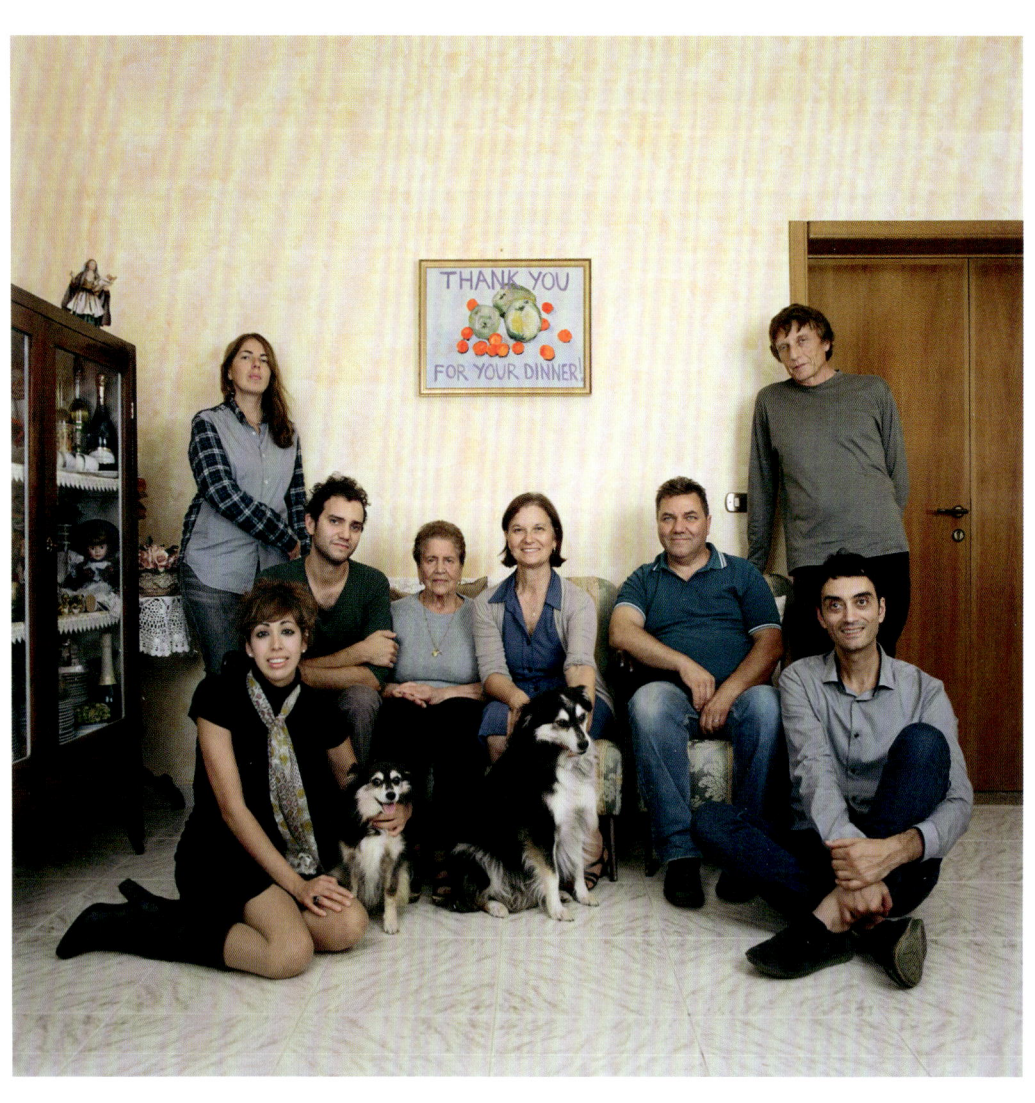

LECCE, ITALY / OCTOBER 16, 2013
Alina Bliumis, Giulia Ciccarese, Orlando, Sofia,
Gianluca Rollo, Nonna Tetta, Mirella Aierba,
Giuseppe Rollo, Francesco Maggiore, Jeff Bliumis

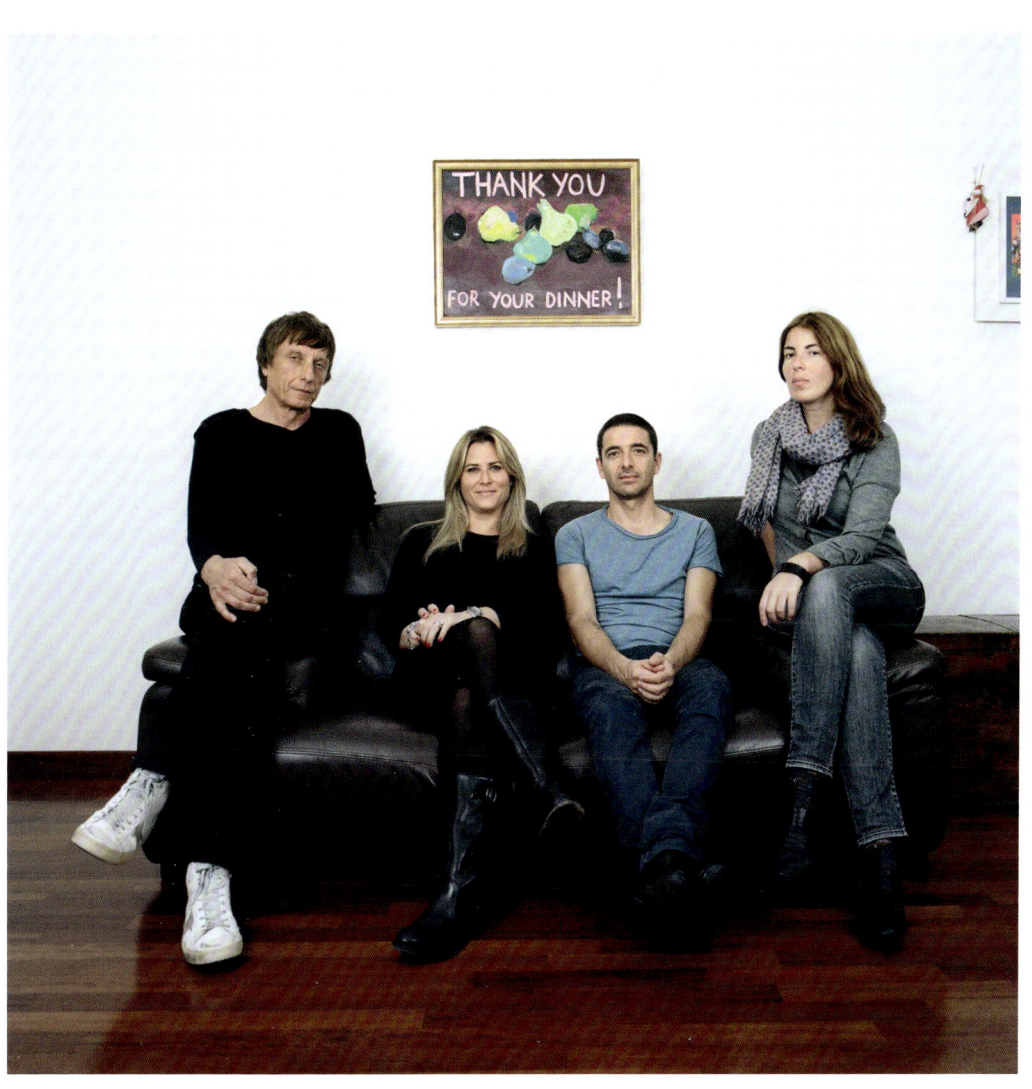

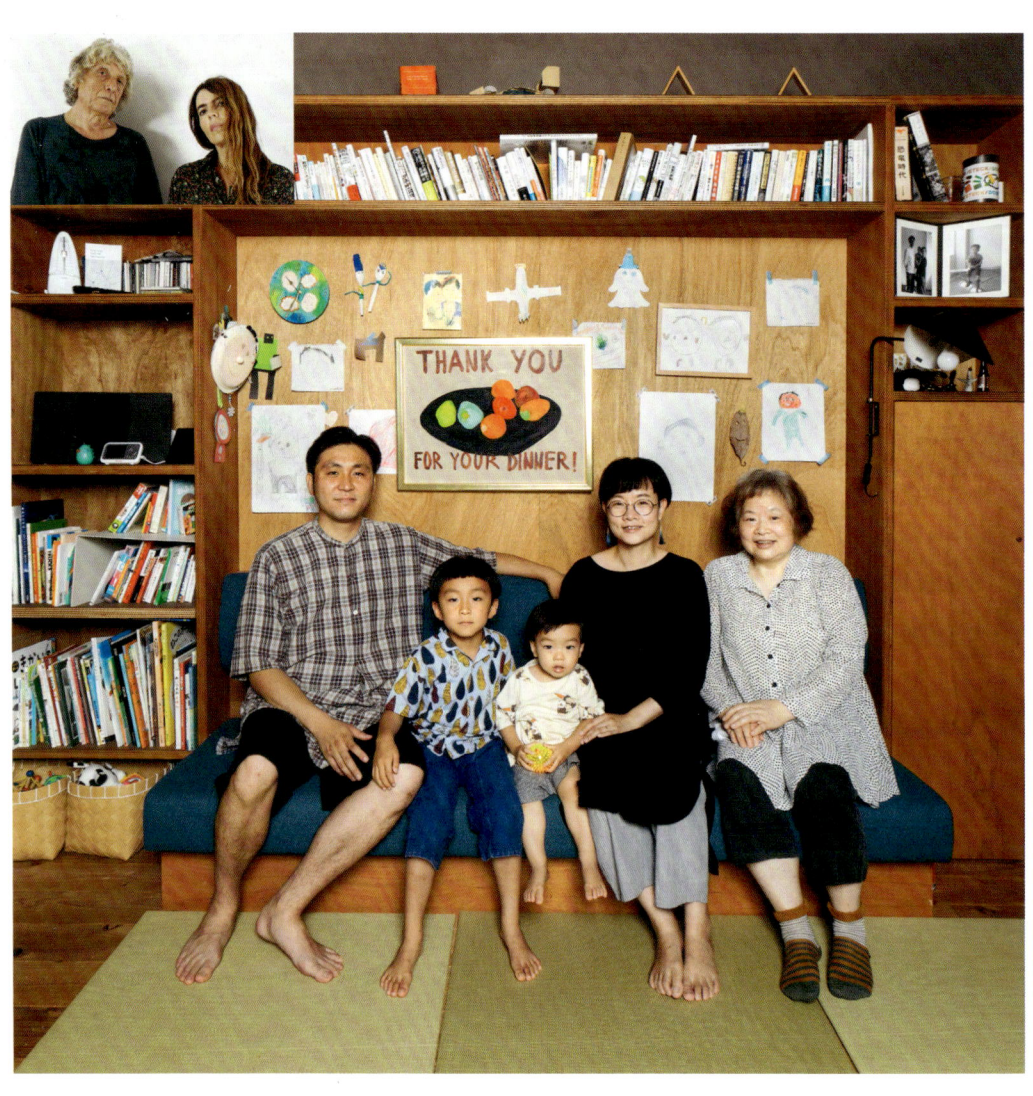

TOKYO, JAPAN / JULY 3, 2021
Mitsuyoshi Miyazaki, Terumichi Miyazaki,
Takumichi Miyazaki, Pinpin Gu, Xiaoqing Zheng,
Alina Bliumis, Jeff Bliumis

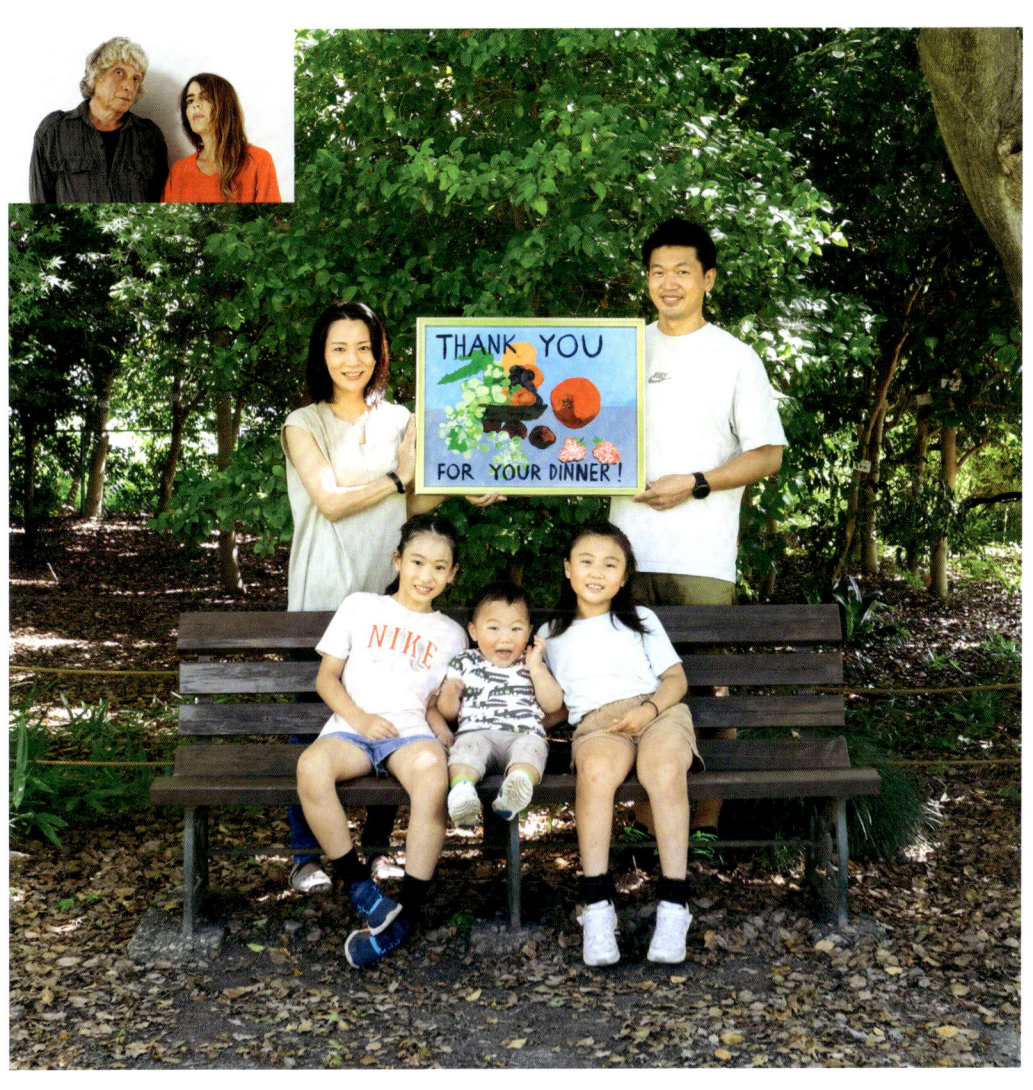

TOKYO, JAPAN / JULY 3, 2021
Naosuke, Ayako, Anne, Kiko, Tomo,
Alina Bliumis, Jeff Bliumis

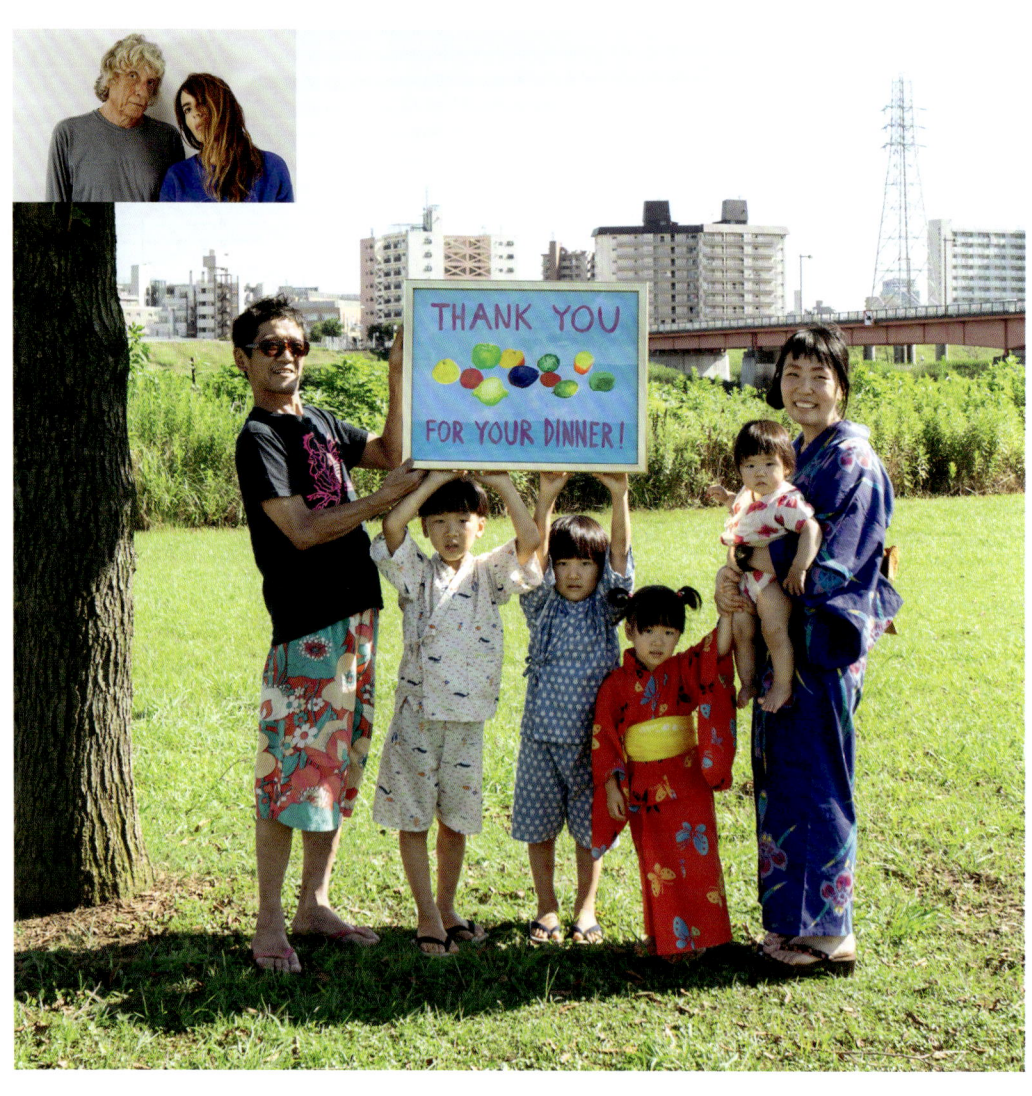

TOKYO, JAPAN / JULY 3, 2021
Hayashi Shinji, Yui, Chiyo, Yano, Waka,
Suzu, Alina Bliumis, Jeff Bliumis

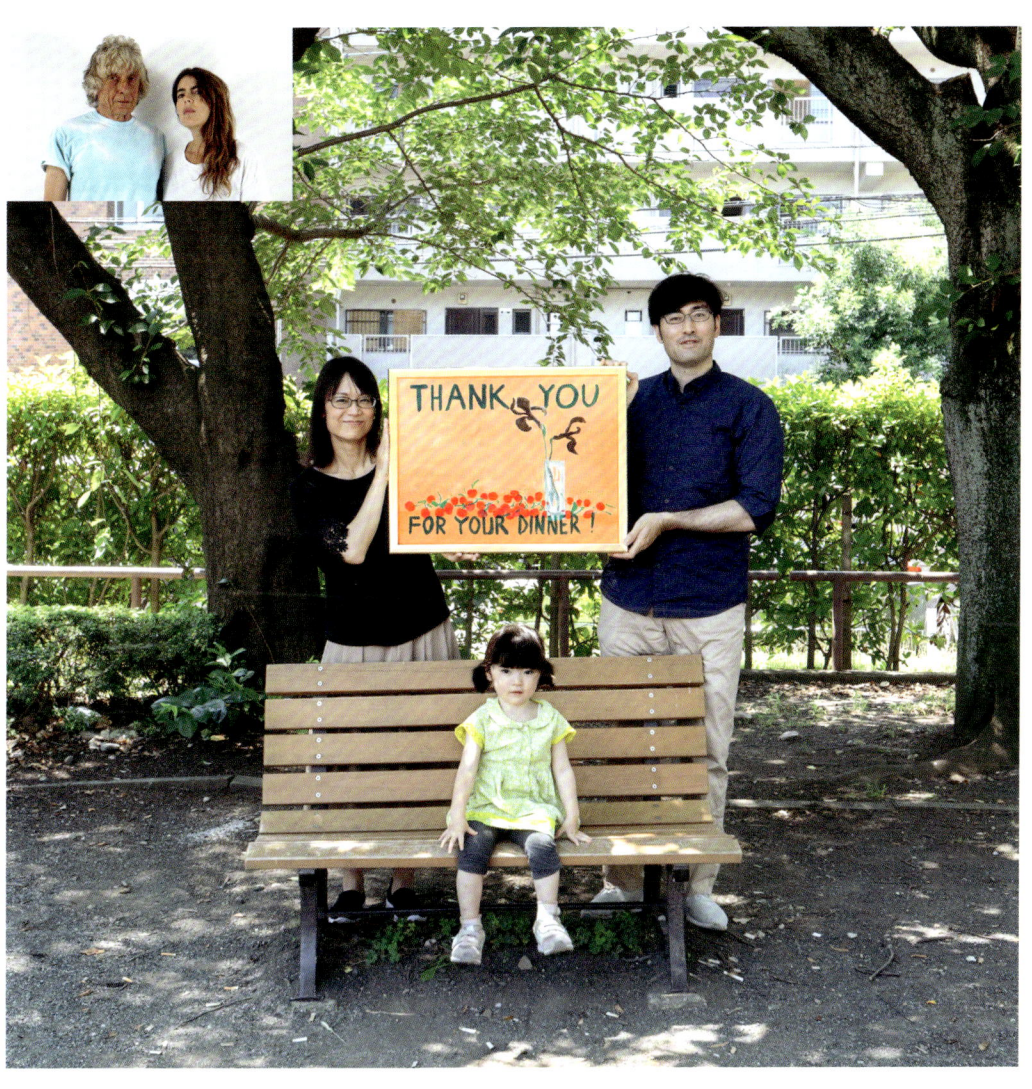

TOKYO, JAPAN / JULY 4, 2021
Sakura Family, Maki, Aki, Tsumugi,
Alina Bliumis, Jeff Bliumis

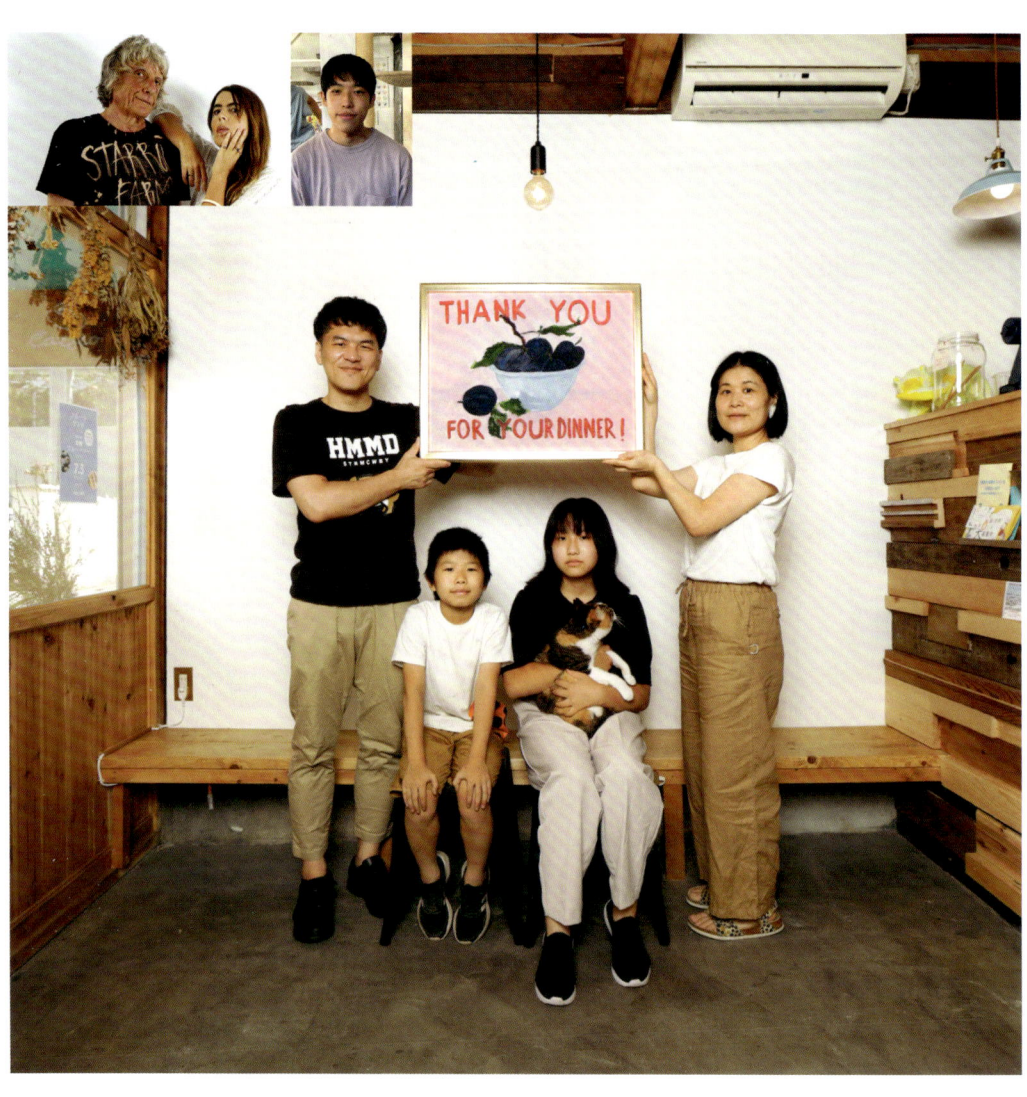

TOKYO, JAPAN / JULY 4, 2021
Hiroshi Abe, Naoko Abe, Haruki Abe, Nico Abe,
Kousuke Abe, Alina Bliumis, Jeff Bliumis

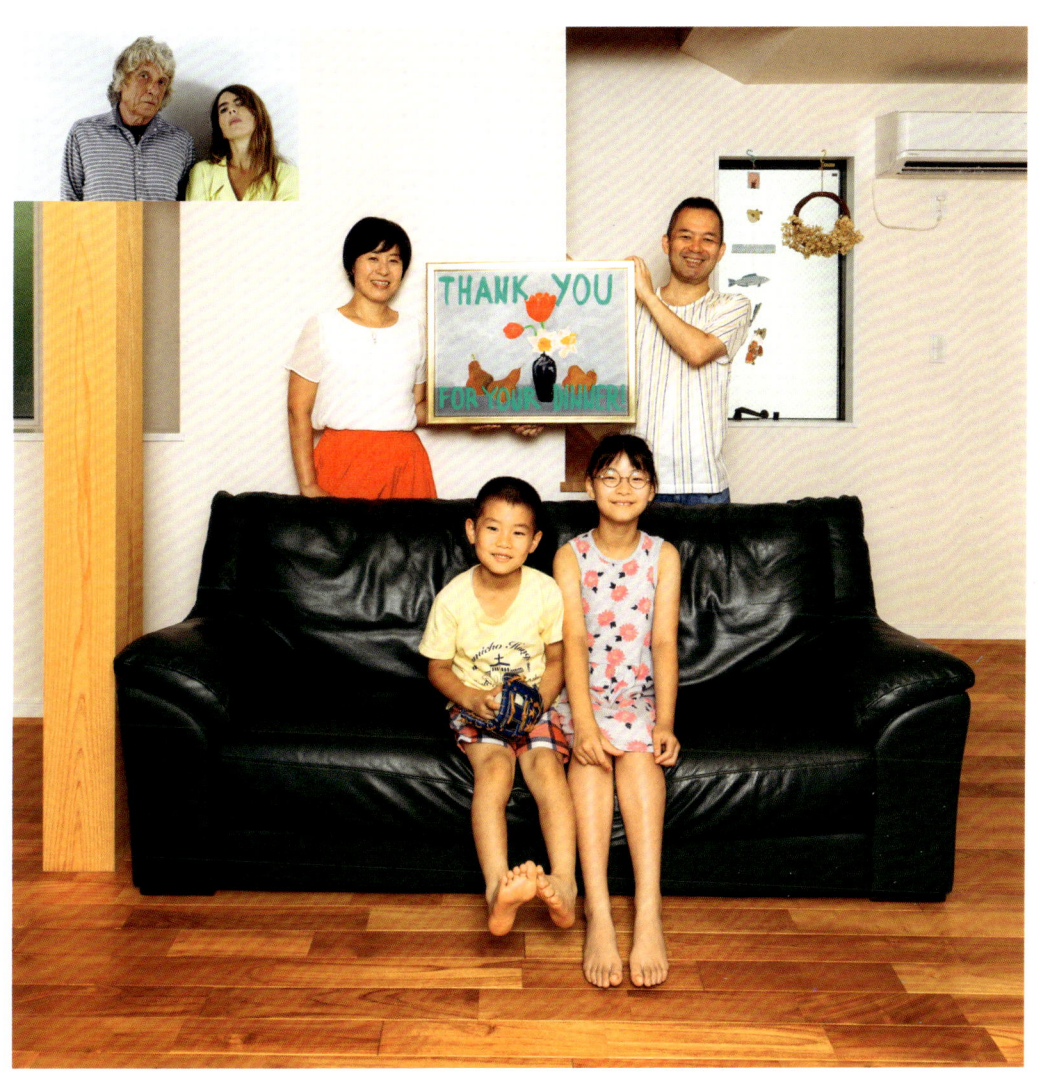

TOKYO, JAPAN / JULY 4, 2021
The Kaneoyas, Alina Bliumis, Jeff Bliumis

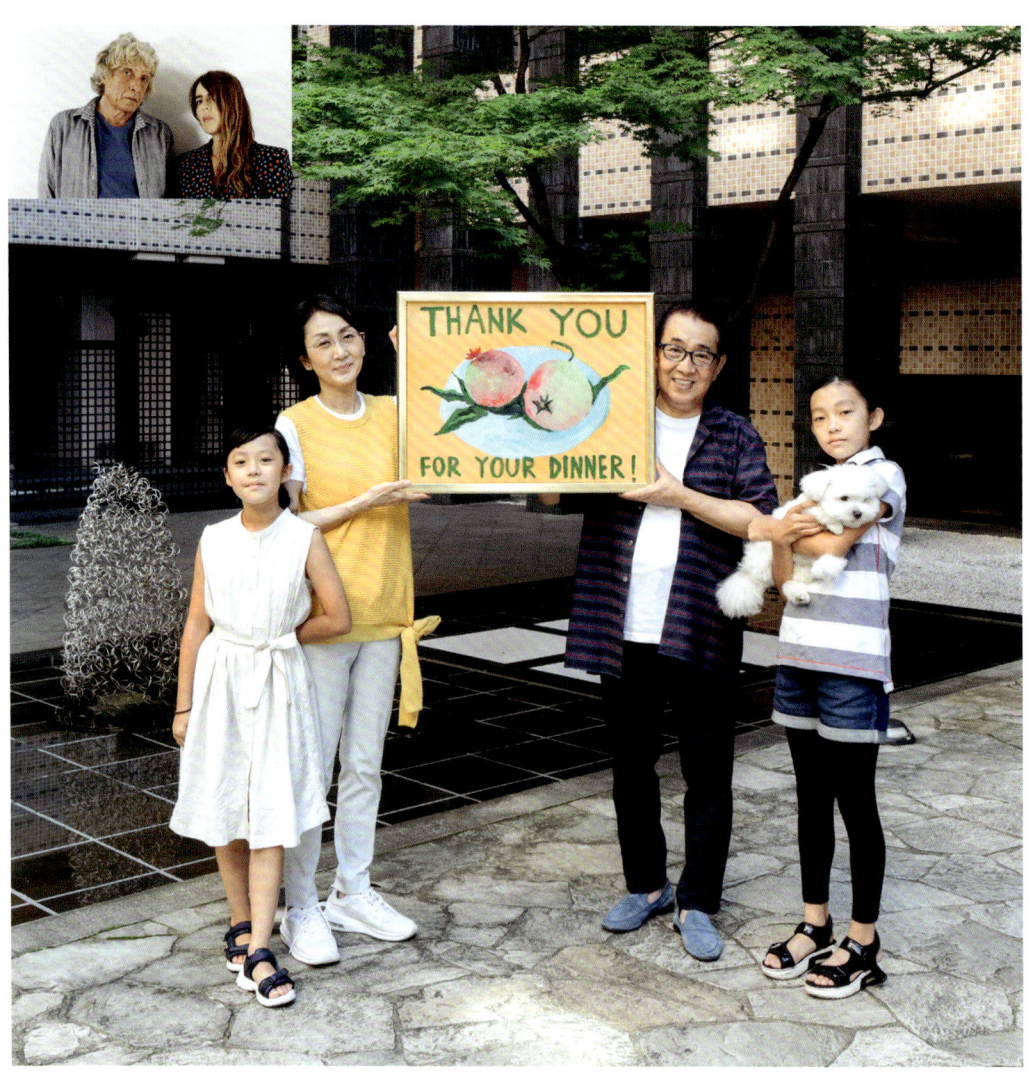

TOKYO, JAPAN / JULY 10, 2021
Shimpei, Yumi, Fukumi, Ayami, Wito,
Alina Bliumis, Jeff Bliumis

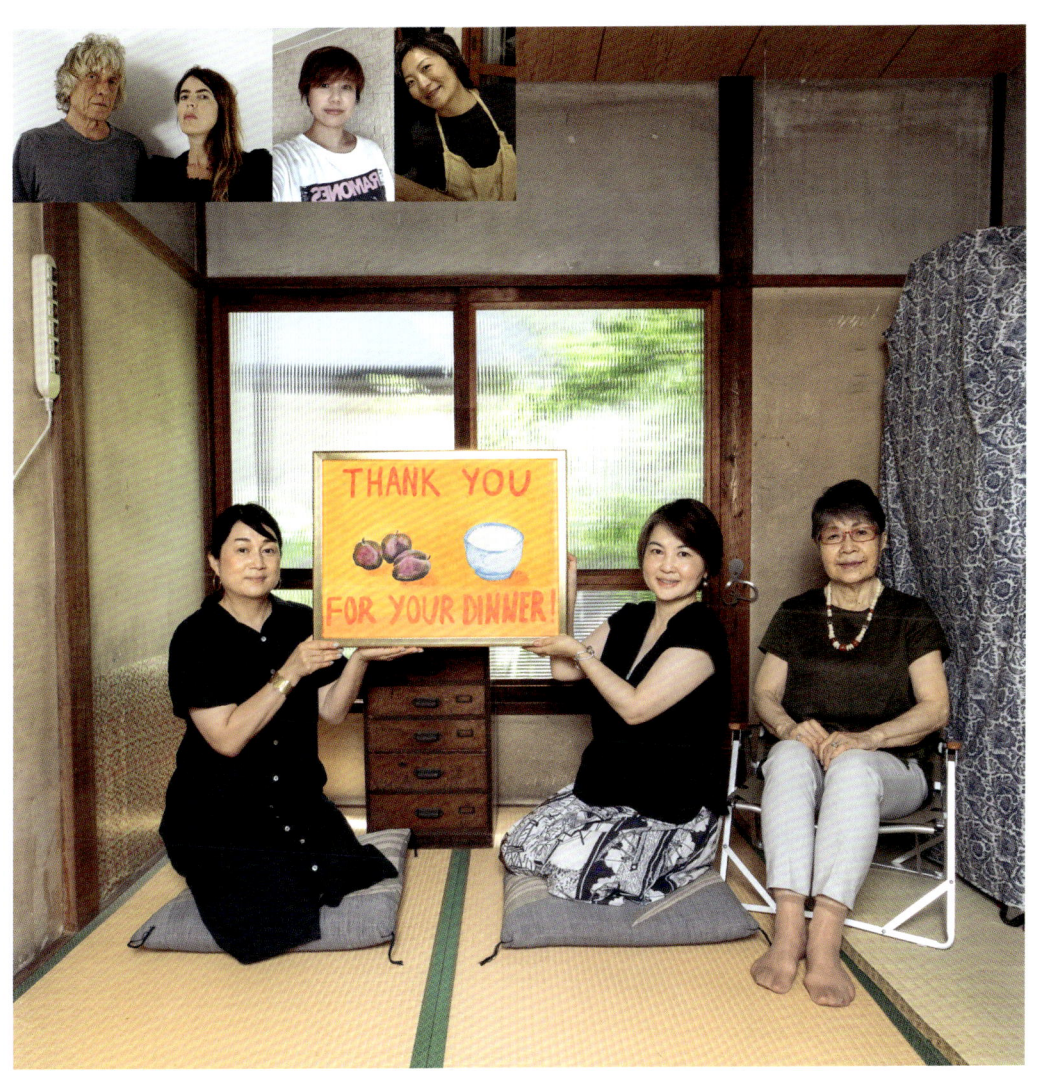

TOKYO, JAPAN / JULY 10, 2021
Suzuki Family, Ms. Minami, Ms. Takahashi,
Ms. Akutsu, Alina Bliumis, Jeff Bliumis

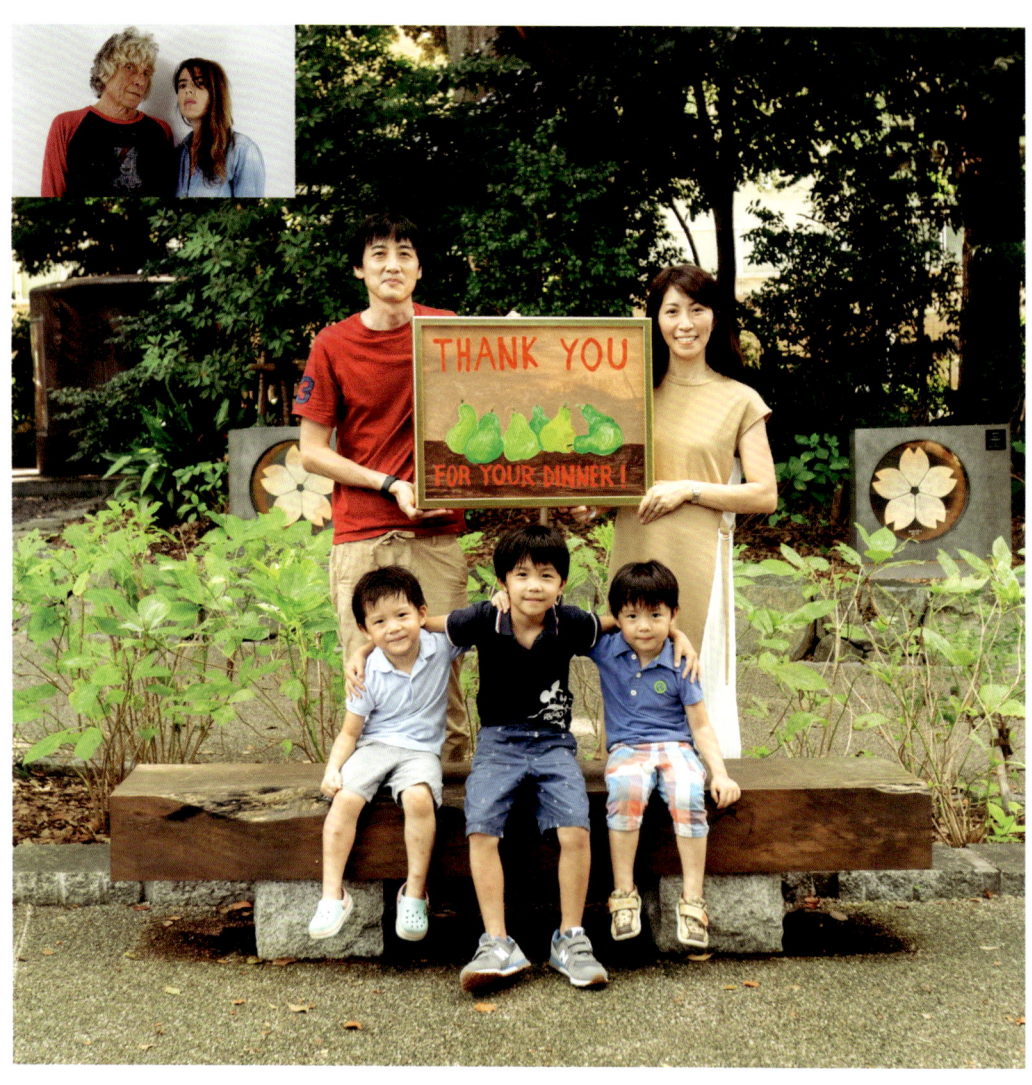

TOKYO, JAPAN / JULY 11, 2021
Horibe Family, Alina Bliumis, Jeff Bliumis

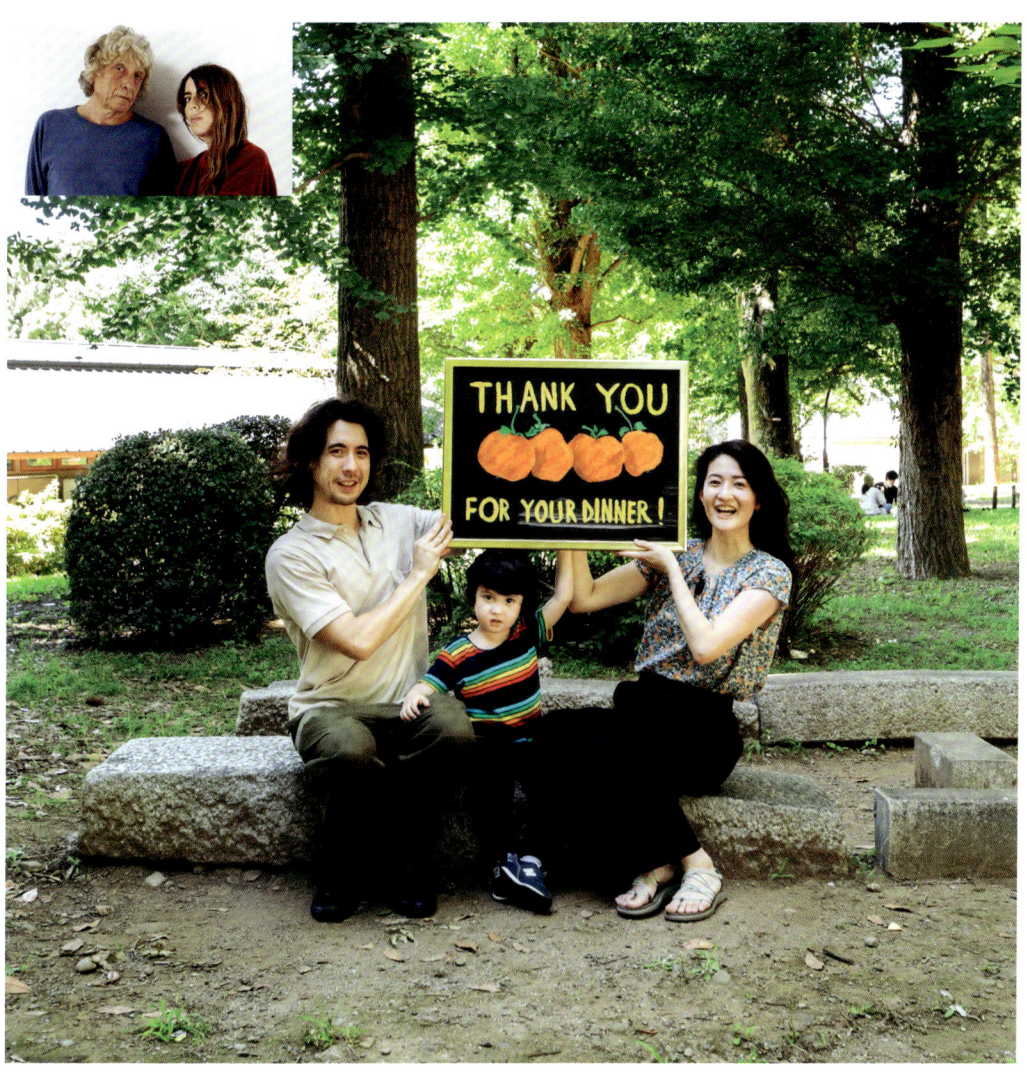

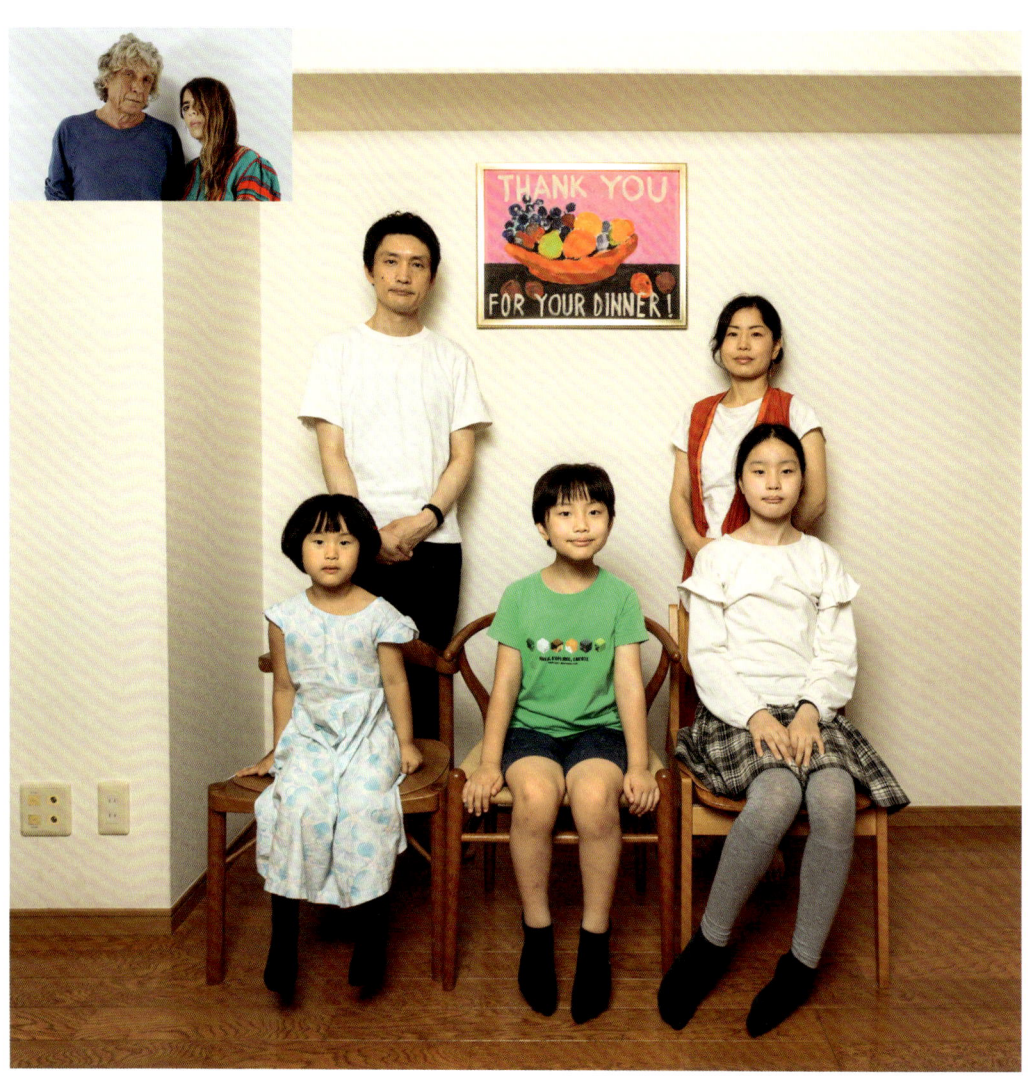

TOKYO, JAPAN / JULY 18, 2021
Kawasaki Family, Alina Bliumis, Jeff Bliumis

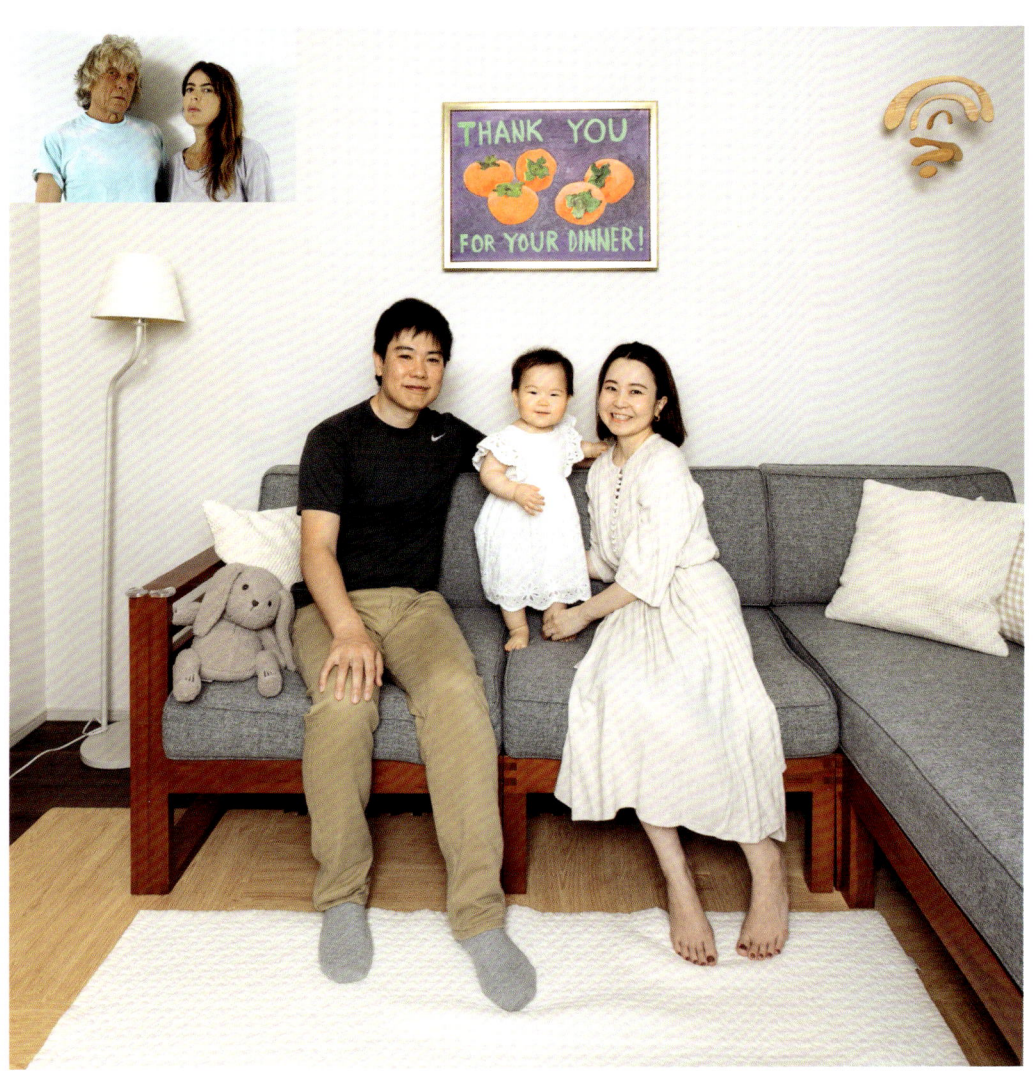

TOKYO, JAPAN / JULY 18, 2021
Tomomi Numakura, Mima, Mayuko,
Alina Bliumis, Jeff Bliumis

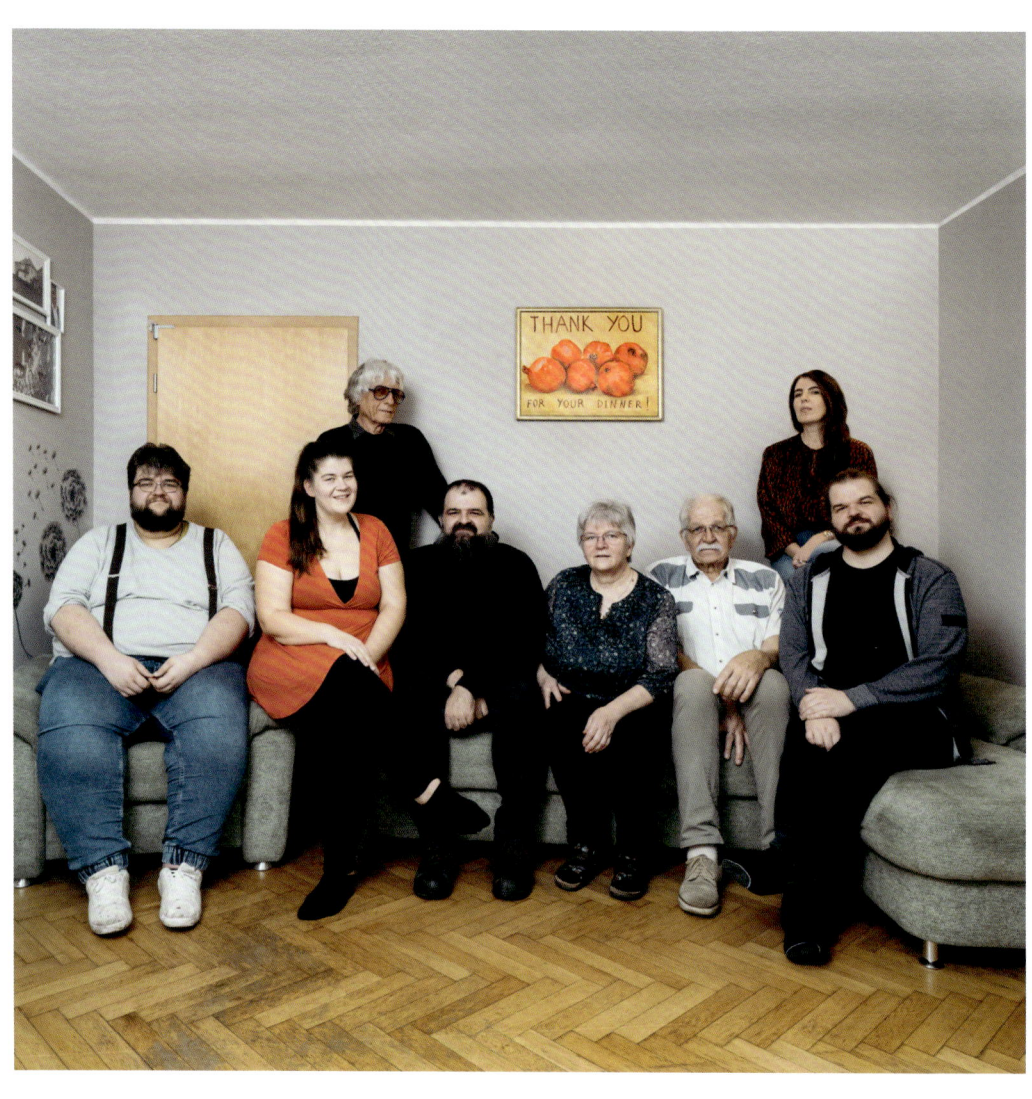

SELM, GERMANY / FEBRUARY 2, 2025
Sven Hoppe, Marc Hoppe, Jeff Bliumis,
Björn Hoppe, Heike Hoppe, Hans Hoppe,
Silke Hoppe, Alina Bliumis

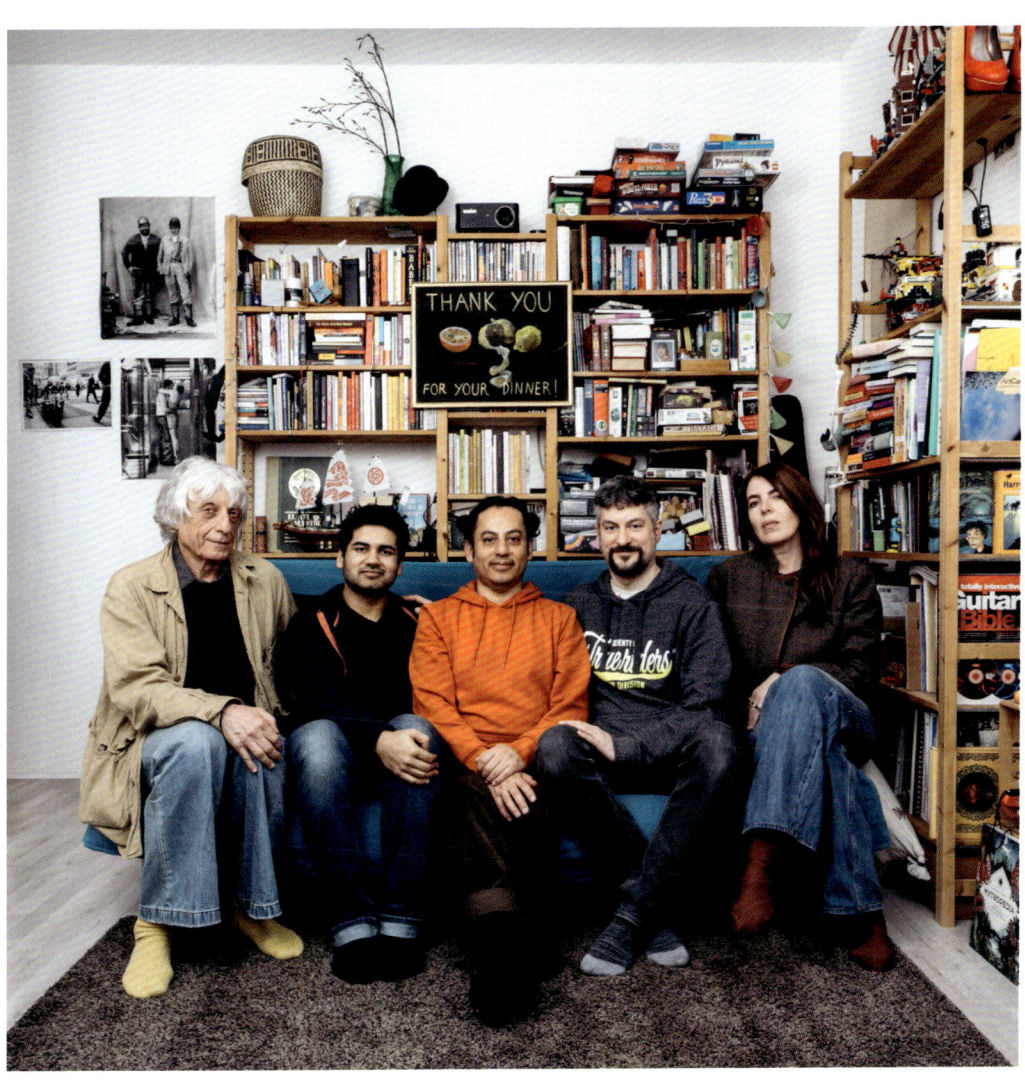

BOCHUM, GERMANY / FEBRUARY 2, 2025
Jeff Bliumis, Aakash Rajawat, Alexis Rodríguez
Suárez, Torben Müller, Alina Bliumis

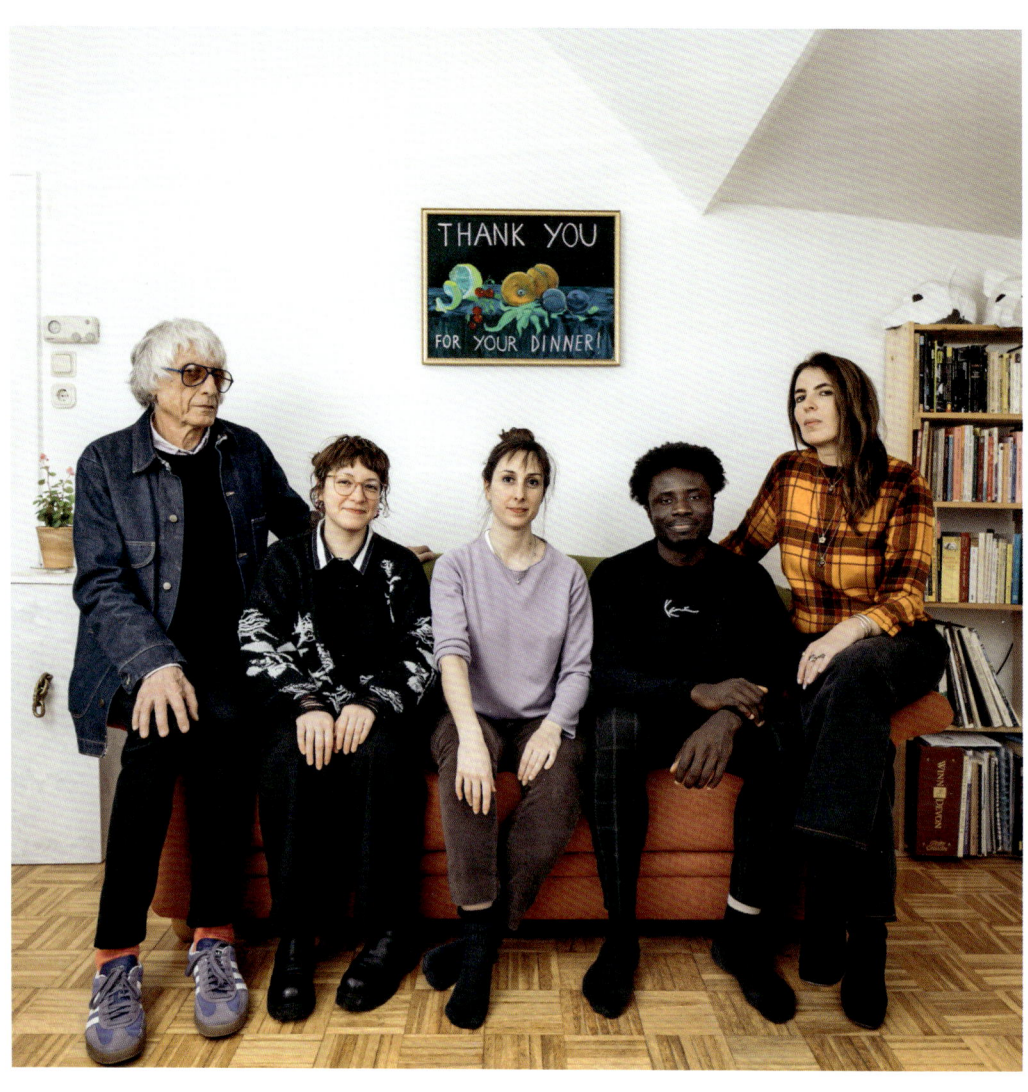

DORTMUND, GERMANY / FEBRUARY 4, 2025
Jeff Bliumis, Florencia Alonso, Elena Tilli,
Charles Osen Mensah, Alina Bliumis

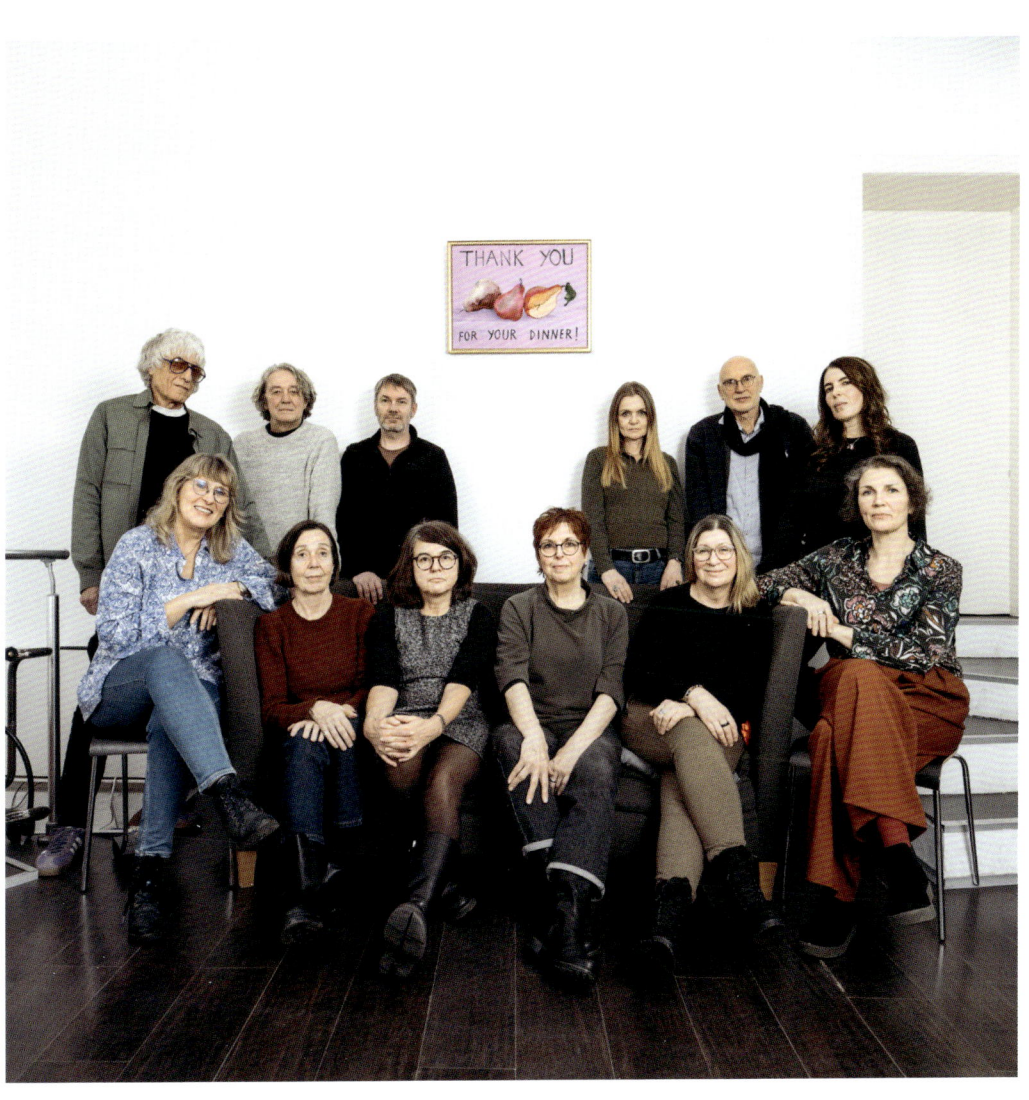

DORTMUND, GERMANY / FEBRUARY 5, 2025
Jeff Bliumis, Gerhard Gruschchyz, Andreas Gutz,
Silke Hempel, Wolfgang Niehall, Alina Bliumis,
Susanne Requardt, Birgit Mattern, Anke König,
Cornelia Studt, Heike Wulf, Ina Rateniek

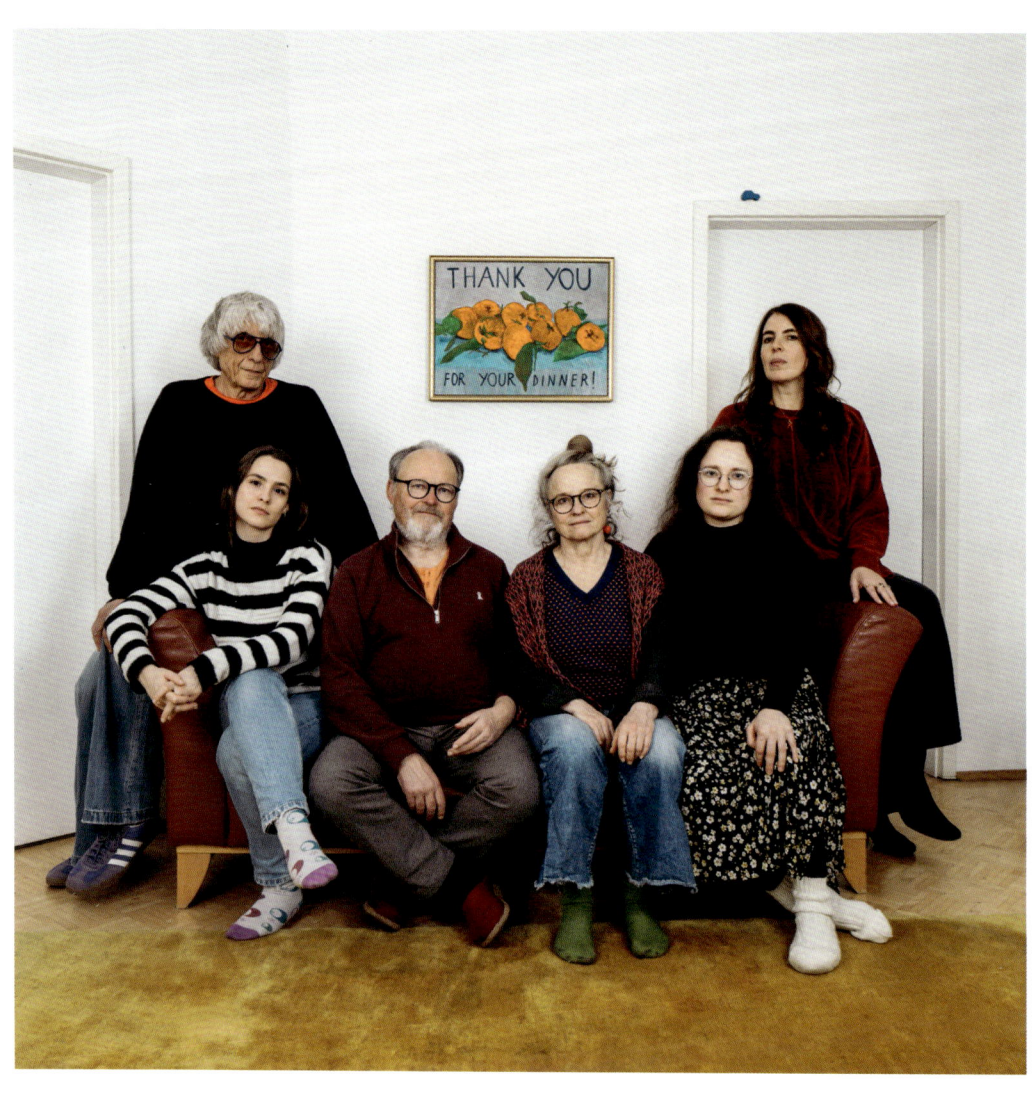

DORTMUND, GERMANY / FEBRUARY 6, 2025
Jeff Bliumis, Cleo Victoria Wägemann,
Hans-Peter Krüger, Susanne Requardt,
Judith Grytzka, Alina Bliumis

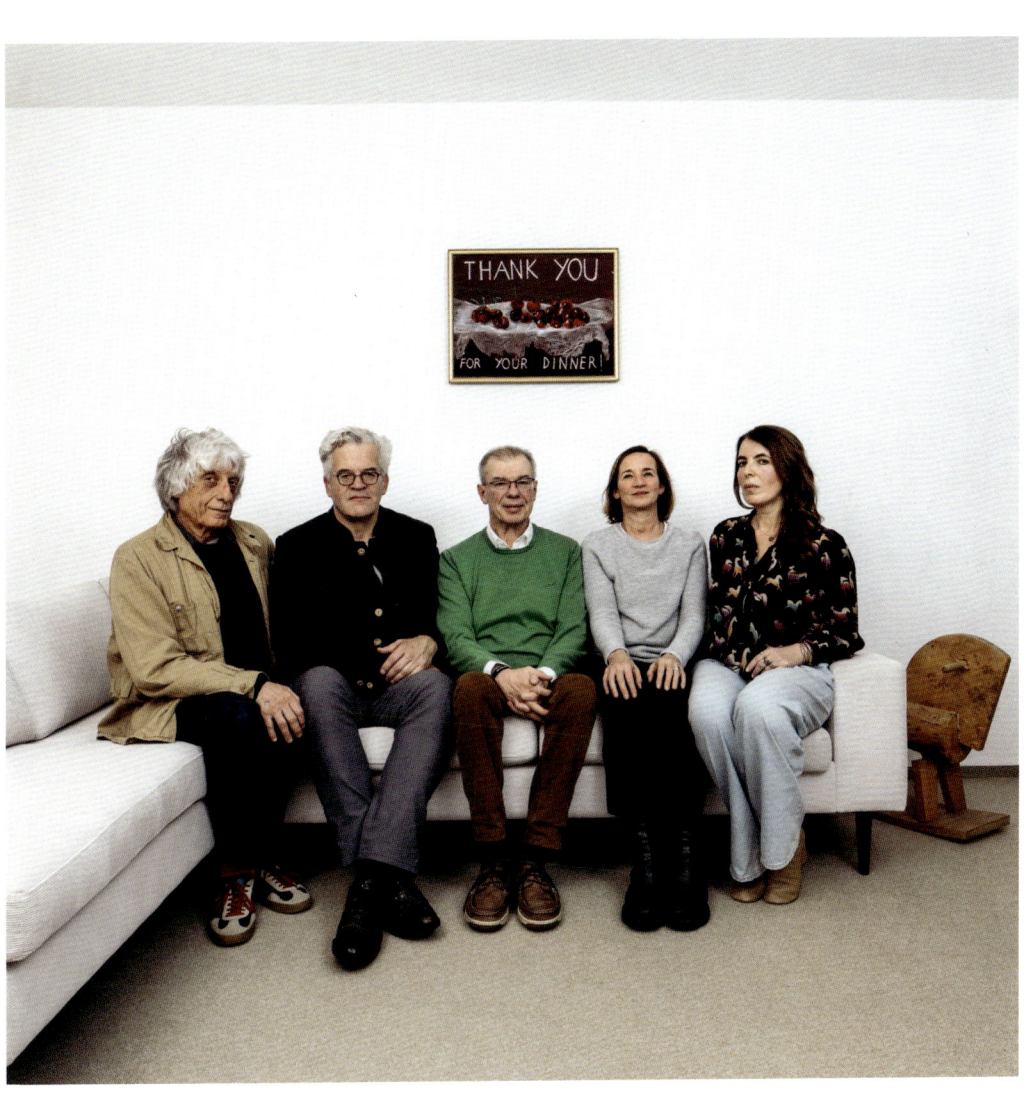

DORTMUND, GERMANY / FEBRUARY 7, 2025
Jeff Bliumis, Timotheus Hofsommer zu Waldweben,
Christian Heinrich Brand, Barbara Geschwinde,
Alina Bliumis

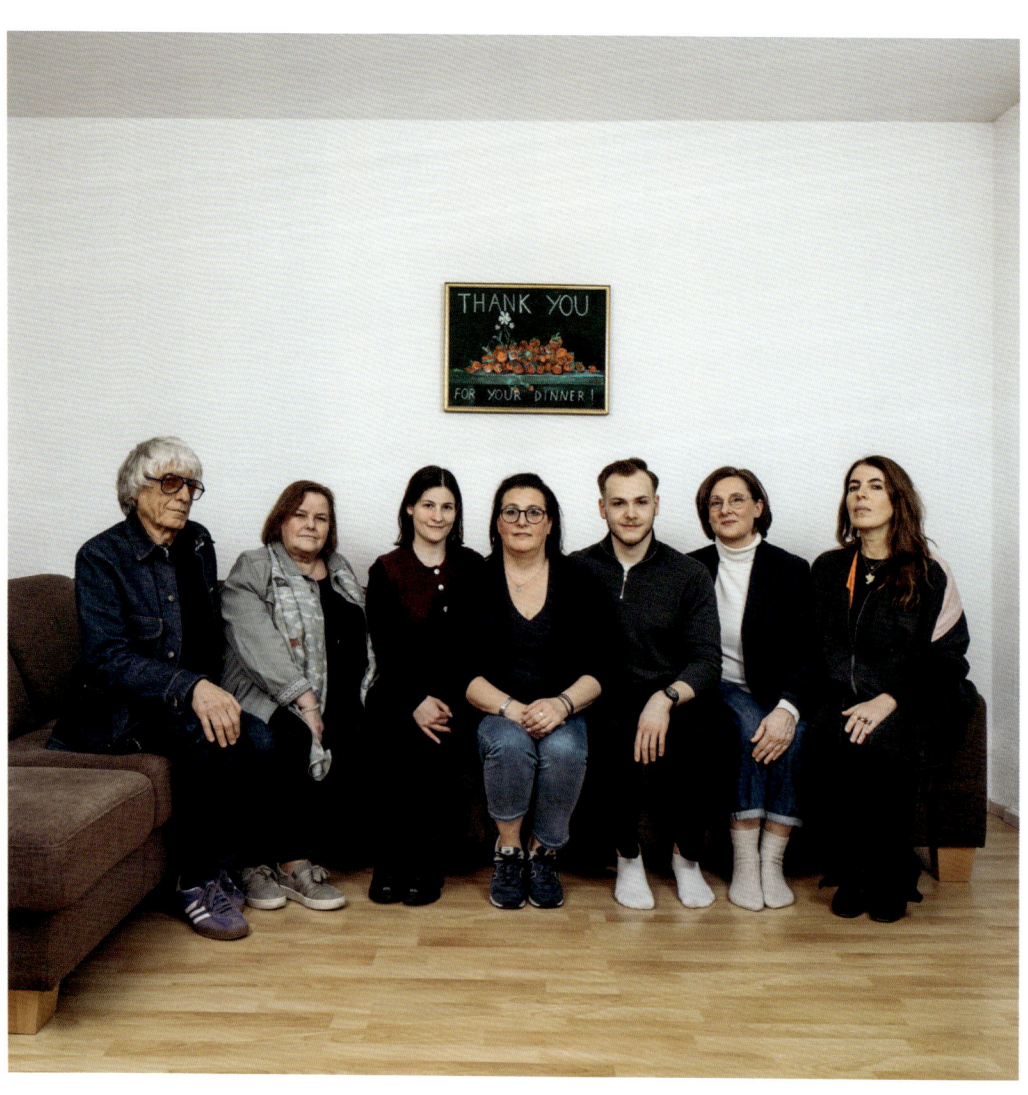

DORTMUND, GERMANY / FEBRUARY 9, 2025
Jeff Bliumis, Ana Schellongowski, Lena Reiss,
Britta Reiss, Tom Reiss, Uta Lemmens, Alina Bliumis

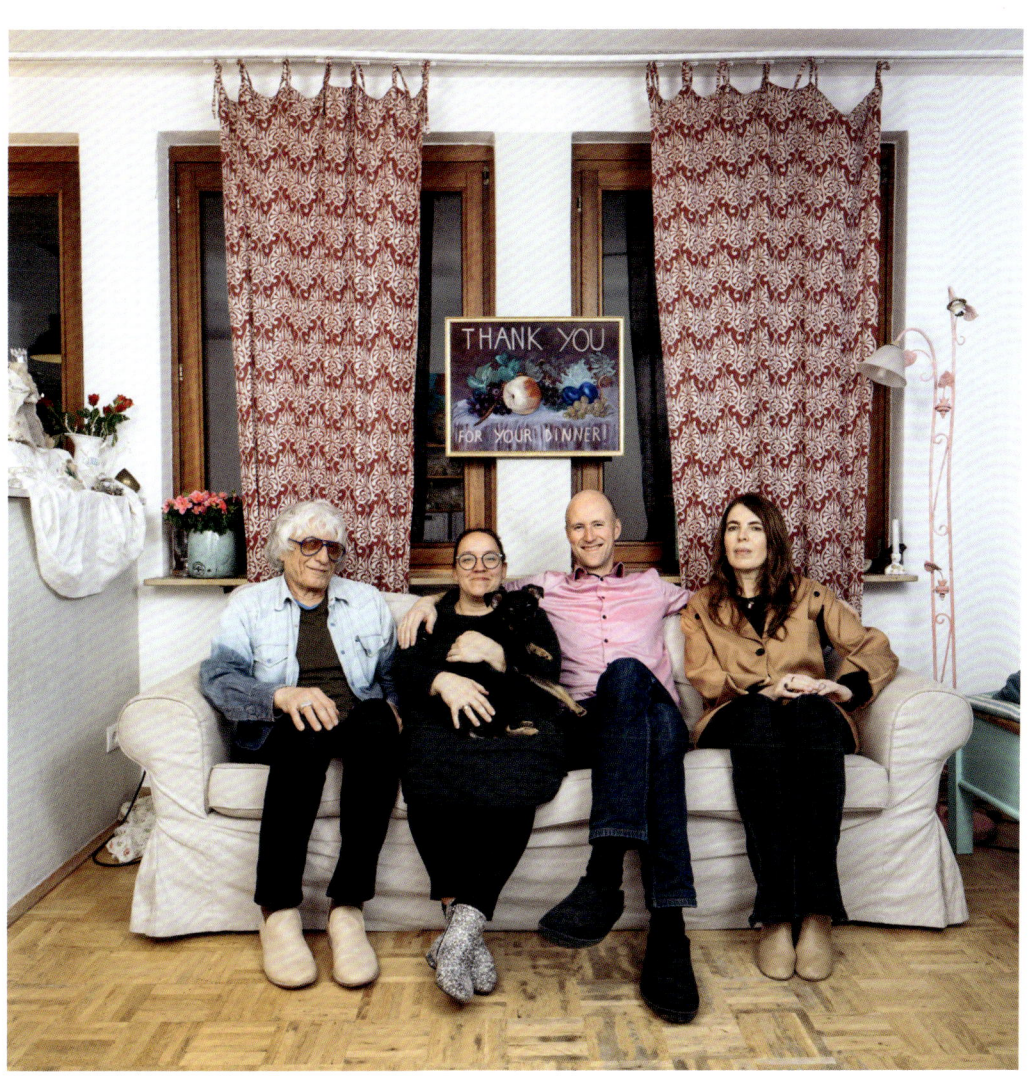

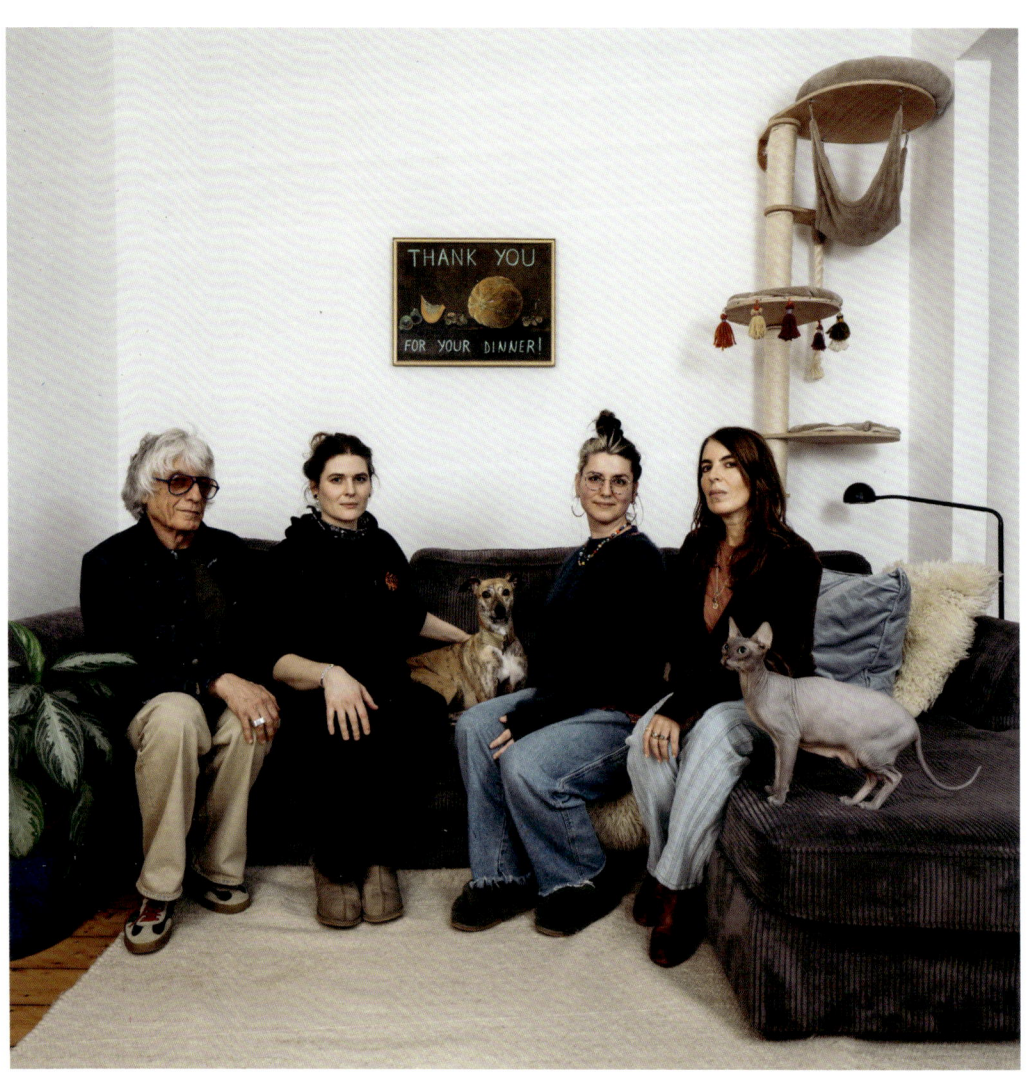

DORTMUND, GERMANY / FEBRUARY 12, 2025
Jeff Bliumis, Lisa Müller, Lioba Sombetzki,
Ouzo, Fiona, Alina Bliumis

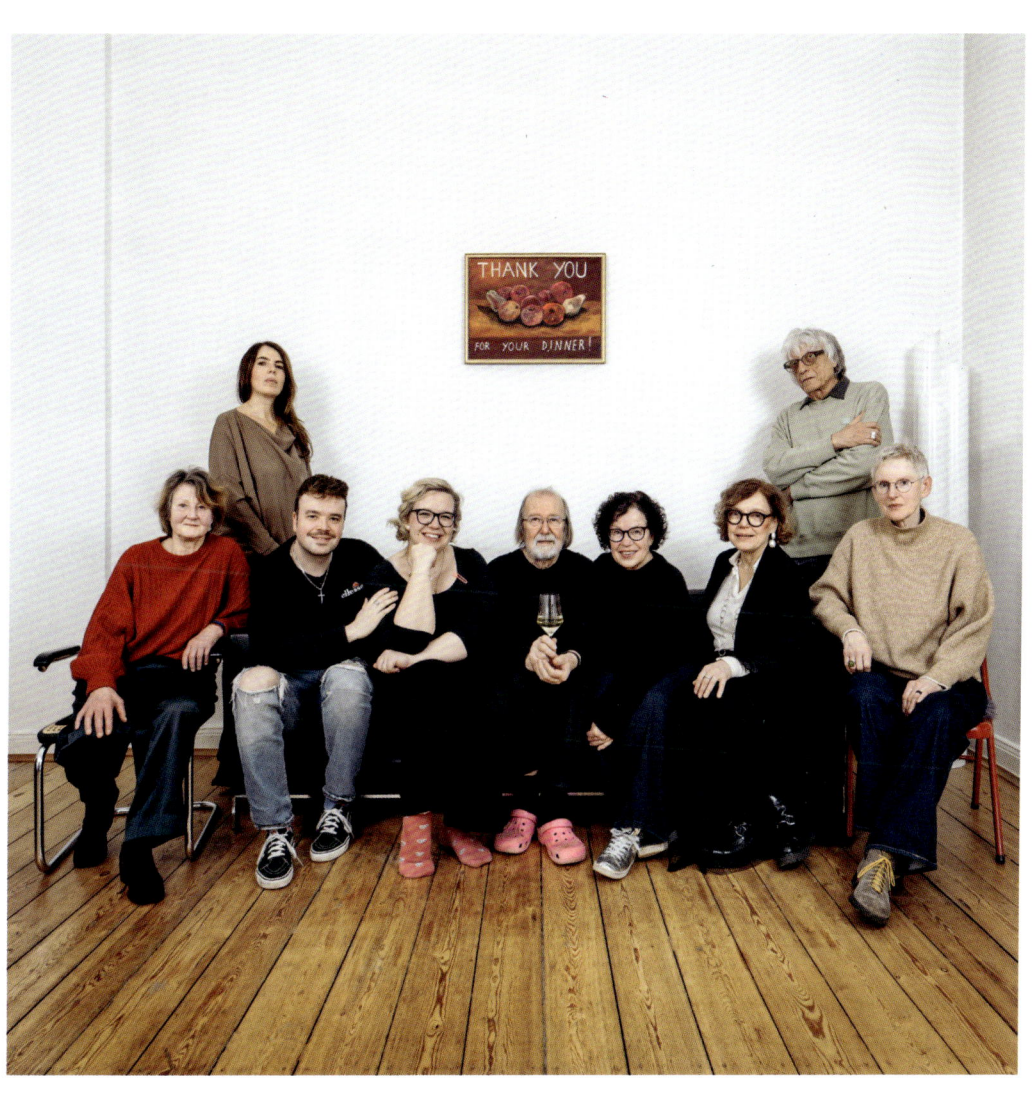

WITTEN, GERMANY / FEBRUARY 13, 2025
Alina Bliumis, Cornelia Hedwig Böhme,
Jonas Planken, Maika Letizia Wolff,
Prof. Dr. Manfred H. Wolff, Dagmar Wolff,
Ruth Hansen, Susanne Stähli, Jeff Bliumis

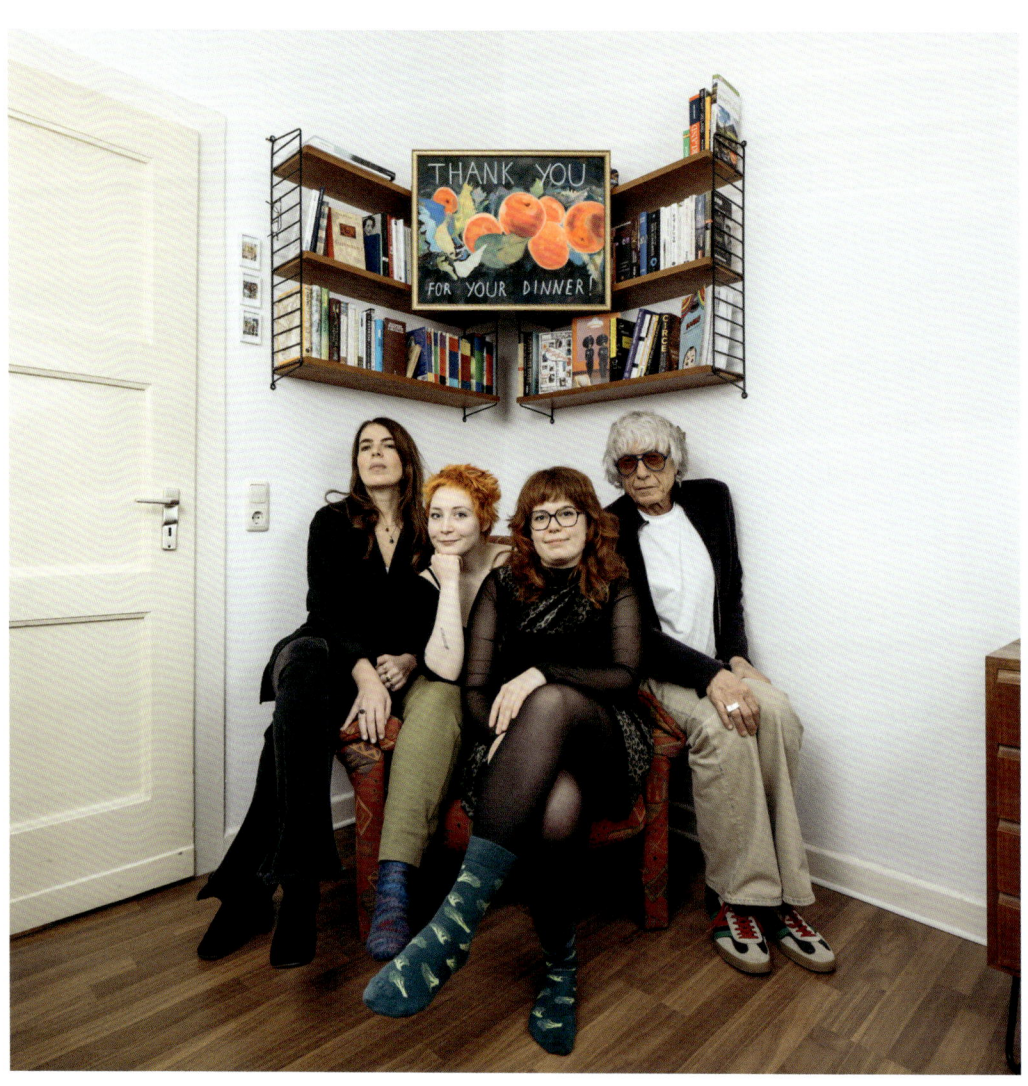

DORTMUND, GERMANY / FEBRUARY 14, 2025
Alina Bliumis, Melina Hyllo, Alina Mathiak,
Jeff Bliumis

Diary

In early March 2008, we placed
the following call for participation
in a local Bat Yam newspaper:

בעל ואישה צוות אמן הם
מציע ציור בתמורה ל-
הזמנה לארוחת ערב
משפחתית. נא לשלוח מייל
או התקשר למידע נוסף.

"Husband and wife artist team is
offering a painting in exchange for
an invitation to a family dinner.
Please email or call for more info."
Between April 7 and 12, we had
dinners with six families all across
Bat Yam and Tel Aviv.

Anfang März 2008 schalteten wir
den folgenden Teilnahmeaufruf in einer
Lokalzeitung aus Bat Yam:
„Künstler*innenteam-Ehepaar bietet
ein Gemälde im Austausch für eine Einladung zum Familienabendessen. Für
weitere Informationen bitte telefonisch
oder per E-Mail melden."
Zwischen dem 7. und 12. April besuchten
wir sechs Familien in Bat Yam und
Tel Aviv.

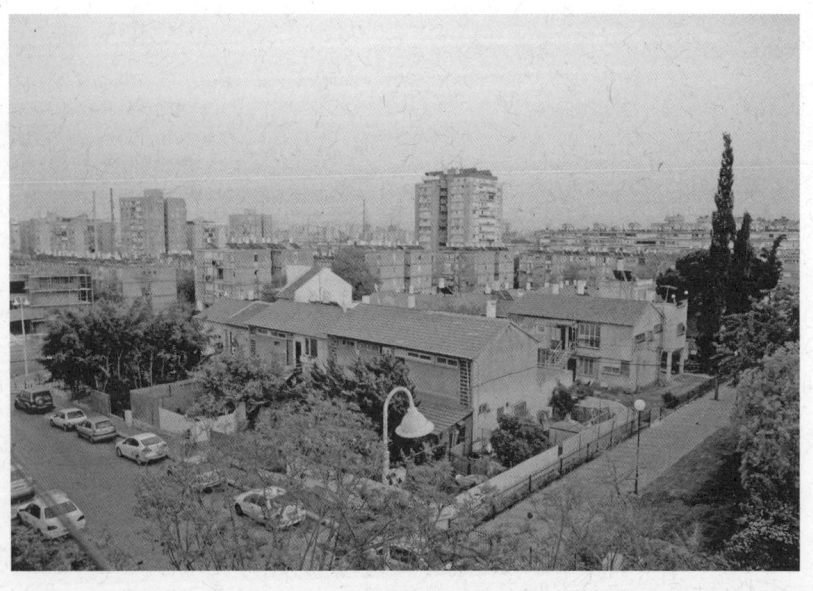

We arrived in Bat Yam early and in the few days we spent hanging out there, we learned that the city has a mixed reputation.

Funnily enough, our first host was a local policeman, Roni. During the dinner over baba ganoush, hummus, labneh, honey-glazed chicken, Israeli wine, soda, and pita bread, he assured us that "everything is under control" and his colleagues "are working very hard to keep the city safe." He is very proud to be a resident of Bat Yam, but his biggest pride is his family: his wife Ada and their two sons, Snir and Tal.

Ada is an office administrator with a real passion for art. Though she never had a formal art education, she loves to paint and, in her words, "to make her life more beautiful." Her subject matter varies from Steve McCurry's iconic *National Geographic* cover from 1985 featuring the "Afghan girl" Sharbat Gula to Knuckles the Echidna from the *Sonic the Hedgehog* cartoon. ✓ P. 19

Wir kamen früh in Bat Yam an und in den wenigen Tagen, die wir dort verbrachten, erfuhren wir, dass die Stadt einen zwiespältigen Ruf genießt.

Wie es der Zufall will, war unser erster Gastgeber ein örtlicher Polizist namens Roni. Während des Abendessens — es gab Baba Ganoush, Hummus, Labneh, honigglasiertes Hühnchen, israelischen Wein, Limonade und Pita-Brot — versicherte er uns, dass „alles unter Kontrolle" ist und seine Kolleg*innen „sehr hart daran arbeiten, die Stadt sicher zu halten". Er ist sehr stolz darauf, in Bat Yam zu leben, aber sein größter Stolz ist seine Familie: seine Frau Ada und ihre beiden Söhne Snir und Tal.

Ada arbeitet als Bürokauffrau und hat eine echte Leidenschaft für Kunst. Obwohl sie nie eine formale Kunstausbildung genossen hat, liebt sie es zu malen und, wie sie sagt, „ihr Leben schöner zu machen". Ihre Motive reichen von Steve McCurrys ikonischem *National-Geographic*-Cover aus dem Jahr 1985, auf dem das „afghanische Mädchen" Sharbat Gula zu sehen ist, bis zu Knuckles the Echidna aus der Spielreihe *Sonic the Hedgehog*. ✓ S. 19

The next day, we visited the home of Guri, Shiri, and their son Nadav. Shiri's sister Roni also joined us for dinner. Guri and Shiri both studied in the US and recently returned to Israel. The family lives in a ground-floor open-plan apartment with a big outdoor garden inhabited by colorful characters.

As hosts, they were easygoing and everyone took their turn in holding little Nadav.

Given his degree in architecture, planning, and preservation, Guri was optimistic about Bat Yam's potential, since it's a multicultural costal town with a beautiful beach not far from Tel Aviv. ✓ P. 20

Am nächsten Tag besuchten wir das Zuhause von Guri, Shiri und ihrem Sohn Nadav. Shiris Schwester Roni kam ebenfalls zum Abendessen. Guri und Shiri hatten beide in den USA studiert und waren kürzlich nach Israel zurückgekehrt. Die Familie lebt in einer Erdgeschosswohnung mit offener Küche und einem großen Garten voll bunter Figuren.

Als Gastgeber waren sie sehr entspannt und wechselten sich beim Halten des kleinen Nadavs ab.

Guri hatte Architektur, Stadtplanung und Denkmalschutz studiert und war deshalb optimistisch hinsichtlich des Potenzials von Bat Yam, da es eine multikulturelle Küstenstadt mit einem schönen Strand unweit von Tel Aviv ist. ✓ S. 20

Guri's Meatballs

1 ½ pounds ground turkey or beef
(YOU COULD USE VEAL TO BE AUTHENTIC—
BUT I'M NOT A FAN OF VEAL)

1 cup freshly chopped parsley
1 onion, grated
(ASK YOUR HUSBAND TO DO THIS IF GRATER + ONION =
YOU CRYING LIKE A BABY)

4 large garlic cloves, minced
1 large egg
3–4 tablespoons breadcrumbs
salt and ground pepper to taste
1 teaspoon sumac
1 teaspoon cumin

For tahini:
1 cup tahini paste
(I USE JOYVA)

4 cloves garlic
¼ cup fresh lemon juice
¾ cup water
1 cup chopped parsley
salt to taste

Combine all ingredients for meatballs
and then shape into oval-shaped balls.

Heat a few tablespoons of vegetable oil in a
frying pan—you are frying, not deep frying. Fry on high
until firm and golden brown. Be sure to flip them
frequently so they don't burn on one side.

Meanwhile, put all the tahini ingredients except for the
parsley in the food processor and blend until smooth.
If it's too thick, add water.

Add the chopped parsley.
Plate the meatballs, then drizzle with tahini.

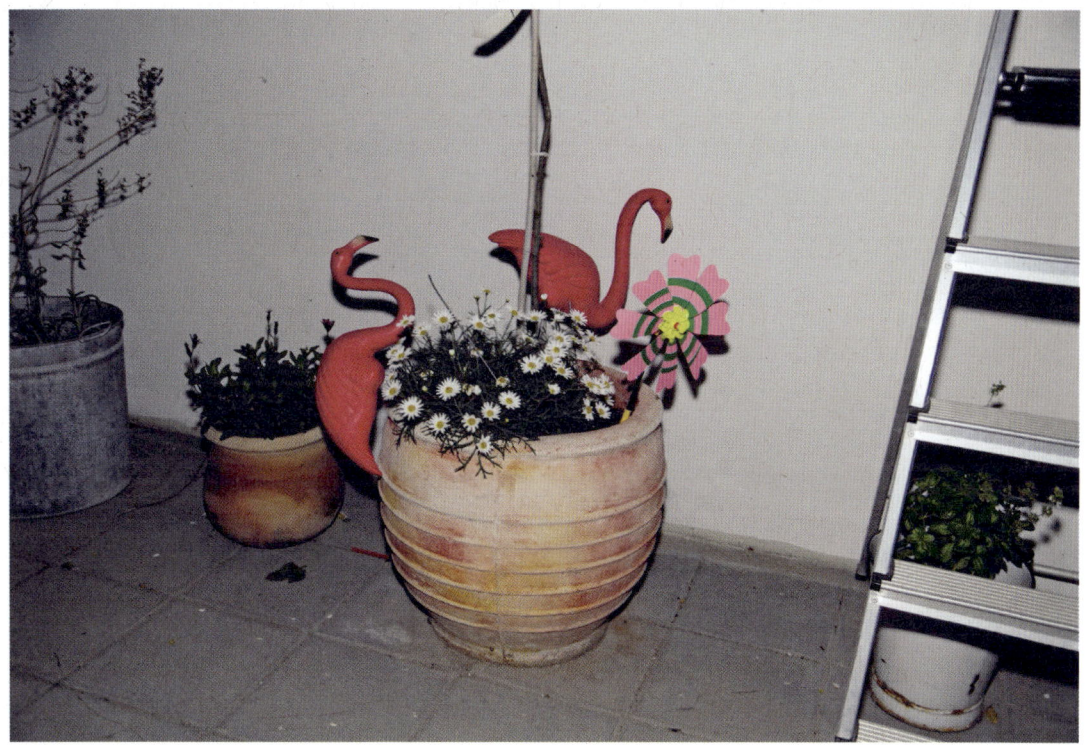

DINNER 2   COLORFUL CHARACTERS   FARBENFROHE CHARAKTERE

DINNER 2   GURI'S MEATBALLS   GURIS FLEISCHBÄLLCHEN

On the following day, we visited Michal in a Tel Aviv high-rise. Her cousin and two friends joined us.

We all sat comfortably around the coffee table eating salads, hummus, and vegetable soup, talking and drinking wine. The conversation was flowing from all directions with several topics being discussed at the same time, interrupted by laughs and cheers of l'chaim. The evening ended with a chocolate cake, baked specially for this occasion by Michal's mother Mila.

We had a chance to see Michal later that year in New York and kept in touch afterward. She is happily married with two kids now.

↙ P. 21

Am folgenden Tag besuchten wir Michal in einem Hochhaus in Tel Aviv. Ihre Cousine und zwei Freund*innen schlossen sich uns an.

Wir saßen gemütlich um den Couchtisch herum, aßen Salate, Hummus und Gemüsesuppe, plauderten und tranken Wein. Die Gespräche sprudelten aus allen Richtungen, mehrere Themen wurden gleichzeitig diskutiert, unterbrochen von Gelächter und fröhlichen L'Chaim-Rufen. Der Abend endete mit einem Schokoladenkuchen, den Michals Mutter Mila eigens für diesen Anlass gebacken hatte.

Später im Jahr trafen wir Michal in New York wieder und blieben danach in Kontakt. Heute ist sie glücklich verheiratet und hat zwei Kinder.

↙ S. 21

Next day we visited Miki, a theater producer living by herself in a small apartment in Tel Aviv. Her brother Ron joined us. He had just come back from army service and lives alone. Miki is interested in meeting new people and traveling. She's an active member of the couchsurfing movement.

IN HER WORDS: "I hosted about 100 people on this couch, and I visited twenty-three countries and never slept in a hotel ..."

Miki prepared some dishes, bought some, and we just talked and talked. By the end of the evening, Ron was happy to get a free meal, and Miki was happy to have a reason to clean her house and stock her fridge for the week—their words, not ours.

Am nächsten Tag besuchten wir Miki, eine Theaterproduzentin, die allein in einer kleinen Wohnung in Tel Aviv lebt. Ihr Bruder Ron schloss sich uns an. Er war gerade vom Militärdienst zurückgekehrt und lebt allein. Miki interessiert sich für neue Begegnungen und Reisen. Sie ist ein aktives Mitglied der Couchsurfing-Community.

IN IHREN WORTEN: „Ich habe auf diesem Sofa etwa 100 Menschen beherbergt und ich habe 23 Länder bereist, ohne je in einem Hotel zu übernachten ..."

Miki bereitete einige Gerichte zu, ein paar waren auch schon fertig gekauft, und wir redeten einfach stundenlang. Am Ende des Abends — so sagten die beiden selbst — war Ron froh, ein kostenloses Essen bekommen zu haben, und Miki freute sich über den guten Grund, ihre Wohnung geputzt und ihren Kühlschrank aufgefüllt zu haben.

MIKI: "I'm single and don't have a partner or kids of my own.
My family only includes my mother and my brother, and unfortunately I'm not in contact with them much these days. So, I guess I'm my own unit now. It was fine when I lived in Germany, but in Israel it is a bit unusual, to put it mildly.

And about food—it's kind of funny—I've started this insane recipe collection, folders and folders and folders divided into orderly categories. However, I don't think that I have even once cooked anything from that huge recipe book. In general, I don't cook. I live alone and I don't even have an oven and definitely no special utensils or kitchenware.

In reality, I go to the supermarket once every couple of weeks, buy lots of food, stock up, and eat it slowly. I also eat out a lot, a few times a week. So, that's how I deal with the topic of food in my everyday life." ↙ P. 22

MIKI: „Ich bin Single und habe weder einen Partner noch Kinder.
Meine Familie besteht nur aus meiner Mutter und meinem Bruder, aber leider habe ich heutzutage kaum Kontakt zu ihnen. Also bin ich wohl jetzt meine eigene kleine Einheit. Als ich in Deutschland lebte, war das kein großes Thema, aber in Israel ist das — gelinde gesagt — etwas ungewöhnlich.

Was das Essen angeht — das ist irgendwie lustig —, habe ich angefangen, eine völlig verrückte Rezeptsammlung anzulegen: Ordner über Ordner, fein säuberlich in Kategorien unterteilt. Aber ehrlich gesagt habe ich noch nie etwas daraus gekocht. Eigentlich koche ich generell nicht. Ich lebe allein, habe keinen Backofen und schon gar keine speziellen Küchengeräte.

In Wirklichkeit gehe ich alle paar Wochen in den Supermarkt, kaufe jede Menge Essen, lege mir Vorräte an und esse das dann nach und nach. Außerdem gehe ich ein paar Mal pro Woche auswärts essen. So handhabe ich das Thema Essen in meinem Alltag." ↙ S. 22

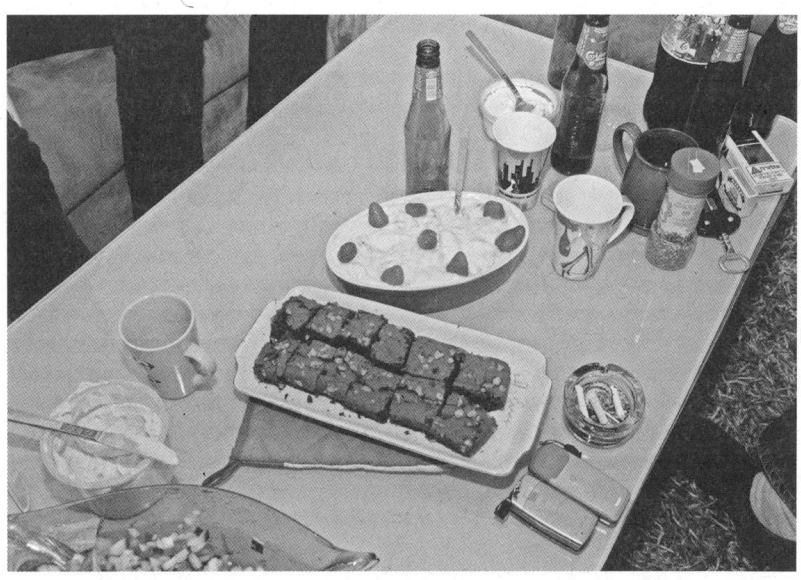

On the next day, we were invited to a Shabbat dinner at Avigial's home in Bat Yam. Her ex-husband, their daughter, their son with his fiancée, and two close friends joined us.

Like a well-orchestrated performance: tablecloths, candle lighting, blessings, wine, challah. Countless dishes came in a steady stream from the kitchen to the table and were passed around with love, hugs, and laughter.

At the end of the evening, the family gathered together to sing "Shalom Aleichem." ⤪ P. 23

Am nächsten Tag waren wir zu einem Schabbat-Essen bei Avigial in Bat Yam eingeladen. Ihr Ex-Mann, ihre Tochter, ihr Sohn mit seiner Verlobten und zwei enge Freund*innen kamen dazu.

Es war wie eine gut inszenierte Performance: Tischtücher, Kerzenlicht, Segenssprüche, Wein, Challah. Unzählige Gerichte kamen in einem stetigen Strom aus der Küche auf den Tisch und wurden mit Liebe, Umarmungen und Gelächter herumgereicht.

Am Ende des Abends versammelte sich die Familie und sang „Shalom Aleichem". ⤪ S. 23

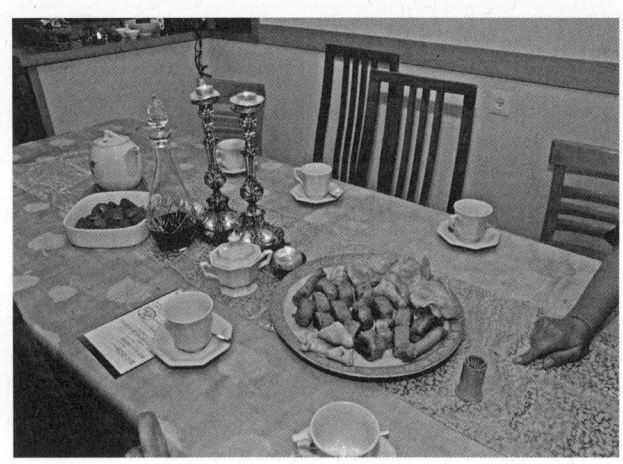

On the last day, we visited Diana, Andrey, and their daughter Masha in Bat Yam.

The family recently moved from Russia, and just like many other immigrants they seek to assimilate while holding on to their native dishes: Olivier salad, herring, potatoes, beet salad, and pickled tomatoes.

As newcomers, it hasn't been easy for this young family—simultaneously studying and making a living. But they make sure their child isn't ever aware of their difficulties and has the best childhood possible.

⤪ P. 24

Am letzten Tag besuchten wir Diana, Andrey und ihre Tochter Masha in Bat Yam.

Die Familie ist vor kurzem aus Russland zugewandert, und wie viele andere Eingewanderte wollen sie sich assimilieren, während sie an ihren heimischen Gerichten festhalten: Russischer Salat, Hering, Kartoffeln, Rote-Beete-Salat und eingelegte Tomaten.

Als Neuankömmlinge hat es die junge Familie nicht leicht — sie müssen gleichzeitig studieren und ihren Lebensunterhalt verdienen. Aber sie sorgen dafür, dass ihr Kind von den Schwierigkeiten nichts mitbekommt und die bestmögliche Kindheit hat. ⤪ S. 24

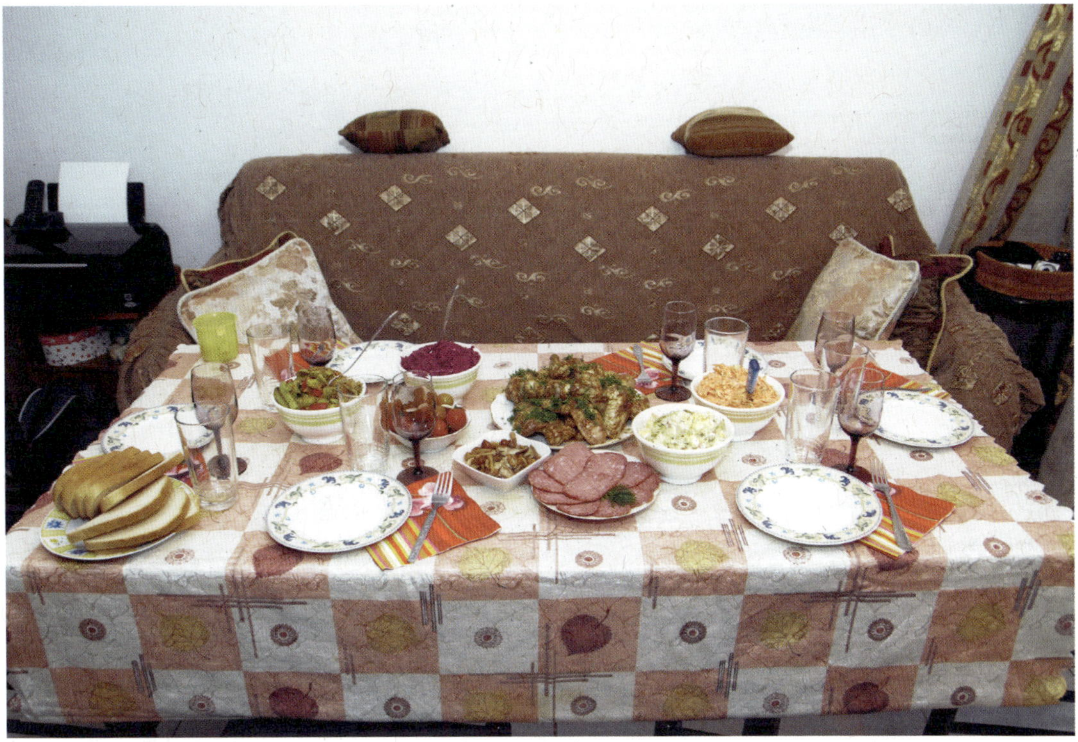

DINNER 6   HOLDING ON TO THEIR NATIVE DISHES   AN HEIMISCHEN GERICHTEN FESTHALTEN

DINNER 6   MASHA

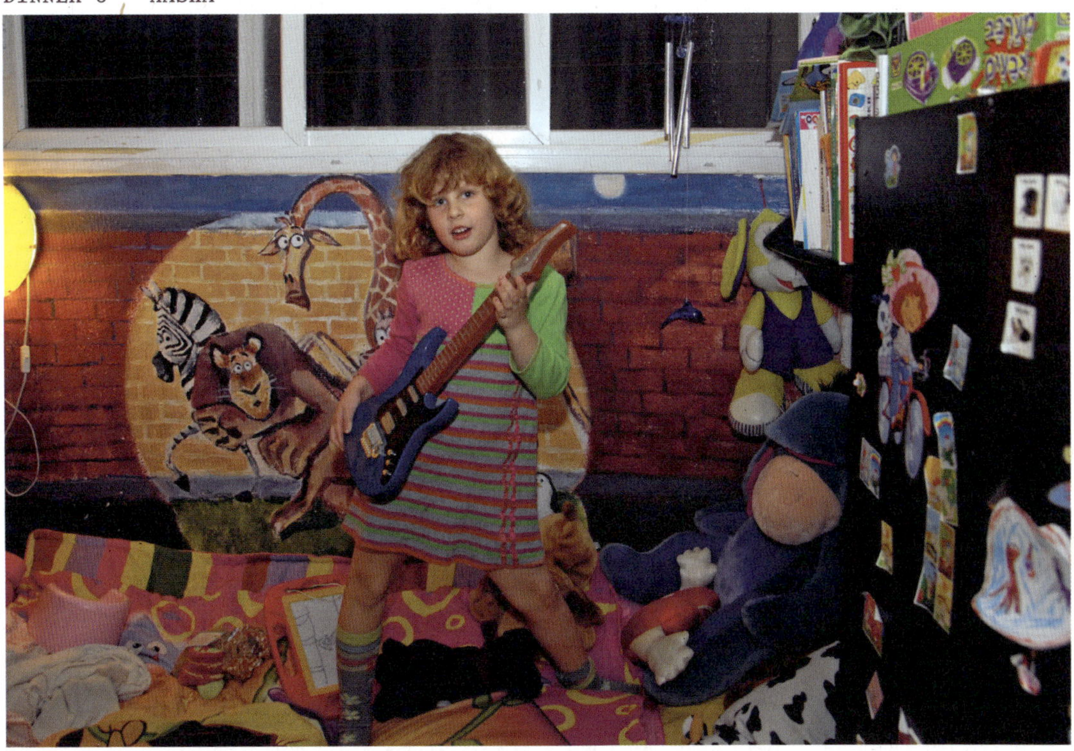

In early March 2012, we placed the following call for participation to Bronx residents via flyers and social networking sites:

(Bronx, NY, 2012)

Husband and wife artist team is offering a painting in exchange for an invitation to a family dinner. Please email or call for more info.

Between March 24 and May 6, we had meals with thirteen families all over the Bronx.

Anfang März 2012 riefen wir Bewohner*innen der Bronx über Flugblätter und soziale Netzwerke zur Teilnahme auf: „Künstler*innenteam–Ehepaar bietet ein Gemälde im Austausch für eine Einladung zum Familienabendessen. Für weitere Informationen bitte telefonisch oder per E-Mail melden."
Zwischen dem 24. März und dem 6. Mai aßen wir mit dreizehn Familien in der ganzen Bronx zu Abend.

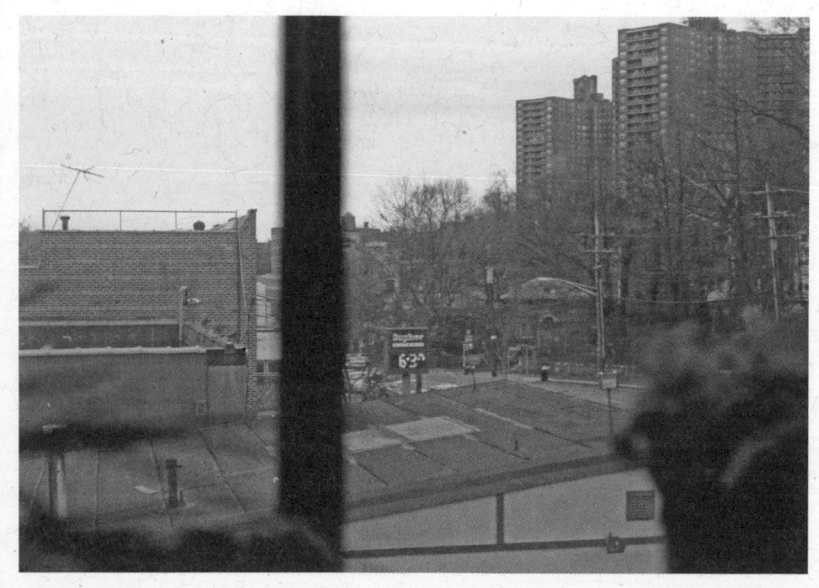

Our hosts are Bohdan, Liliya, and their three kids in a two-story building in Riverdale. Liliya greeted us at the door, while Bohdan was in a store getting few more things for the dinner. Their five-year-old son Pavlo was busy talking to a Superman on a toy phone. The apartment was a temporary residence provided by his employer, the Embassy of Ukraine in New York.

Later, their two teenage daughters and guests arrived and gathered around the table with pickles, salads, cold cuts, and a rotisserie chicken. After dinner, Bohdan played techno-trance tracks he composed and their daughters were dancing in the kitchen. ↙ P. 25

Unsere Gastgeber*innen sind Bohdan, Liliya und ihre drei Kinder. Sie leben in einem zweistöckigen Haus in Riverdale. Liliya begrüßte uns an der Tür, während Bohdan noch ein paar Dinge für das Abendessen einkaufte. Ihr fünfjähriger Sohn Pavlo war damit beschäftigt, über ein Spielzeugtelefon mit einem Superman zu sprechen. Die Wohnung war ein vorübergehender Wohnsitz, bereitgestellt von seiner Arbeitsstelle, der ukrainischen Botschaft in New York.

Später trafen die beiden Töchter im Teenageralter und die Gäste ein und versammelten sich um den Tisch voll mit Essiggurken, Salaten, Aufschnitt und einem Brathähnchen.

Nach dem Essen spielte Bohdan von ihm komponierte Techno-Trance-Tracks, und die Töchter tanzten in der Küche. ↙ S. 25

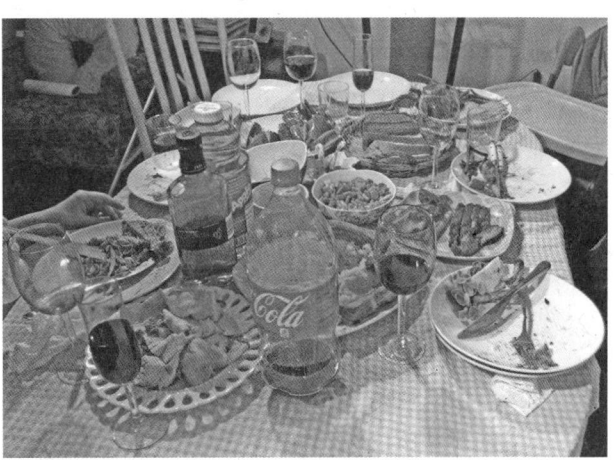

We visited Laura and her daughters, Emma and Josel, in a high-rise modern building overlooking the Hudson River. Her husband works late during the week, so the girls often have dinner without him. Laura cooked honey-glazed chicken, oven-roasted butternut squash, tomato salad, bok choy, and rice. The daughters helped in the kitchen. ↙ P. 26

Wir besuchten Laura und ihre Töchter Emma und Josel in einem modernen Hochhaus mit Blick auf den Hudson River.

Ihr Mann arbeitet unter der Woche lang, so dass die Mädchen oft ohne ihn zu Abend essen. Laura kochte honigglasiertes Hühnchen, gerösteten Butternusskürbis, Tomatensalat, Pak Choi und Reis. Die Töchter halfen in der Küche. ↙ S. 26

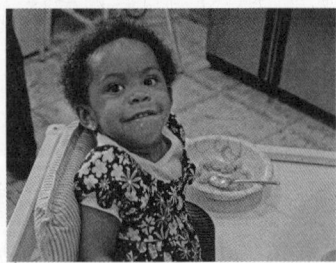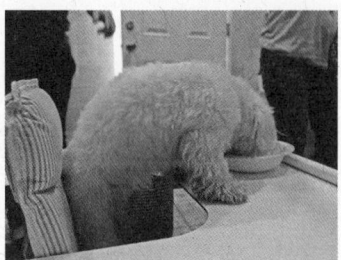

We were invited by Sulma and Maurice to the house of Sulma's mother on Homer Avenue. The house was big enough to fit all the guests: Sulma's godmother, friends, and co-workers. The godmother was cooking in the kitchen, smashing plantains in a wooden mortar.

Sulma served a classic Garifuna dish, hudut, consisting of fish cooked in a coconut broth and served with mashed plantains. The Garifuna are descendants of West African, Central African, Island Carib, and Arawak people with a big diaspora in the US. After cheering for her co-worker's twins' birthdays, we were ready for the next step—dance lessons to Garifuna music. ↙ P. 27

Wir wurden von Sulma und Maurice in das Haus von Sulmas Mutter in der Homer Avenue eingeladen. Das Haus war groß genug, um alle Gäste unterzubringen: Sulmas Patin, Freund*innen und Kolleg*innen. Die Patentante kochte in der Küche und zerstampfte Kochbananen in einem hölzernen Mörser.

Sulma servierte ein klassisches Garifuna-Gericht, Hudut, aus Fisch, der in einer Kokosnussbrühe gekocht und mit zerdrückten Kochbananen serviert wird. Die Garifuna sind Nachfahr*innen von westafrikanischen, zentralafrikanischen und karibischen Kalinago- und Arawak-Gruppen mit einer großen Diaspora in den USA.

Nachdem wir auf den Geburtstag der Zwillinge einer Kollegin angestoßen hatten, waren wir bereit für den nächsten Schritt — Tanzstunden zu Garifuna-Musik. ↙ S. 27

We visited Maiysha, her husband, and their sons, Jahsaia and Lohan. The family lives in an apartment building near the Yankee Stadium. Maiysha is a doula. Her husband is a musician. Everyone gathered around the kitchen table and served themselves pasta from the pot. ↙ P. 28

Wir besuchten Maiysha, ihren Ehemann und ihre Söhne Jahsaia und Lohan. Die Familie lebt in einem Mehrfamilienhaus in der Nähe des Yankee Stadium. Maiysha ist Doula. Ihr Mann ist Musiker. Alle versammelten sich um den Küchentisch und nahmen sich Nudeln direkt aus dem Topf. ↙ S. 28

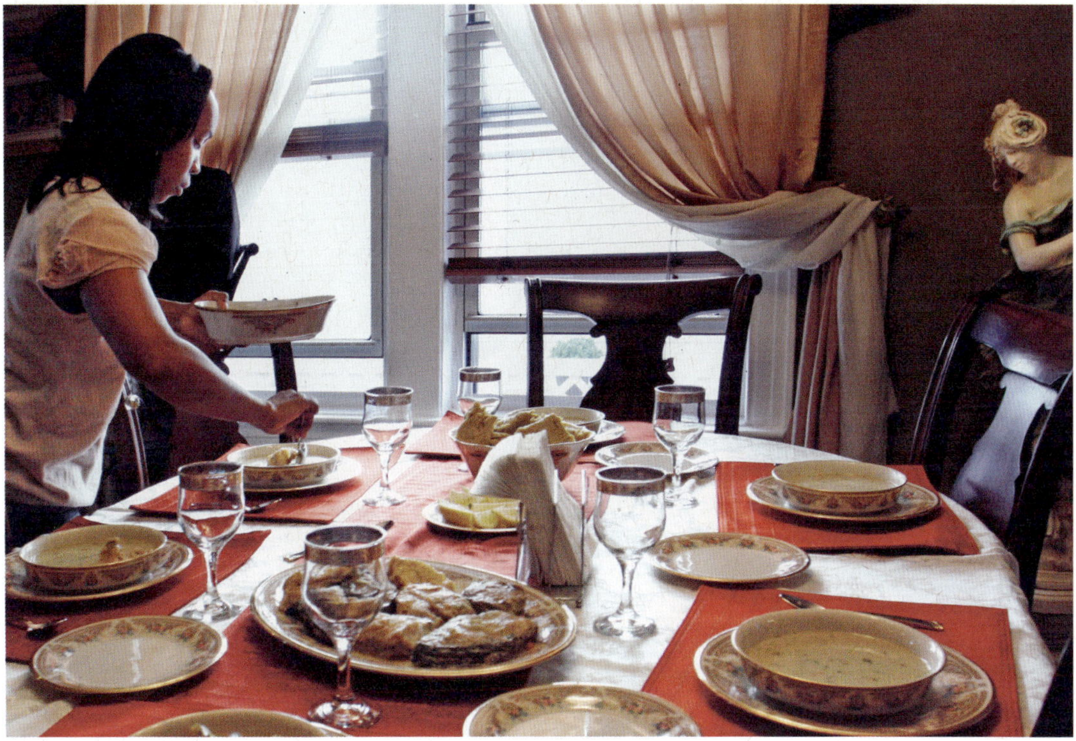

DINNER 9   SERVING HUDUT   HUDUT SERVIEREN

DINNER 9   DANCE PARTNER   TANZPARTNER

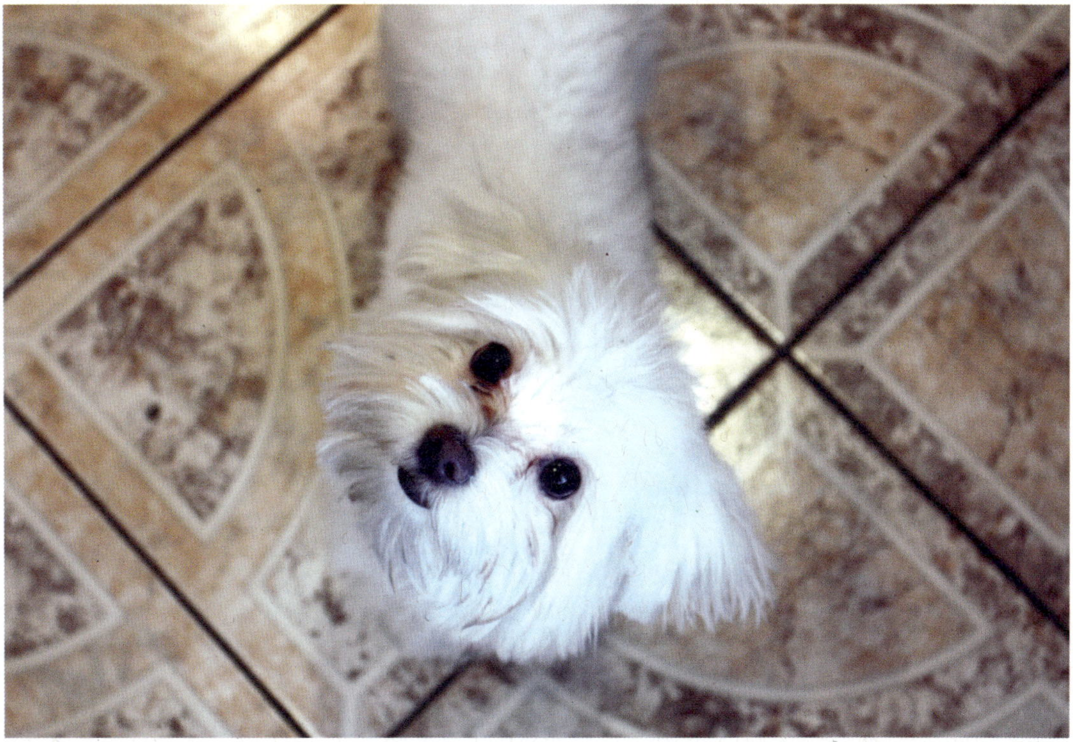

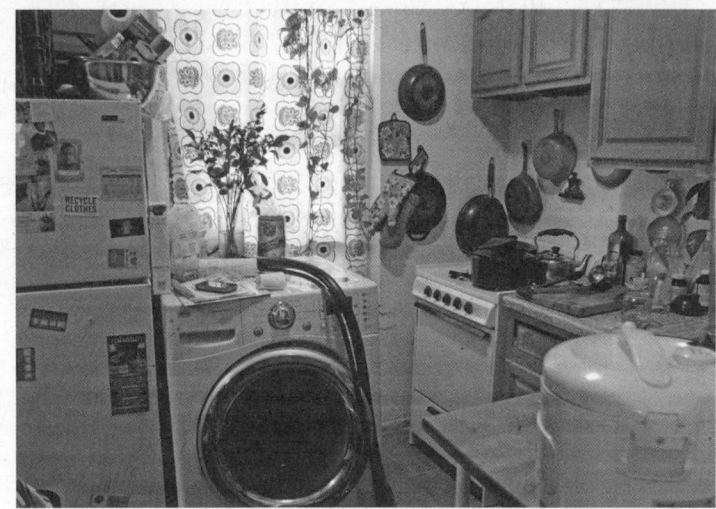

DINNER 11   APRIL 15, 2012

We visited Ed and Gayle in a single-family house in Woodlawn, an Irish-American neighborhood at the very north
end of the Bronx.
The living room on the first floor was occupied by two major
structures: a huge dollhouse belonging to their daughter
Charlotte and a bird cage belonging to two parakeets, Betty
and Lothar.

Gayle likes to cook new dishes. That
evening was her take on Thai cuisine.
For our family portrait, Betty and
Lothar took their place on a wood
shelf. ↙ P. 29

Wir besuchten Ed und Gayle in einem Einfamilienhaus
in Woodlawn, einem irisch–amerikanischen Viertel am
nördlichsten Ende der Bronx.
Das Wohnzimmer im Erdgeschoss wurde von zwei
großen Objekten dominiert: einem riesigen Puppen-
haus, das ihrer Tochter Charlotte gehörte, und einem
Vogelkäfig mit zwei Wellensittichen, Betty und Lothar.
Gayle kocht gerne neue Gerichte. An diesem Abend
servierte sie ihre Interpretation der thailändischen
Küche. Für unser Familienporträt nahmen Betty und
Lothar ihren Platz auf einem Holzregal ein. ↙ S. 29

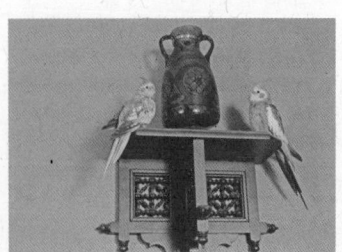

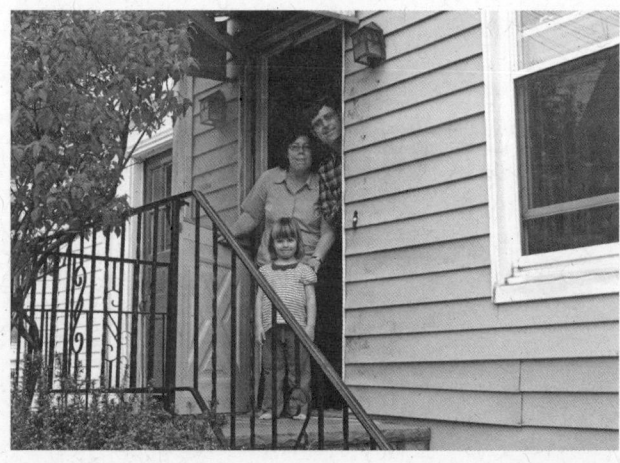

We visited the home of Nicole, Luis, and their daughter Briana in the Unionport section of the Bronx. Nicole is the founder of the family lifestyle site BronxMama. Luis is a chef at the Yankee Stadium food court. Briana introduced us to her goldfish while Luis cooked ravioli and chicken.

Shazia T. Khan from NY1 joined us to do a TV segment about our project. In his interview with Shazia, Luis mentioned that at first, he was concerned about strangers—two starving artists—coming to his house.

↙ P. 30

Wir besuchten das Zuhause von Nicole, Luis und ihrer Tochter Briana im Unionport-Viertel der Bronx.

Nicole ist die Gründerin einer Familien-Lifestyle-Internetseite — bronxmama.com. Luis ist Koch in der Küche des Yankee Stadium. Briana stellte uns ihren Goldfisch vor, während Luis Ravioli und Hühnchen zubereitete.

Shazia T. Khan von NY1 kam dazu, um einen TV-Beitrag über unser Projekt zu drehen. In seinem Interview mit Shazia erwähnte Luis, dass er anfangs Bedenken hatte, Fremde — zwei hungrige Künstler*innen — zu sich nach Hause einzuladen.
↙ S. 30

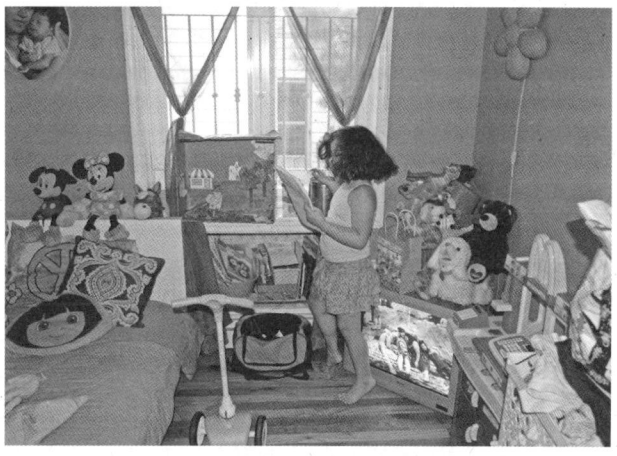

The next day, we visited the Hebrew Home senior housing community at Riverdale. We were to have dinner in the cafeteria with seven residents—six women and one man. Dinner included vegetable soup, spinach and cheese lasagna, and ice cream.

At our table, most conversations took place one-on-one rather than in groups, but sometimes comments flew across the table: "B., you are talking too much" or "She is always saying that, don't believe her."

After the dinner, one of the residents, Alice, invited us to see her room with cutouts of butterflies around her bed, a black-and-white picture of Martin Luther King delivering his "I Have a Dream" speech hung next to Obama delivering his "Change Has Come" speech.

↙ P. 31

Am nächsten Tag besuchten wir die Seniorenwohnanlage Hebrew Home in Riverdale. Wir sollten in der Cafeteria mit sieben Bewohner*innen — sechs Frauen und einem Mann — zu Abend essen.

Das Abendessen bestand aus Gemüsesuppe, Spinat-Käse-Lasagne und Eiscreme. An unserem Tisch fanden die meisten Gespräche eher eins zu eins statt in der Gruppe statt, aber gelegentlich flogen Kommentare quer über den Tisch: „B., du redest zu viel" oder „Das sagt sie immer, glaub ihr nicht."

Nach dem Essen lud uns Alice, eine der Bewohnerinnen, in ihr Zimmer ein. Rund um ihr Bett hingen ausgeschnittene Schmetterlinge als Deko, ein Schwarz-Weiß-Bild von Martin Luther King während seiner „I Have a Dream"-Rede hing neben einem Bild von Obama bei seiner „Change Has Come"-Rede.
↙ S. 31

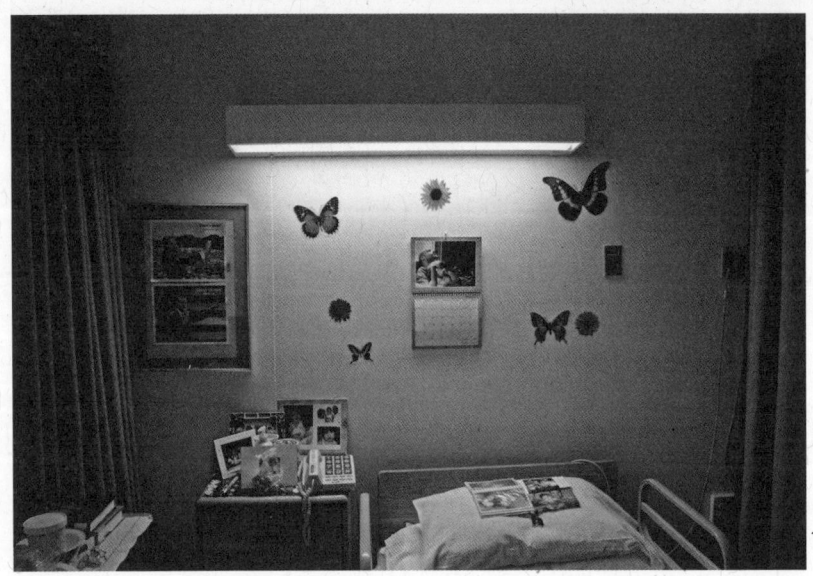

We were invited by Judy to join her friends, Mierle and Jack, and her daughter's family visiting from Philadelphia for Shabbat dinner in an old single-family house in Riverdale. We couldn't take any photographs after sunset. The only photo we took was a family portrait. Judy cooked a sorrel soup. Her recipe was exactly like our families'. To our surprise, Mierle turned to be Mierle Laderman Ukeles, an artist, whom we greatly admire.

MIERLE LADERMAN UKELES, "MANIFESTO FOR MAINTENANCE ART," 1969

"I am an artist.
I am a woman.
I am a wife.
I am a mother.
(Random order)
I do a hell of a lot of washing, cleaning, cooking, renewing, supporting, preserving, etc. Also, (up to now separately) I 'do' Art. Now I will simply do these everyday things, and flush them up to consciousness, exhibit them, as Art."
↙ P. 32

Judy lud uns ein zu einem Schabbat–Abendessen mit ihren Freund*innen Mierle und Jack sowie der Familie ihrer Tochter, die zu Besuch aus Philadelphia war. Das Essen fand in einem alten Einfamilienhaus in Riverdale statt. Nach Sonnenuntergang durften wir keine Fotos mehr machen. Das einzige Bild, das wir aufnahmen, war ein Familienporträt. Judy kochte eine Sauerampfersuppe. Ihr Rezept war genau wie das unserer Familien.
Zu unserer Überraschung stellte sich heraus, dass ihre Freundin Mierle tatsächlich Mierle Laderman Ukeles war — eine Künstlerin, die wir sehr bewundern.

MIERLE LADERMAN UKELES, „MANIFESTO FOR MAINTENANCE ART", 1969

„Ich bin eine Künstlerin. Ich bin eine Frau. Ich bin eine Ehefrau.
Ich bin eine Mutter (in zufälliger Reihenfolge). Wovon ich wahnsinnig viel mache: Ich wasche, putze, koche, erneuere, unterstütze, bewahre usw. Außerdem ‚mache' ich (bisher parallel) Kunst.
Jetzt werde ich diese alltäglichen Dinge einfach machen und sie ins Bewusstsein spülen, sie ausstellen, als Kunst." ↙ S. 32

We visited Sasha, Kendra, and their two daughters for a lunch in a single-family home in the Jerome Park neighborhood.
Sasha met us holding his younger daughter. His older daughter was preparing place cards for the table. Sasha grew up in Manhattan and moved to the Bronx to start a charter school, and Kendra is a teacher at that school.
Kendra was setting the table with a healthy choice of salads and vegetables. ↙ P. 33

Wir besuchten Sasha, Kendra und ihre beiden Töchter zum Mittagessen in einem Einfamilienhaus im Stadtteil Jerome Park.
Sasha begrüßte uns mit seiner jüngeren Tochter auf dem Arm. Seine ältere Tochter bereitete Platzkarten für den Tisch vor. Sasha wuchs in Manhattan auf und zog in die Bronx, um eine Charter-Schule zu gründen. Kendra ist Lehrerin an dieser Schule.
Kendra deckte den Tisch mit einer gesunden Auswahl an Salaten und Gemüse. ↙ S. 33

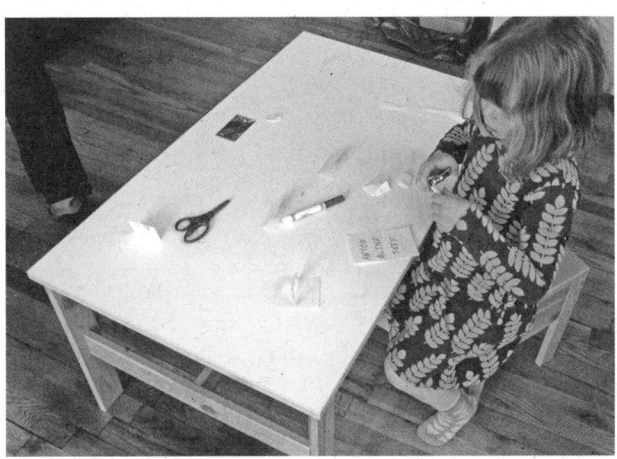

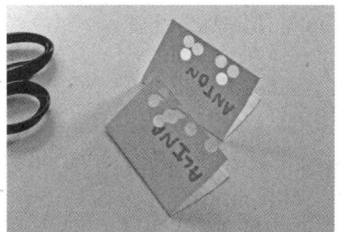

DINNER 16

Later in the day, we visited Alicia for a dinner, who was a five-minute drive away. Alicia is an artist. Her work often involves social issues. She lives with her Netherlands-born husband and two daughters. Her brother and her two friends joined us.
With many conversations around the table, time passed quickly, and it was time for a family portrait. With this dynamic group, it was not easy to get everyone to sit still. ↙ P. 34

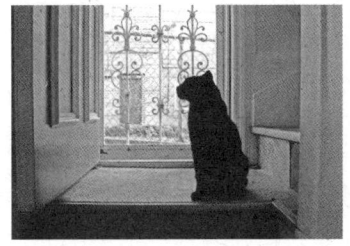

Später am Tag besuchten wir Alicia zum Abendessen, die nur fünf Minuten entfernt wohnte. Alicia ist Künstlerin. Ihre Arbeit beschäftigt sich oft mit sozialen Themen. Sie lebt zusammen mit ihrem in Holland geborenen Ehemann und ihren zwei Töchtern. Ihr Bruder und zwei Freunde schlossen sich uns an.
Bei den vielen Gesprächen am Tisch verging die Zeit wie im Flug, bis es Zeit war für ein Familienporträt. Mit dieser dynamischen Gruppe war es nicht leicht, alle dazu zu bekommen, stillzuhalten. ↙ S. 34

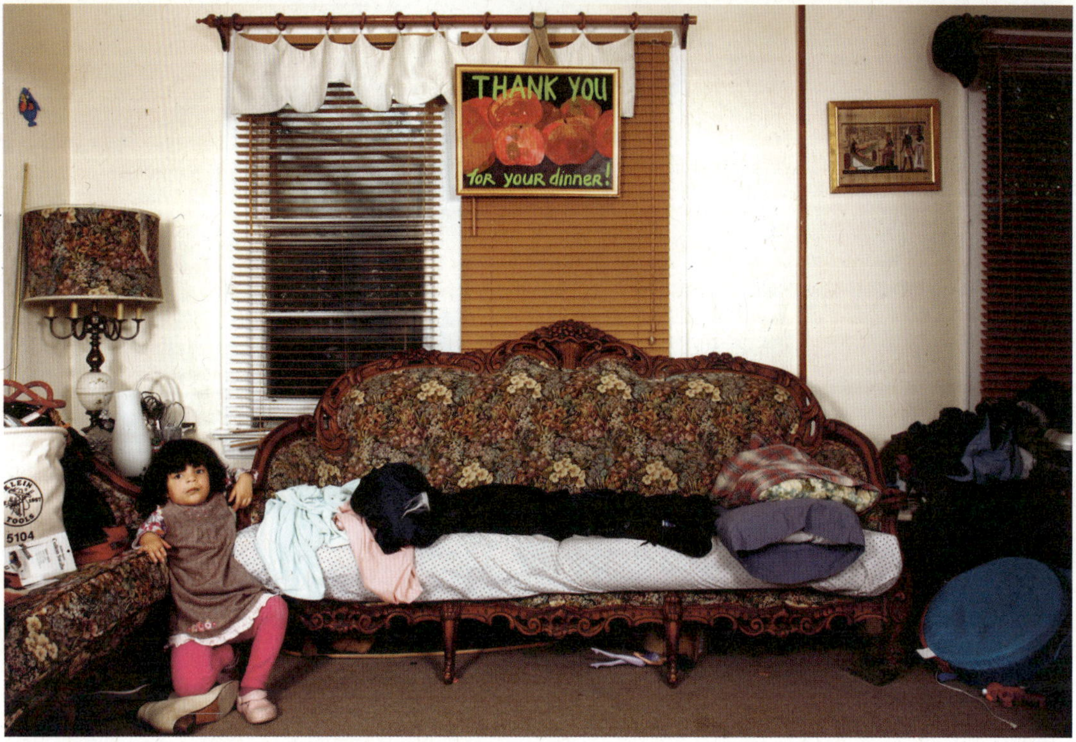

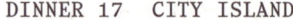

DINNER 16 TIME FOR A FAMILY PORTRAIT   ZEIT FÜR EIN FAMILIENPORTRÄT

DINNER 17 CITY ISLAND

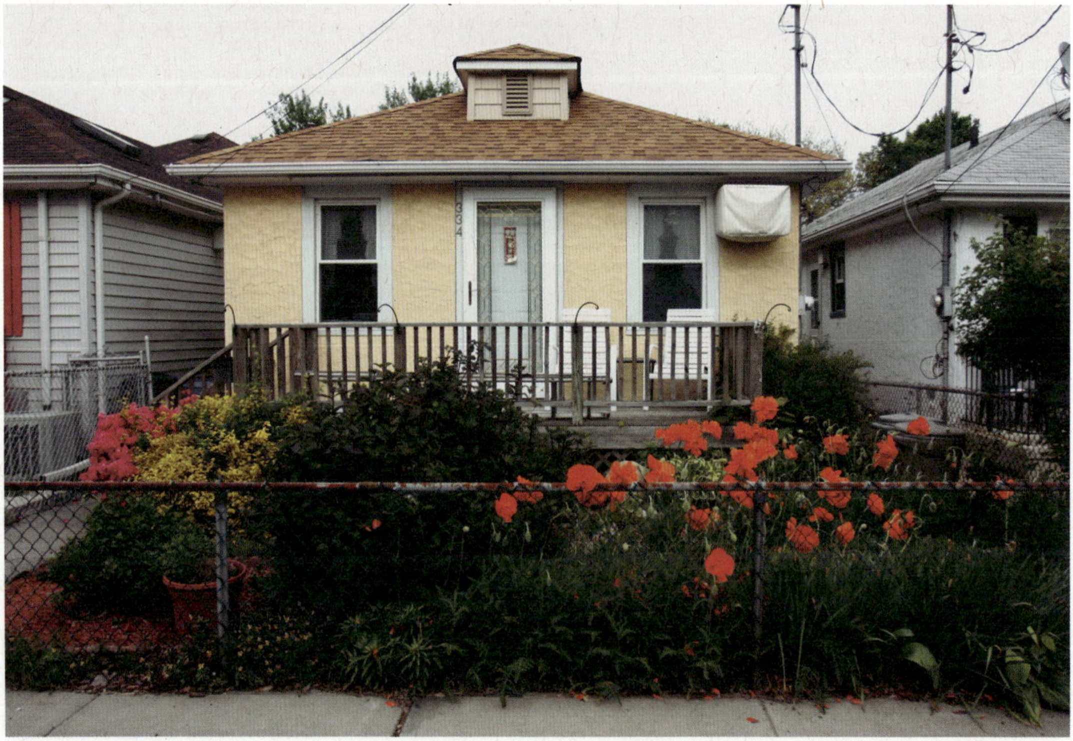

We were invited by Beatrice and Manny "Megman" Oquendo to the home of his parents, Paco and Noemi, on City Island. It was our first visit to the island. City Island is a small island at the extreme western end of Long Island Sound, about 1.5 miles long by 0.5 miles wide, a real gem that looks more like a fishing village than a Bronx neighborhood.

Francisco "Paco" Lugovina is a Buddhist priest, community organizer, activist, and one of the long-time residents of City Island, known as "clam diggers," who try to preserve the island's culture in the face of newcomers, called "mussel suckers." ↙ P. 35

Wir wurden von Beatrice und Manny „Megman" Oquendo in das Haus seiner Eltern, Paco und Noemi, auf City Island eingeladen. Es war unser erster Besuch auf der Insel. City Island ist eine kleine Insel am äußersten westlichen Ende des Long Island Sound, etwa 2,4 km lang und 0,8 km breit — ein echtes Juwel, das eher wie ein Fischerdorf als ein Viertel der Bronx wirkt. Francisco „Paco" Lugovina ist ein buddhistischer Priester, Community-Organizer, Aktivist und einer der langjährigen Bewohner von City Island, die als „clam diggers" (Muschelgräber*innen) bekannt sind. Sie versuchen, die Kultur der Insel gegen die Neuankömmlinge, die „mussel suckers" (Muschelsauger*innen), zu bewahren. ↙ S. 35

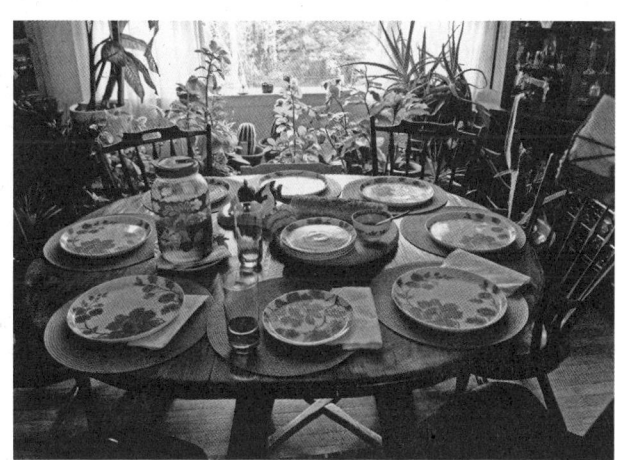

The next day, we visited the single-family home of Israel, Sandra, and their sons, Andres and Xavier. Israel is a history and social science teacher, and Sandra is the principal of a Bronx high school.
Sandra was helping in the kitchen while their boys set the table with colorful mats. Israel's passion is cooking. The menu included ceviche, green salad, stuffed chicken, and rice. ↙ P. 36

Am nächsten Tag besuchten wir das Einfamilienhaus von Israel, Sandra und ihren Söhnen Andres und Xavier. Israel ist Lehrer für Geschichte und Sozialwissenschaften und Sandra ist Direktorin einer High School in der Bronx.
Sandra half in der Küche, während die Jungs den Tisch mit bunten Platzsets deckten. Israels Leidenschaft ist das Kochen. Auf dem Speiseplan standen Ceviche, grüner Salat, gefülltes Huhn und Reis. ↙ S. 36

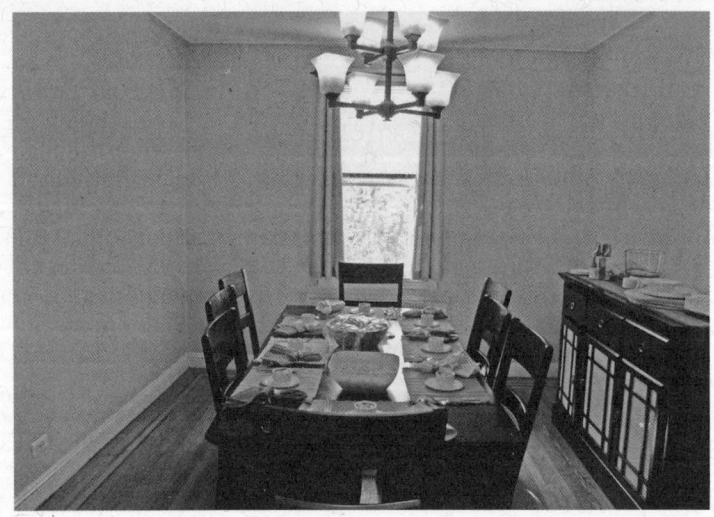

For dinner that day, we had to travel across the Bronx to visit an apartment building near the Yankee Stadium where Thailand-born Manaswinee lives with her husband Hector and their four kids.

Manaswinee, an employee of the Bronx Botanical Garden, is involved in all kinds of local initiatives from kayaking on the East River to bring attention to the poor water quality to running local elementary school bake sales. Hector, a Vietnam War veteran, is a maintenance worker at the Statue of Liberty. Manaswinee cooked Thai food, and we all enjoyed it. ✓ P. 37

Zum Abendessen an diesem Tag mussten wir quer durch die Bronx zu einem Wohnhaus in der Nähe des Yankee Stadium fahren, wo die in Thailand geborene Manaswinee mit ihrem Ehemann Hector und ihren vier Kindern lebt.
Manaswinee, eine Mitarbeiterin des Bronx Botanical Garden, engagiert sich in allen möglichen lokalen Initiativen — von Kajakfahrten auf dem East River, um auf die schlechte Wasserqualität aufmerksam zu machen, bis hin zu Charity–Kuchenverkäufen an örtlichen Grundschulen. Hector, ein Vietnamkriegsveteran, arbeitet als Hausmeister an der Freiheitsstatue. Manaswinee kochte thailändisches Essen, das uns allen sehr schmeckte. ✓ S. 37

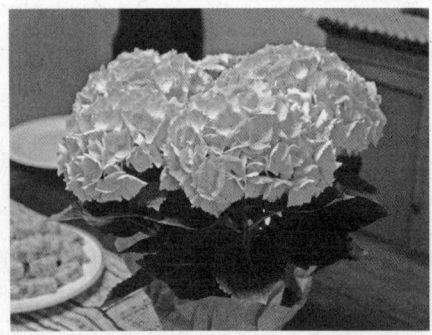

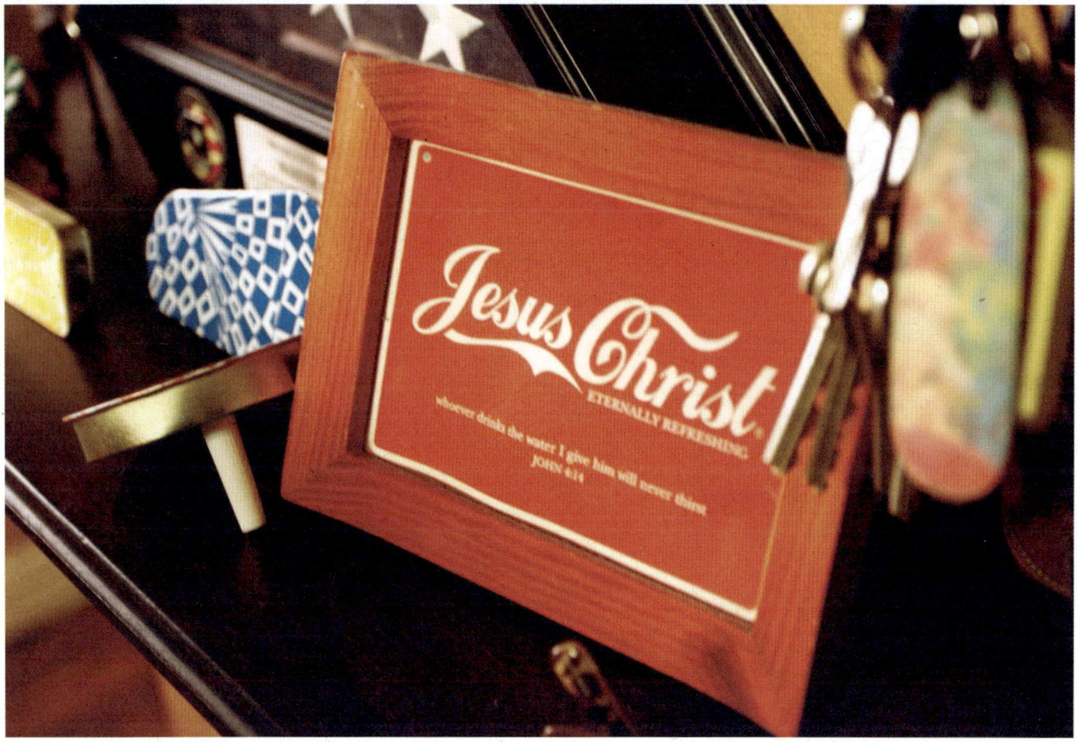

DINNER 19   HECTOR'S DESK   HECTORS SCHREIBTISCH

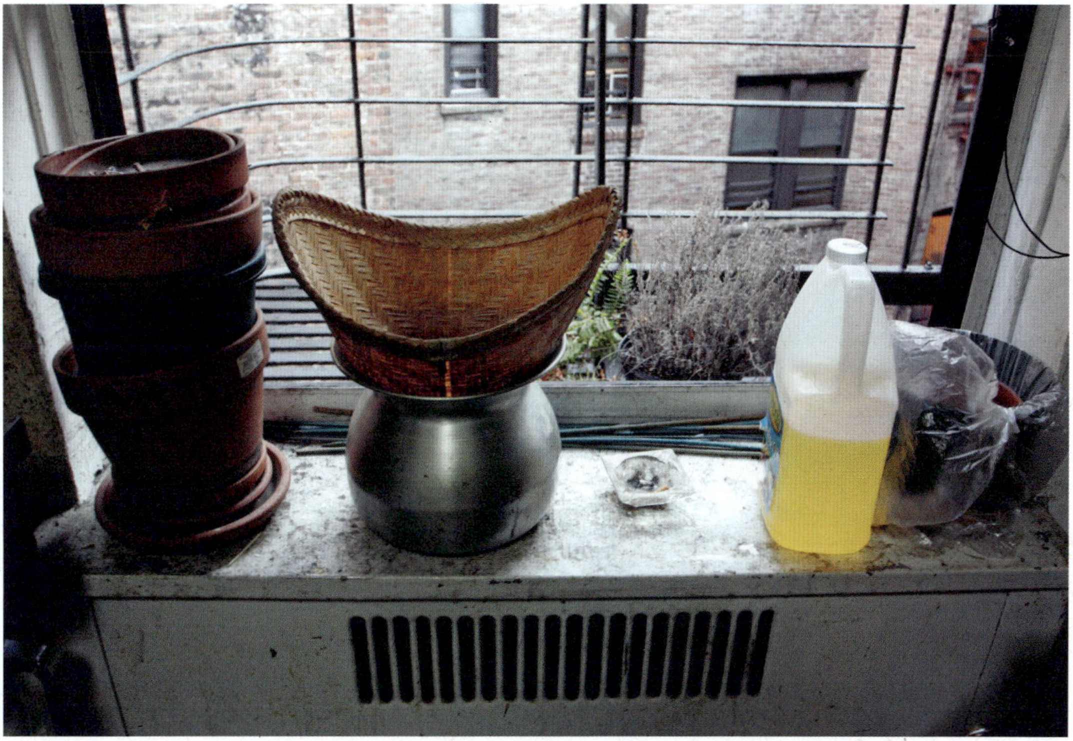

In early August 2013, we placed
the following call for participation
to Beijing residents via social
networking sites:

夫妻藝術家團隊會提供一
幅繪畫作品，來換取一次家庭晚餐
的邀請。如需了解更多詳情，
請發送郵件或致電聯繫。

"Husband and wife artist team is
offering a painting in exchange for
an invitation to a family dinner.
Please email or call for more info."
Between September 13 and 21,
we had meals with ten families
all over Beijing.

Anfang August 2013 riefen wir die
Einwohner*innen Pekings über soziale
Netzwerke zur Teilnahme auf:
„Künstler*innenteam–Ehepaar bietet ein
Gemälde im Austausch für eine Einladung
zum Familienabendessen. Für weitere
Informationen bitte telefonisch oder per
E-Mail melden."
Zwischen dem 13. und 21. September
haben wir mit zehn Familien in ganz
Peking zu Abend gegessen.

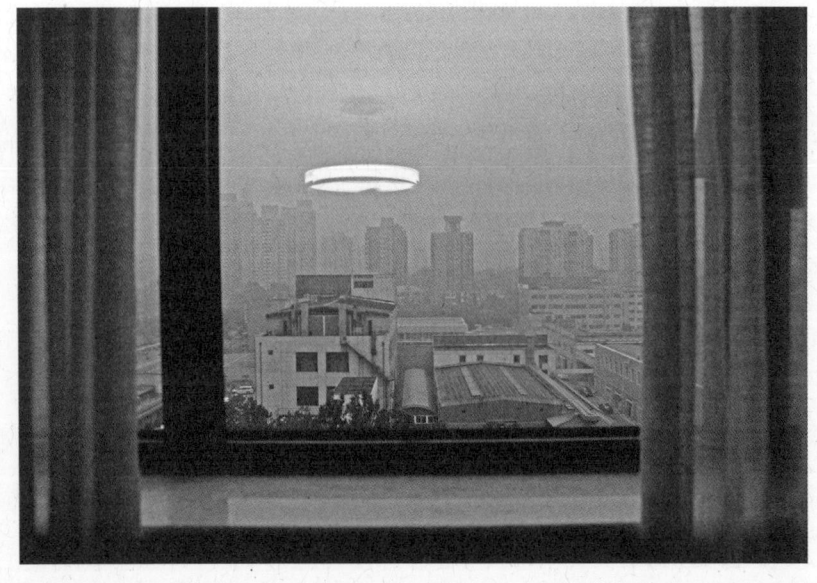

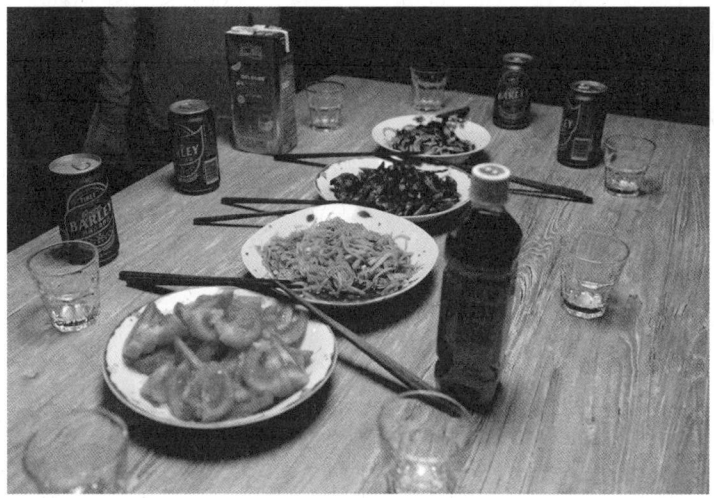

Mr. Cheng, Yang Xue Li and their teenage son, Cheng Tao Ning, greeted us in a modern apartment in the central part of the city.

Cheng Tao Ning is encouraged to learn English. Many Chinese parents see it as a necessary skill for success. The family was surprised to hear that many schools in New York are integrating Chinese language classes, considering it to be a key to success as well.

That day we had to rely on the help of a translator, Ms. Zeng, who joined us in the evening. The meal included many vegetable dishes, followed by homemade dumplings. Sliced tomatoes sprinkled with sugar were new to us.

After we gifted our "Thank You" painting to the family, Mr. Cheng added his signature on the back of the painting, emphasizing his active collaboration on the project.

Time to go, and it is not even dark outside. Beijingers eat their dinners early. ↙ P. 38

Herr Cheng, Yang Xue Li und ihr jugendlicher Sohn, Cheng Tao Ning, begrüßten uns in einer modernen Wohnung im Zentrum der Stadt.

Cheng Tao Ning wird ermutigt, Englisch zu lernen. Viele chinesische Eltern betrachten das als Grundvoraussetzung für den Erfolg. Die Familie war überrascht, als sie erfuhr, dass viele Schulen in New York Chinesischunterricht einführen und dies ebenfalls als Schlüssel zum Erfolg betrachten.

An diesem Tag waren wir auf die Hilfe einer Übersetzerin, Frau Zeng, angewiesen, die sich uns am Abend anschloss. Das Essen bestand aus vielen Gemüsegerichten, gefolgt von hausgemachten Dumplings. Mit Zucker bestreute Tomatenscheiben waren neu für uns.

Nachdem wir der Familie unser „Dankeschön"-Gemälde überreicht hatten, fügte Herr Cheng seine Unterschrift auf der Rückseite des Bildes hinzu. Er unterstrich damit seine aktive Mitarbeit an dem Projekt.

Zeit zu gehen, und draußen ist es noch nicht einmal dunkel. Die Menschen in Peking essen früh zu Abend.
↙ S. 38

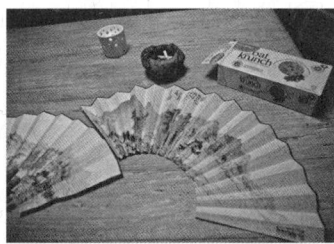

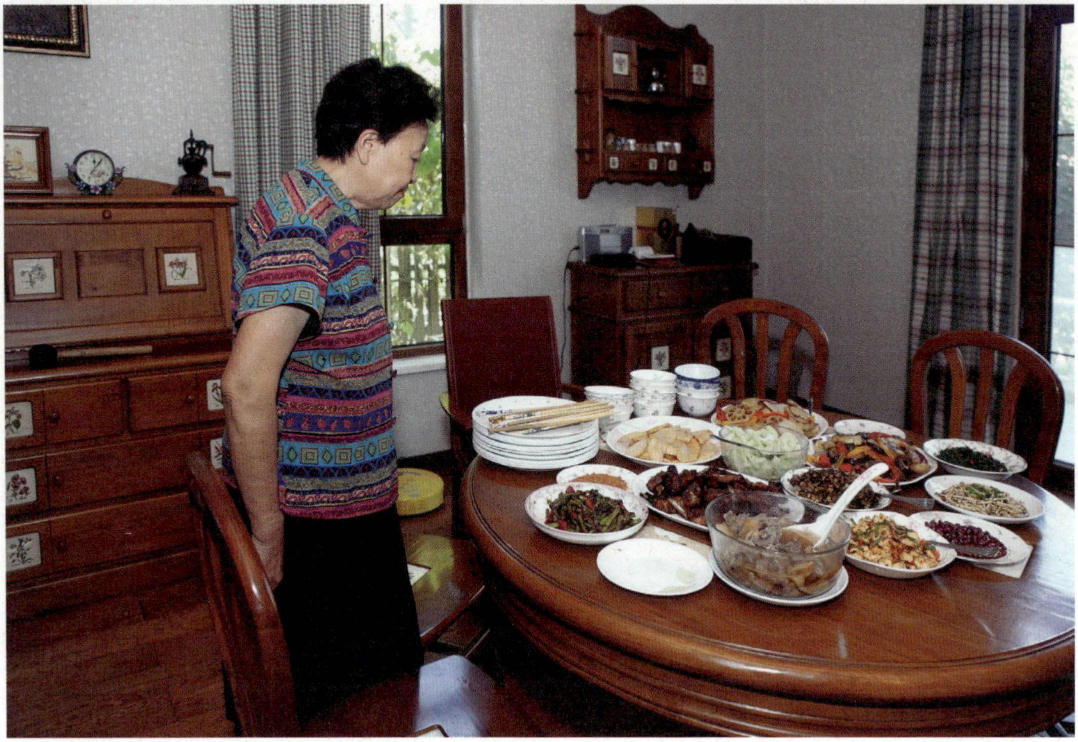

DINNER 21   FINAL TOUCHES ON THE FEAST   DER LETZTE SCHLIFF FÜR DAS FESTMAHL

DINNER 22   SLIPPERS ARE A MUST   HAUSSCHUHE SIND PFLICHT

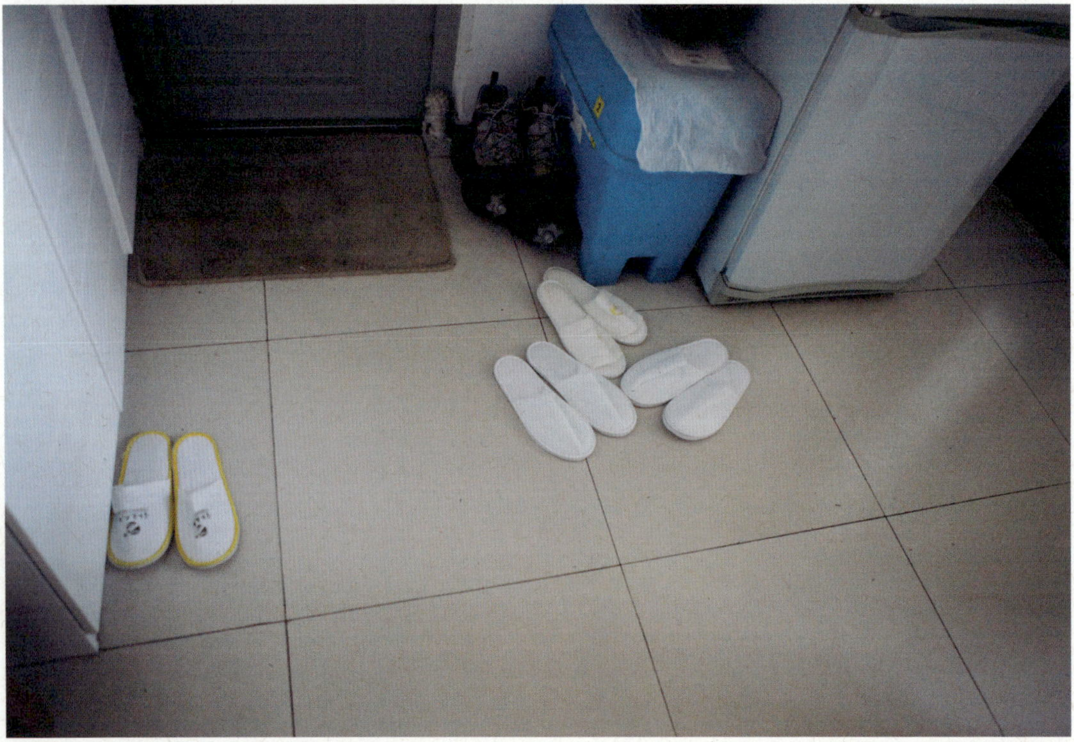

In the afternoon, we meet Sanguo Cheng, his wife Yanhong Kong, and his mother-in-law Ji Qiong Yang in their house in the suburbs of Beijing.

We started with a tea ceremony lead by Sanguo Cheng. Meanwhile Ji Qiong Yang was putting the final touches on preparing the feast with the help of other guests. Ji Qiong Yang made her signature squash and pumpkin soup, using vegetables she grows in her garden.

We were about to go, but not without presents, and here was an important lesson to learn. You have to be careful about what you praise in a Chinese household, because a host may end up giving it to you as a gift. We left with two ceramic jars of tea that we praised during the tea ceremony. ✓ P. 39

Am Nachmittag treffen wir Sanguo Cheng, seine Frau Yanhong Kong und seine Schwiegermutter Ji Qiong Yang in ihrem Haus in einem Vorort von Peking.

Wir begannen mit einer Teezeremonie, die von Sanguo Cheng geleitet wurde. Währenddessen gab Ji Qiong Yang mit Hilfe anderer Gäste dem Festmahl den letzten Schliff. Ji Qiong Yang kochte ihre Spezialität: eine Kürbissuppe, für die sie Gemüse aus ihrem Garten verwendet.

Wir waren im Begriff zu gehen, aber nicht ohne Geschenke, und dabei lernten wir eine wichtige Lektion. Man muss aufpassen, was man in einem chinesischen Haushalt lobt, denn es kann sein, dass der Gastgeber es einem am Ende schenkt. Wir gingen mit zwei Keramik-Teedosen nach Hause, die wir während der Teezeremonie gelobt hatten. ✓ S. 39

Later that day, we reached the apartment of Li Zhiyan and Liu Wenbin in a five-story panel building in the central part of the city.
Li Zhiyan greeted us at the door, slippers are a must.
The host Liu Wenbin was busy in the kitchen. There were two parts of the kitchen: the original kitchen and an expanded kitchen in the glass-walled balcony, where there was an extra stove with an exhaust. Liu Wenbin moved quickly between two spaces, utilizing both. The family has a garden just outside of Beijing, where they grow vegetables to use fresh, pickled, or canned. Jeff tried their homemade 80 proof vodka.

Liu Wenbin has to travel because of his engineering work. He mentioned that his last trip was to Italy, but when we started praising Italian cuisine, he quickly replied that he only tried it once during his seven-day trip. He didn't like it and ate Chinese food for the rest of his stay.
✓ P. 40

Später am Tag erreichten wir die Wohnung von Li Zhiyan und Liu Wenbin in einem fünfstöckigen Plattenbau im Zentrum der Stadt.
Li Zhiyan begrüßte uns an der Tür, Hausschuhe waren ein Muss.
Der Gastgeber Liu Wenbin war in der Küche beschäftigt. Es gab zwei Teile der Küche: die ursprüngliche Küche und eine erweiterte Küche auf dem verglasten Balkon, wo es einen zusätzlichen Herd mit Abzug gab. Liu Wenbin bewegte sich flink zwischen den Bereichen hin und her und nutzte beide. Die Familie hat einen Garten etwas außerhalb von Peking, in dem sie Gemüse anbaut, das sie frisch, eingelegt oder eingekocht verwendet. Jeff probierte ihren selbstgemachten 80-prozentigen Wodka.
Liu Wenbin muss wegen seiner Arbeit als Ingenieur viel reisen. Er erwähnte, dass seine letzte Reise nach Italien ging, aber als wir anfingen, die italienische Küche zu loben, antwortete er schnell, dass er sie nur einmal während seiner siebentägigen Reise probiert habe. Er mochte sie nicht und aß für den Rest seines Aufenthalts chinesisches Essen. ✓ S. 40

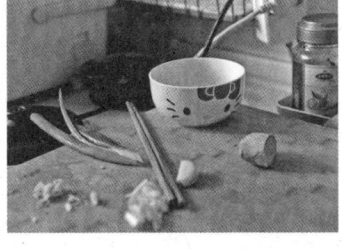

The next day, we planned to visit a husband and wife in a newly constructed building complex.

It turned out to be just Carol; her husband had to go on an emergency business trip.

During our visit, we felt that we indirectly met her whole family: Her husband through their wedding photographs. Her father, who lives in another province, through the folded newspaper boats that he makes for his daughter and mails to her. The boats are good for storing fruit pits during the meal. And Carol's mother, through her recipes that her daughter followed. ↙ P. 41

Am nächsten Tag wollten wir ein Ehepaar in einem neu erbauten Wohnkomplex besuchen. Es stellte sich heraus, dass nur Carol zu Hause war; ihr Ehemann hatte eine dringende Geschäftsreise antreten müssen.

Während unseres Besuchs hatten wir das Gefühl, ihre ganze Familie indirekt kennenzulernen: Ihren Ehemann durch ihre Hochzeitsfotos. Ihren Vater, der in einer anderen Provinz lebt, durch die gefalteten Zeitungsschiffchen, die er für seine Tochter bastelt und ihr zuschickt. Diese Boote sind gut dafür geeignet, während des Essens Obstkerne zu verstauen. Und Carols Mutter lernten wir durch die Rezepte kennen, denen ihre Tochter folgte. ↙ S. 41

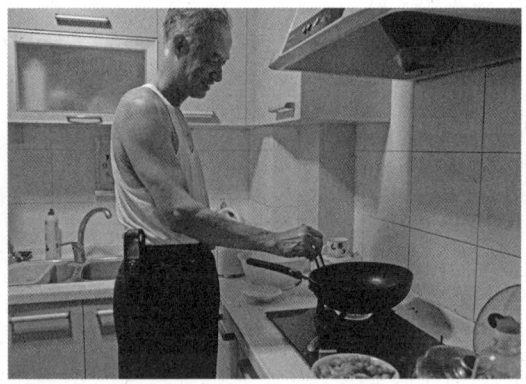 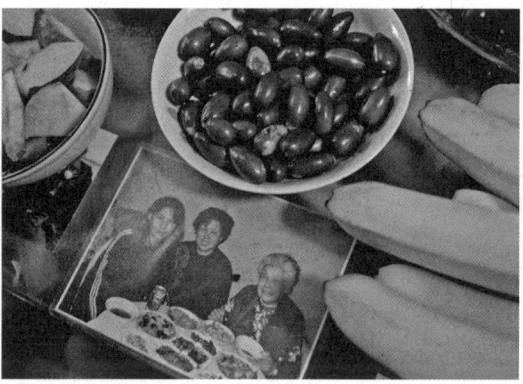

Later that day, we visited Hanjun Guo and her family: her husband HaoXiang Chen, her sister Shengli Liu, and her niece Wei Zhai. As with a few other families we visited, both husband and wife were cooking alongside each other. The family joke is that Hanjun Guo would spend all day in the kitchen and HaoXiang Chen will cook something in five minutes and everyone would love his dishes better.

Hanjun Guo's parents are both traditional Chinese artists, so her house is full of their art, books, and antiques. Nonetheless, she is social media savvy. While we were still at the table, our photos appeared on her blog. ↙ P. 42

Später besuchten wir Hanjun Guo und ihre Familie: ihren Ehemann HaoXiang Chen, ihre Schwester Shengli Liu und ihre Nichte Wei Zhai. Wie bei einigen anderen Familien, die wir besuchten, kochten Ehemann und Ehefrau nebeneinander. Es ist eine alte Geschichte in der Familie, dass Hanjun Guo den ganzen Tag in der Küche verbringt, während HaoXiang Chen in fünf Minuten etwas kocht, das allen besser schmeckt.

Die Eltern von Hanjun Guo sind beide traditionelle chinesische Künstler*innen, daher ist ihr Haus voll mit deren Kunst, Büchern und Antiquitäten. Trotzdem ist sie äußerst versiert, was die sozialen Medien betrifft. Noch während wir am Tisch saßen, erschienen unsere Fotos auf ihrem Blog. ↙ S. 42

Hanjun's Shredded Pork
with Green Peppers

300 grams pork tenderloin
100 grams green peppers
5 grams salt
1 gram MSG
10 grams mixture of cornstarch and water
100 grams cooking oil
1 egg white
10 grams cooking wine
25 grams water

Cut the meat into thin strips 6 cm
long and 0.3 cm thick and wide.
Put in a bowl. Add 1 g of salt and stir until
mixture becomes sticky. Add the egg white
and dry cornstarch and mix well.

Cut the green peppers into strips of similar size to the meat.

Heat the oil to 110–135°C and
stir-fry the pork strips until they are done.
Take out and drain off the oil.

Put 25 g of oil in the wok and
stir-fry the strips of green peppers for one minute.
Add the shredded pork, cooking wine, salt, MSG,
and water and bring to boiling point. Put in the mixture
of cornstarch and water to thicken the sauce.

Take out and serve.

Next day we went to meet Shao Jun, her husband Dai Jing, her son Dai Mingyang, her father Shao Yingzhi, and her mother Du Shuhua. Shao Jun met us outside so she could lead the way through her building complex, since it was hard to navigate. The family lives in a modern high-rise with a view of a park, which is considered a luxury in Beijing. Her mother decorated the interior in a traditional style with dark wood and red accents, even her colorful handmade slippers matched the style. The dinner consisted of thin pancakes with various meat and vegetable fillings, and a homemade fermented, mildly alcoholic rice drink, jiuniang, similar to an unfiltered rice wine.
After the meal, Du Shuhua shared her new hobby with us: playing guzheng, a zither-type instrument. Impressive! ↙ P. 43

Am nächsten Tag trafen wir Shao Jun, ihren Ehemann Dai Jing, ihren Sohn Dai Mingyang, ihren Vater Shao Yingzhi und ihre Mutter Du Shuhua. Shao Jun Shao Jun holte uns draußen ab, um uns den Weg durch ihren etwas unübersichtlichen Gebäudekomplex zu zeigen. Die Familie wohnt in einem modernen Hochhaus mit Blick auf einen Park, was in Peking als Luxus gilt. Ihre Mutter hat die Wohnung in einem traditionellen Stil mit dunklem Holz und roten Akzenten eingerichtet, sogar ihre bunten, handgefertigten Hausschuhe passten zu diesem Stil. Das Abendessen bestand aus dünnen Pfannkuchen mit verschiedenen Fleisch- und Gemüsefüllungen sowie einem selbstgemachten fermentierten, leicht alkoholischen Reisgetränk namens Jiuniang, das einem ungefilterten Reiswein ähnelt.
Nach dem Essen teilte Du Shuhua ihr neues Hobby mit uns: das Spielen der Guzheng, eines zitherähnlichen Instruments. Beeindruckend! ↙ S. 43

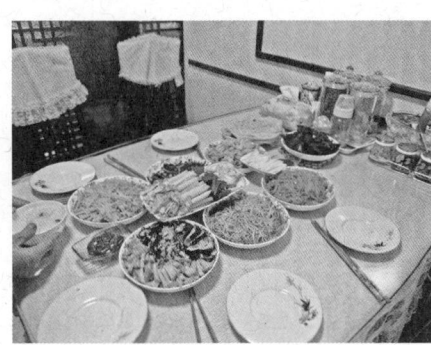

The following day, we met a young family in the Chaoyang District. The hostess Xunbo Guo came downstairs to meet us. Her husband was on his way home from work. Soon Zongxi Zhang arrived bringing some fruits and moon cakes. He placed the moon cakes on a plate and wanted us to try. Our project in China had coincided with The Mid-Autumn Festival, one of the four most important Chinese festivals. Traditionally it is a harvest festival, but nowadays it is like Chinese Thanksgiving. The festival is for lunar worship and moon watching, and moon cakes are regarded as an indispensable delicacy. ↙ P. 44

Am folgenden Tag trafen wir eine junge Familie im Bezirk Chaoyang. Die Gastgeberin Xunbo Guo kam herunter, um uns zu empfangen. Ihr Ehemann war auf dem Heimweg von der Arbeit. Bald traf Zongxi Zhang ein und brachte Früchte und Mondkuchen mit. Er arrangierte die Mondkuchen auf einen Teller und bat uns, sie zu probieren.
Unser Projekt in China fiel mit dem Mittherbstfest zusammen, einem der vier wichtigsten chinesischen Feste. Traditionell ist es ein Erntefest, aber heutzutage ist es eher wie das chinesische Thanksgiving. Das Fest ist der Mondverehrung und der Mondbeobachtung gewidmet, und Mondkuchen gelten als unentbehrliche Delikatesse. ↙ S. 44

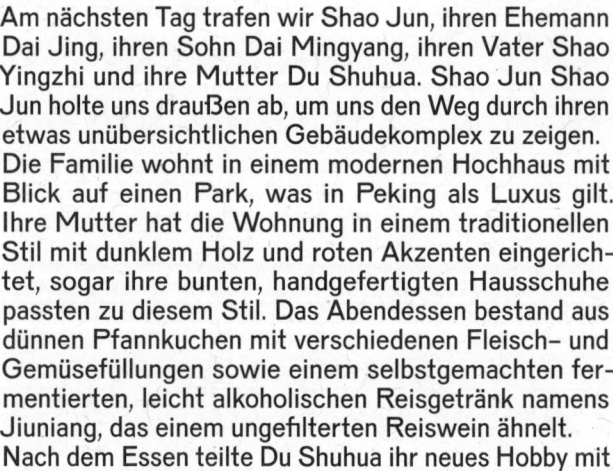

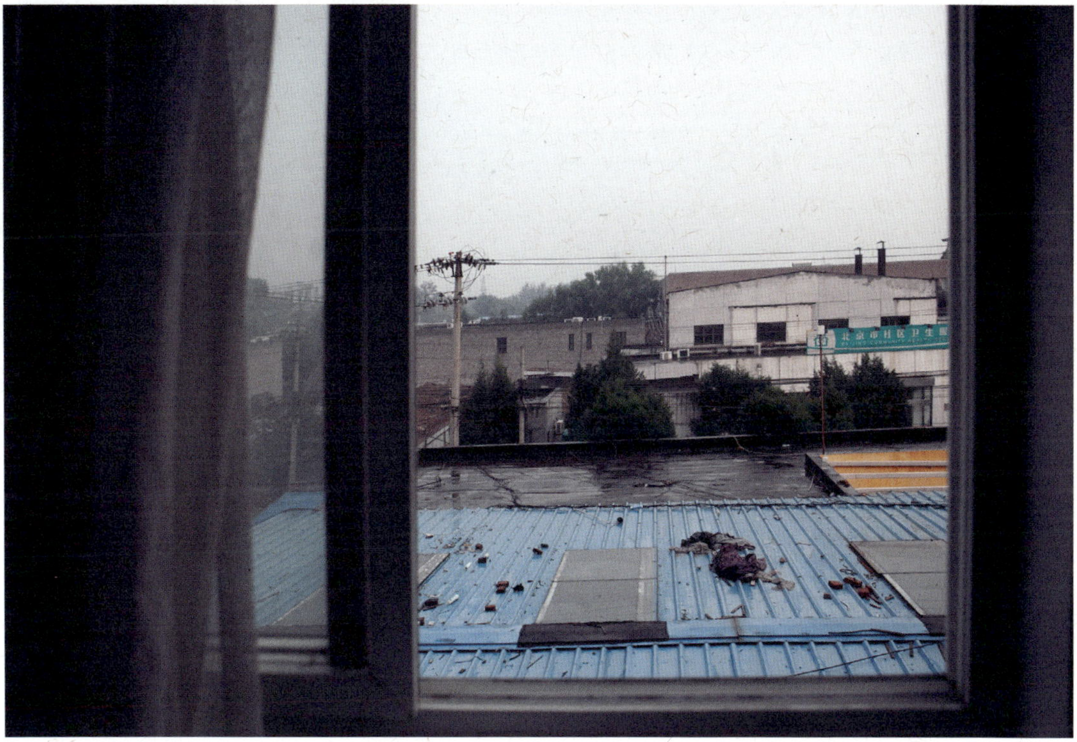

DINNER 26   THE CHAOYANG DISTRICT

DINNER 26   FRUITS AND MOON CAKES

FRÜCHTE UND MONDKUCHEN

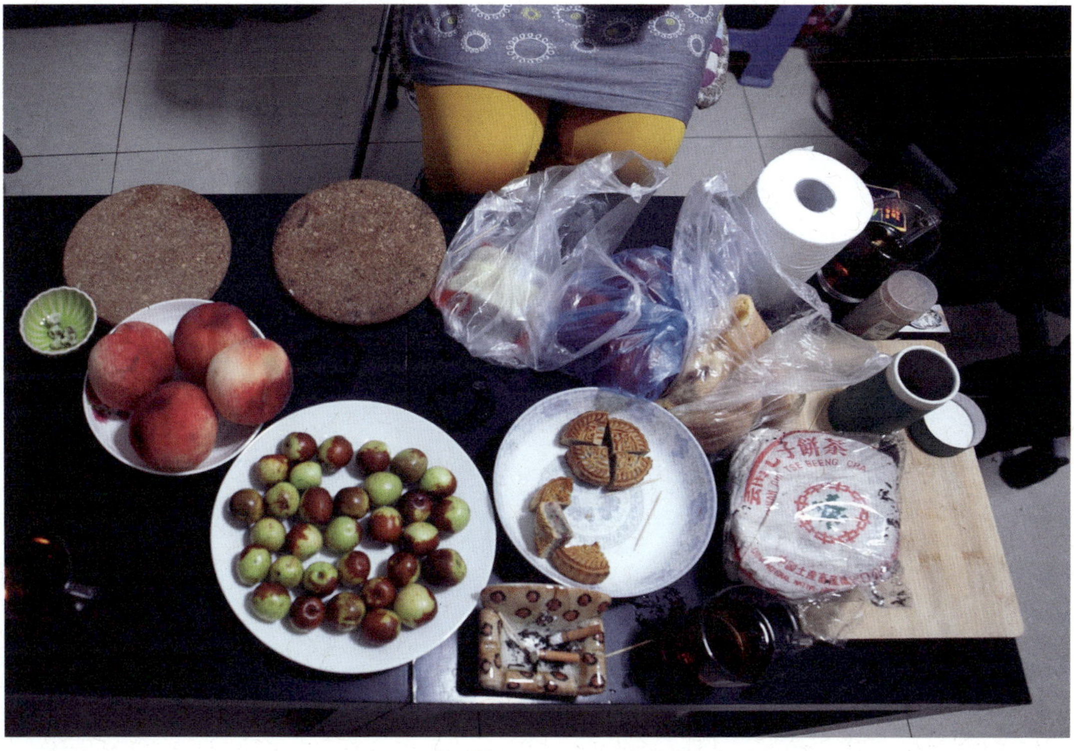

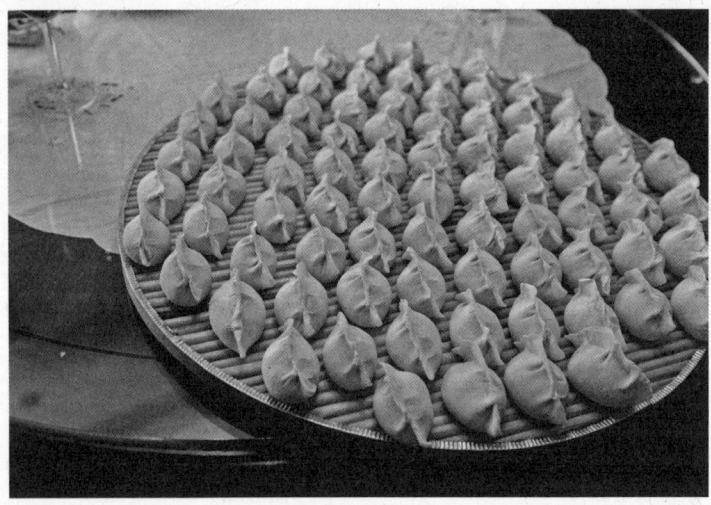

The next day, we had lunch at the home of Mini Li and her husband, Liangjun Xu, just outside of Beijing. Their long-time friends joined us. Mini cooked her signature dish: homemade dumplings.

After lunch we had our first lesson in Mahjong, a nineteenth-century Chinese tile-based game. The symbols are Peng, Bamboos, Dragons, Gang, Flowers, Chi, Eyes, Circles, and Seasons. Alina won. It's what you call "beginner's luck" or "good hosting." ↙ P. 45

Am nächsten Tag waren wir zum Mittagessen bei Mini Li und ihrem Ehemann Liangjun Xu, etwas außerhalb von Peking. Ihre langjährigen Freund*innen schlossen sich uns an. Mini kochte ihre Spezialität, selbstgemachte Dumplings.

Nach dem Mittagessen hatten wir unsere erste Lektion in Mahjong, einem chinesischen Spiel mit Plättchen, das auf den Symbolen Peng, Bambus, Drachen, Gang, Blumen, Chi, Augen, Kreise und Jahreszeiten basiert. Alina gewann. Sowas nennt man „Anfängerglück" oder „gute Gastgeber*innen sein". ↙ S. 45

Later that day we visited a young couple living in a hutong: Cao Chao, a photographer, and Wu Xuan, an illustrator, who just moved to Beijing.

Hutongs are alleys formed by rows of siheyuan, or traditional courtyard residences. Since the mid-twentieth century, the number of Beijing hutongs has dropped dramatically as many have been demolished to make way for new construction. More recently, some hutongs have been designated as protected areas in an attempt to preserve this aspect of Chinese cultural history and have become tourist attractions. The couple lives in a house with two small rooms: one room has a fridge and a sink; the other has a bed, bookshelves, and a dining table. The communal kitchen and bathroom are in two different structures in a courtyard and shared by all the neighbors.

Cao Chao considers himself a gastronome. He loves experimenting with food, and has a blog, Cooked in Hutong.

IN HIS WORDS: "There is an old saying in China: 'shi se xing ye'
(The desire for food and sex is part of human nature).
Shi means food. Se not only refers to sex but also color.
Those two things are my favorite: cooking and picturing
its color.
I think they are the same, both reflect your desire.
Being a gastronome and photographer is the best
choice in my life." ⌐ P. 46

Später an diesem Tag besuchten wir ein junges Paar, das in einem
Hutong lebt: Cao Chao, ein Fotograf, und Wu Xuan, eine Illustratorin,
die gerade nach Peking gezogen waren.
Hutongs sind Gassen, die von Reihen von Siheyuan, traditionellen Häu-
sern mit Innenhöfen, gebildet werden. Seit Mitte des 20. Jahrhunderts
ist die Zahl der Hutongs in Peking drastisch gesunken, da viele abgeris-
sen wurden, um Platz für Neubauten zu schaffen. In letzter Zeit wurden
einige Hutongs als schützenswerte Zonen ausgewiesen, um diesen
Aspekt der chinesischen Kulturgeschichte zu bewahren, und wurden
zu touristischen Attraktionen.
Das Paar lebt in einem Haus mit zwei kleinen Zimmern: ein Zimmer
mit einem Kühlschrank und einem Waschbecken, das andere mit einem
Bett, Bücherregalen und einem Esstisch. Die Gemeinschaftsküche und
das Badezimmer befinden sich in zwei verschiedenen Gebäuden im
Innenhof und werden von allen Nachbar*innen genutzt.
Cao Chao bezeichnet sich selbst als Feinschmecker. Er liebt es, mit
Essen zu experimentieren, und hat einen Blog mit dem Titel „Cooked
in Hutong".

IN SEINEN WORTEN: „Es gibt ein altes Sprichwort in China: ,shi se xing ye' (Das Ver-
langen nach Essen und Sex gehört zur menschlichen Natur).
Shi bedeutet Essen. Se bezieht sich nicht nur auf Sex, sondern
auch auf Farbe. Diese beiden Dinge sind meine Lieblings-
dinge: das Kochen und seine Farben malen.
Ich denke, sie sind gleich, beide spiegeln dein Begeh-
ren wider. Ein Feinschmecker und ein Fotograf zu
sein, ist die beste Wahl in meinem Leben." ⌐ S. 46

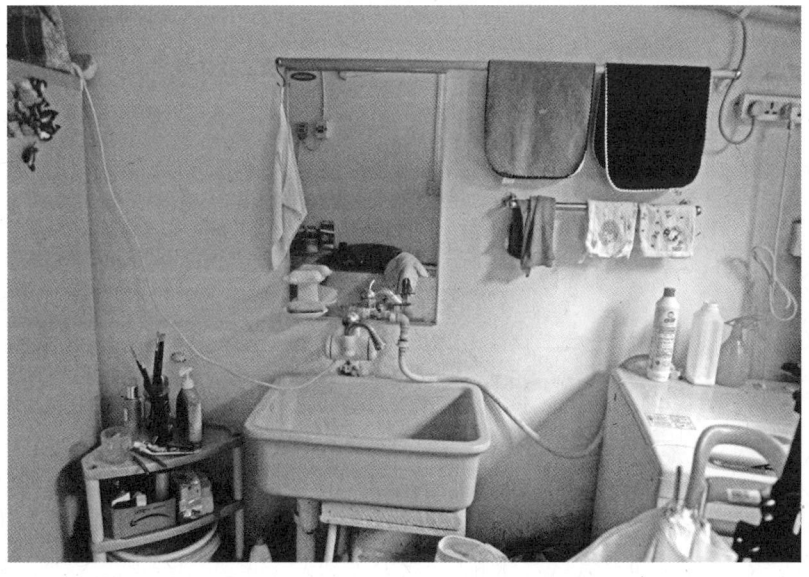

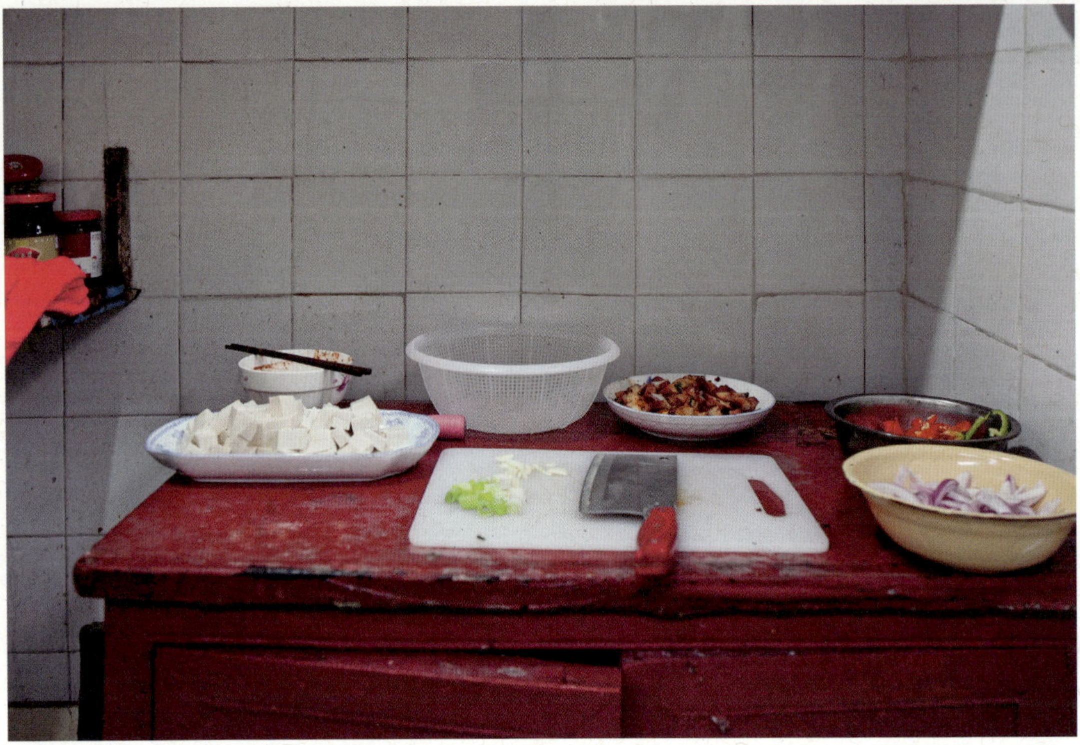

DINNER 28   THE COMMUNAL KITCHEN

DINNER 28   COOKED IN HUTONG

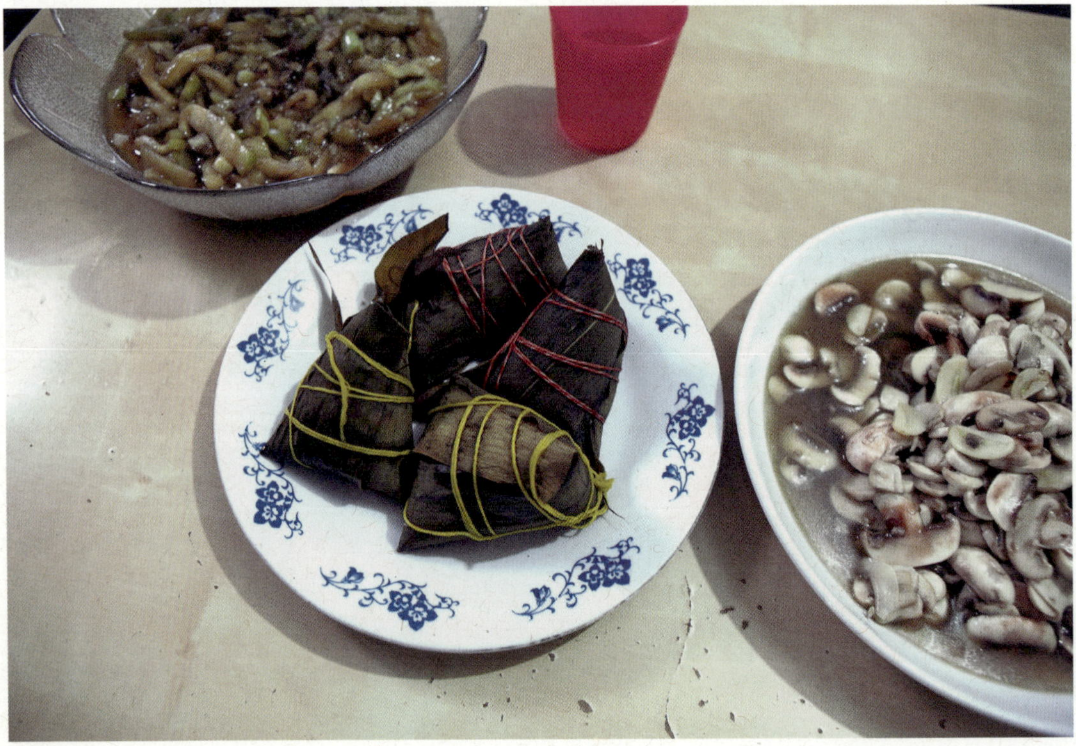

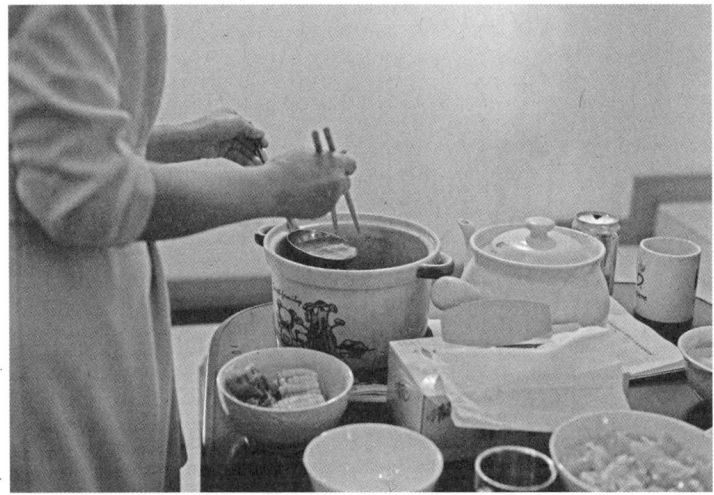

On our last day, we visited Ms. Qiu's apartment on the top floor of a high-rise building in the central part of the city. She is a single mother raising a teenage son, who wasn't there because he takes English classes on the weekends. Ms. Qiu invited her friend, Zhang Hong Ya, also a single mother raising a teenage daughter.

When we arrived, they were both cooking. We started with tea, then Ms. Qiu served a soup and a range of side dishes. Over lunch, both women told us about the challenges of raising children as single mothers in Beijing. ↙ P. 47

An unserem letzten Tag besuchten wir die Wohnung von Frau Qiu im obersten Stockwerk eines Hochhauses im Zentrum der Stadt. Sie ist alleinerziehende Mutter eines Teenagers, der nicht zu Hause war, weil er am Wochenende Englischunterricht hatte. Frau Qiu hatte ihre Freundin Zhang Hong Ya eingeladen, ebenfalls eine alleinerziehende Mutter, die eine Teenager-Tochter großzieht.

Als wir ankamen, waren beide Frauen am Kochen. Wir begannen mit Tee, dann servierte Frau Qiu eine Suppe und eine Auswahl an Beilagen. Während des Mittagessens erzählten uns beide Frauen von den Herausforderungen, ihre Kinder als alleinerziehende Mütter in Peking großzuziehen. ↙ S. 47

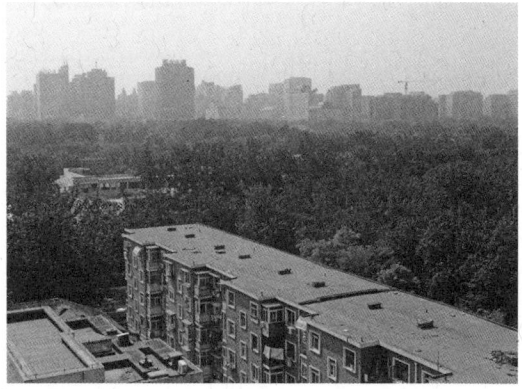

In early September 2013, we placed the following call for participation to Lecce residents via local media, flyers, and social networking sites:

Team di artisti marito e moglie offre un dipinto in cambio di un invito a una cena di famiglia. Si prega di inviare un'e–mail o chiamare per più informazioni.

"Husband and wife artist team is offering a painting in exchange for an invitation to a family dinner. Please email or call for more info." Between October 11 and 17, we had meals with ten families all over Lecce and in the nearby area.

Anfang September 2013 veröffentlichten wir über lokale Medien, Flyer und soziale Netzwerke folgenden Aufruf an die Bewohner*innen von Lecce: „Künstler*innenteam-Ehepaar bietet ein Gemälde im Austausch für eine Einladung zum Familienabendessen. Für weitere Informationen bitte telefonisch oder per E-Mail melden." Zwischen dem 11. und 17. Oktober speisten wir mit zehn Familien in ganz Lecce und der Umgebung.

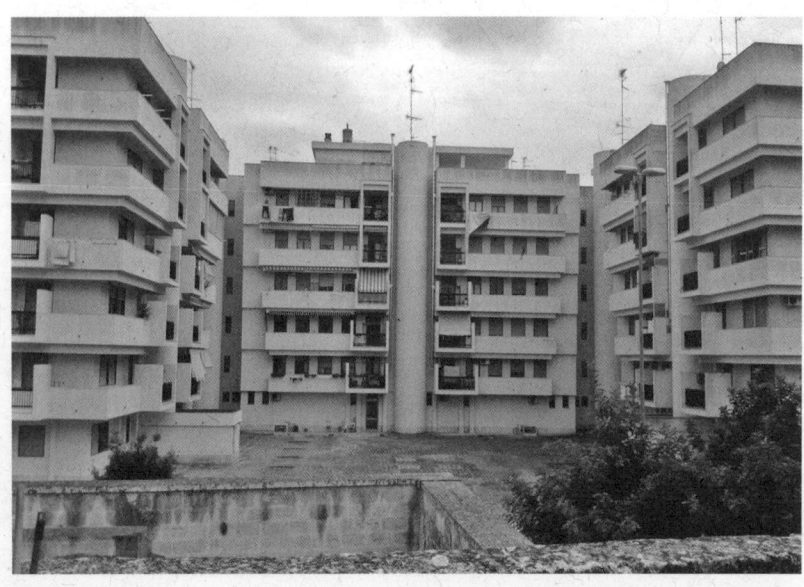

Our hosts, Annarita and Antonio and his brother Nicola joined us that evening. There were countless dishes and plate changes—spaghetti, oysters, beet salad, mozzarella, eggplants, and more. The choice of wine was a social statement by Antonio: Centopassi, Placido Rizzotto, Rosso.

"Centopassi is a label of wines made in Sicily from vines grown on land confiscated from the Mafia. It is produced by the Libera Terra Cooperative, founded by Don Luigi Ciotti, a priest who was the driving force behind a 1995 campaign to change the laws and turn confiscated Mafia property over to social use. He was assassinated by Sicilian Mafia boss Luciano Leggio." ↙ P. 48

Unsere Gastgeber*innen Annarita und Antonio sowie Antonios Bruder Nicola waren an diesem Abend dabei. Es gab unzählige Gerichte und Gänge — Spaghetti, Austern, Rote-Bete-Salat, Mozzarella, Auberginen und mehr. Die Wahl des Weins war ein gesellschaftliches Statement Antonios: Centopassi, Placido Rizzotto, Rosso.

„Centopassi ist ein Weinhersteller aus Sizilien, dessen Trauben auf Land angebaut werden, das der Mafia entzogen wurde. Er wird von der Libera Terra Cooperative produziert, die von Don Luigi Ciotti gegründet wurde, einem Priester, der die treibende Kraft hinter einer Kampagne von 1995 war, die Gesetze zu ändern und beschlagnahmtes Mafia-Eigentum sozialen Zwecken zuzuführen. Er wurde vom sizilianischen Mafiaboss Luciano Leggio ermordet." ↙ S. 48

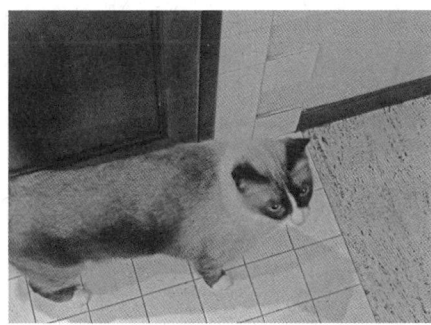

In Lecce, our project was hosted by the Ammirato Culture House. Marcella was in charge of its operations and lived on the second floor of the sixteenth-century villa that was once the home of Renaissance man Scipione Ammirato.
Marcella baked a fish from a local seafood market and made a salad from tomatoes and herbs that she grows on the common terrace. Her plants are "her babies," as she put it. Later that day, her coworkers joined us for the family portrait. ↙ P. 49

In Lecce wurde unser Projekt durch das Ammirato Culture House durchgeführt. Marcella leitete die Einrichtung und lebte im zweiten Stock einer Villa aus dem 16. Jahrhundert, die einst das Haus des Universalgelehrten Scipione Ammirato war.
Marcella bereitete einen Fisch vom örtlichen Fischmarkt im Ofen zu und machte einen Salat aus Tomaten und Kräutern, die sie auf der gemeinsamen Terrasse anbaut. Ihre Pflanzen sind „ihre Babys", wie sie es ausdrückte.
Später gesellten sich ihre Kolleg*innen für das Familienporträt zu uns. ↙ S. 49

Born in Lecce, Alessia rents an apartment near Chiesa Matrice (Mother Church) in the little town of San Pietro in Lama, a fifteen-minute drive from Lecce.

ALESSIA: "The time in the village I'm living in tastes of past ages. Every day, I wake hearing the bell of the church beside my home. Every day, I get the impression that I'm waking up in a Rosi or De Sica movie.

Outside, time stands still. A man is waiting in an old-fashioned car for his wife to come out of the church at the end of the Holy Mass. Everything looks quiet."

Alessia invited her brother, Marco, and her two close friends, Valeria and Antonio, for the dinner. She was trying to stay away from traditional Italian cuisine, leaning instead toward more ethnic-inspired choices of Thai rice with vegetables and chicken.

After dinner, the group went to a bar for a few drinks. ↙ P. 50

Alessia, geboren in Lecce, lebte in einer Mietwohnung in der Nähe der Chiesa Matrice (Mutter–Kirche) im kleinen Ort San Pietro in Lama, etwa 15 Minuten von Lecce entfernt.

ALESSIA: „In dem Dorf, in dem ich lebe, schmeckt die Zeit nach Vergangenheit. Jeden Tag wache ich auf und höre die Glocken der Kirche neben meinem Haus. Jeden Tag habe ich das Gefühl, ich wache in einem Film von Rosi oder De Sica auf.

Draußen scheint die Zeit stillzustehen. Ein Mann wartet in einem altmodischen Auto darauf, dass seine Frau nach der Heiligen Messe aus der Kirche kommt. Alles wirkt ruhig."

Alessia lud ihren Bruder Marco sowie ihre beiden engen Freund*innen Valeria und Antonio zum Abendessen ein. Sie versuchte, sich von der traditionellen italienischen Küche fernzuhalten, und entschied sich stattdessen für thailändischen Reis mit Gemüse und Hühnchen.

Nach dem Essen ging die Gruppe auf ein paar Drinks in eine Bar. ↙ S. 50

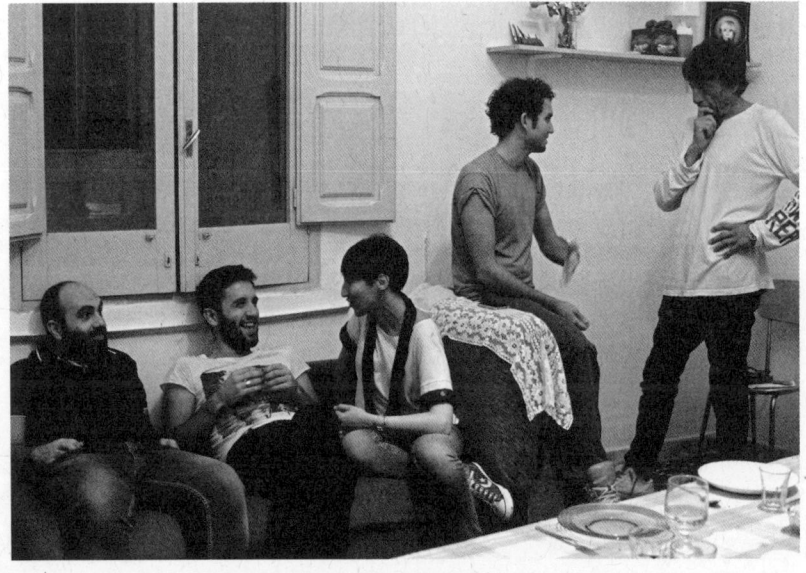

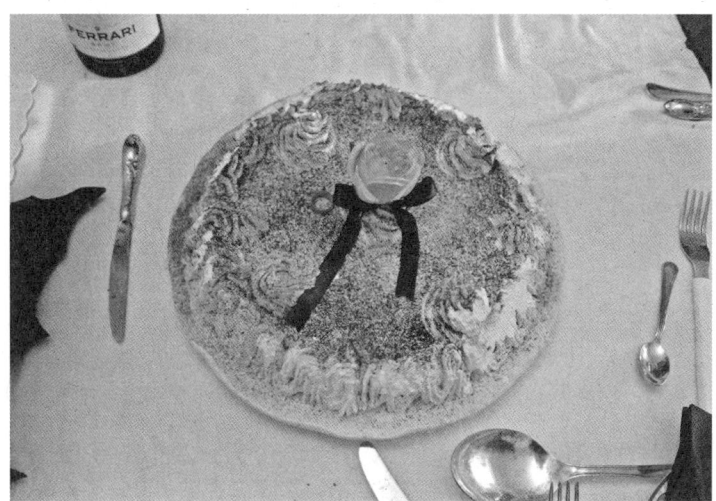

The next day, we visited Nino and Luciana Pomarico. It was a 1 pm lunch—a double birthday celebration of Gaetano Pomarico "Nino" and his friend Franco. The celebration included relatives and friends, old and new. The guests ranged from a Greek Orthodox priest to an Albanian fisherman family. The Pomaricos value traditions, but not formalities. Guests ate, drank, talked, read, and napped.

Nino and Luciana's granddaughter, Nina, lives in New York, but spends summers at her grandparents' house.

NOTE FROM NINA'S PARENTS: "Nina loves to make meatballs. We often make them when she has friends over, and everybody can help. For rolling the meat balls, or another version of it which is called schiacciatine, you roll the ball in your palms and then press the two palms together, like for a small fatty hamburger. We normally bake them in the oven with a bit of oil and white wine. Nina loves getting her hands dirty and working with the sticky texture of ground meat. And it is really helpful to have a group rolling them!" ↙ P. 51

Am nächsten Tag besuchten wir Nino und Luciana Pomarico. Es war ein Mittagessen um 13 Uhr — eine doppelte Geburtstagsfeier für Gaetano Pomarico „Nino" und seinen Freund Franco. Zur Feier kamen Verwandte und Freund*innen, alte wie neue. Die Gäste reichten von einem griechisch–orthodoxen Priester bis zu einer albanischen Fischerfamilie. Die Pomaricos schätzen Traditionen, aber keine Formalitäten. Die Gäste aßen, tranken, redeten, lasen und machten Nickerchen.

Nino und Lucianas Enkelin Nina lebt in New York, verbringt aber die Sommer im Haus ihrer Großeltern.

NOTIZ VON NINAS ELTERN: „Nina kocht unheimlich gerne Fleischbällchen. Wir machen sie oft, wenn sie Freund*innen zu Besuch hat, und alle können mithelfen. Für das Rollen der Fleischbällchen oder einer Variante namens Schiacciatine rollt man die Kugel in den Handflächen und drückt dann die beiden Handflächen zusammen, wie für einen kleinen fetten Hamburger. Normalerweise backen wir sie im Ofen mit etwas Öl und Weißwein. Nina macht gerne ihre Hände schmutzig und liebt es, mit der klebrigen Textur von Hackfleisch zu arbeiten. Und es ist wirklich hilfreich, wenn eine Gruppe beim Rollen hilft!" ↙ S. 51

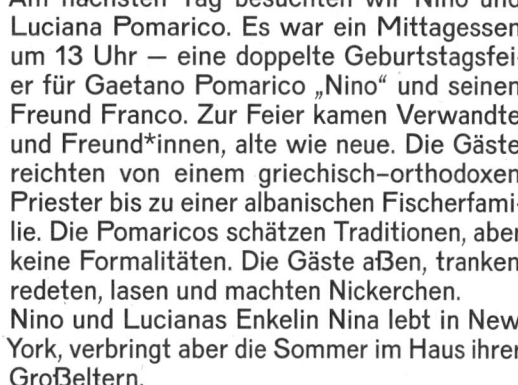

Pomarico's Meatballs

1 pound stale country-style bread
1 ½ cups milk
2 large eggs
½ cup grated pecorino or
Parmigiano Reggiano
1 rib of celery
1 clove garlic, thinly sliced
salt and pepper
1 bay leaf
2 cups basic tomato sauce

Soak stale bread in milk or water; after soaking, remove the hard parts of the bread and squeeze; then add cheese, at least 2 eggs, a little garlic, salt to taste.

Make beautiful balls with the hollow of the hand (not small, but substantial, the size of a walnut.) If intended for adults, you can add a little pepper. I put them in the oven at low temperature for 15 minutes.

Then plunge into boiling tomato sauce that is on the liquid side, because the meatballs absorb a lot of sauce. To flavor the sauce, add a bay leaf and a stalk of celery. It's not as complicated as it looks, and it is easy and suitable for children to have a full meal with only the meatballs.

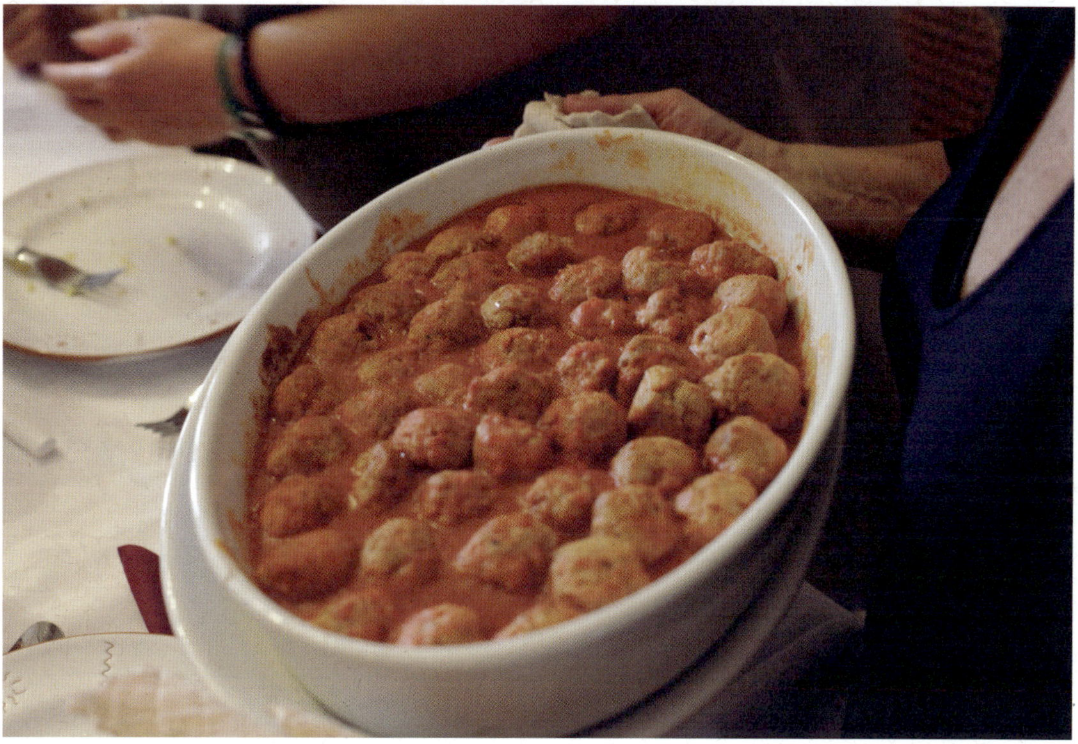

DINNER 33   POMARICO'S MEATBALLS

POMARICOS FLEISCHBÄLLCHEN

DINNER 33   NINA

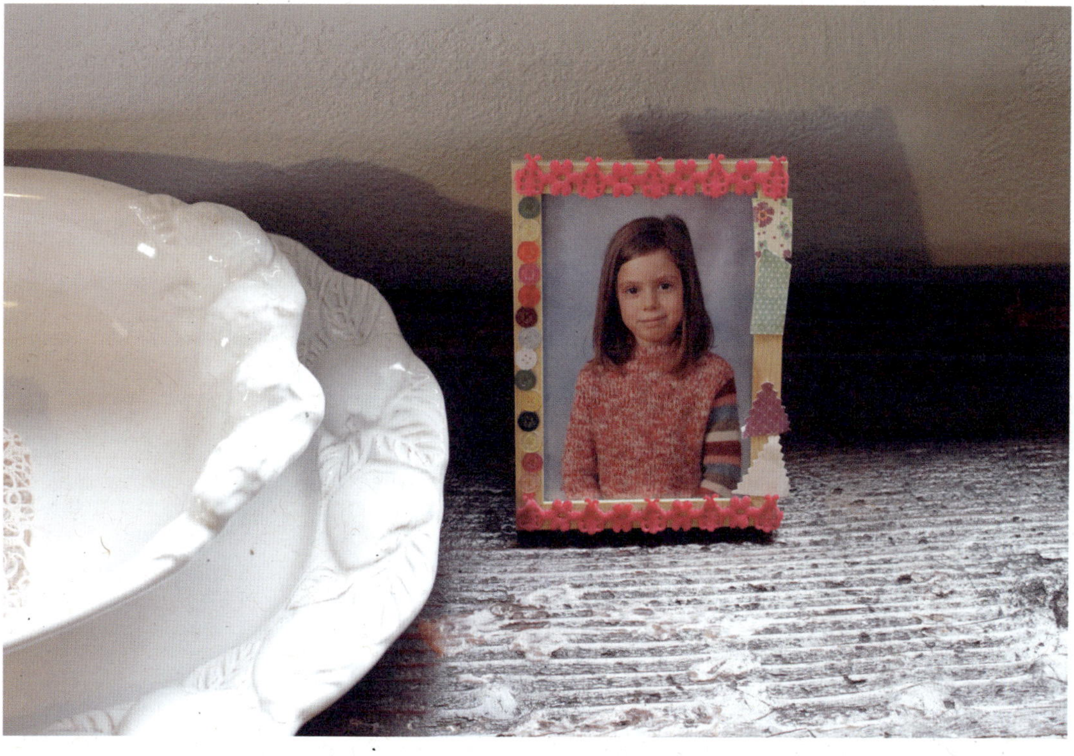

Later that day at 7 pm, we were headed to Gabriele's home.
The artist-turned-banker lives in an old house in a little town
by the sea called Frigole.

Gabriele has a passion for travel. Only last year alone he visited India, Tibet, and traveled 800 kilometers by bike from Santiago de Compostela in Spain to the Pyrenees mountains on the French border.

Gabriele invited a few friends and cooked a staple dish of Lecce region, fave e cicoria, or fava bean purée with chicory.

It was 4 am by the time we left. ↙ P. 52

Später um 19 Uhr waren wir auf dem Weg zu Gabriele. Der ehemalige Künstler, der mittlerweile Banker ist, lebt in einem alten Haus in einem kleinen Küstenort namens Frigole.

Gabriele hat eine Leidenschaft für das Reisen. Allein im letzten Jahr besuchte er Indien und Tibet und radelte 800 Kilometer von Santiago de Compostela in Spanien bis zu den Pyrenäen an der französischen Grenze.

Gabriele lud ein paar Freund*innen ein und kochte ein typisches Gericht der Lecce-Region: Fave e Cicoria, also ein Püree aus Saubohnen mit Chicorée.

Es war 4 Uhr morgens, als wir gingen. ↙ S. 52

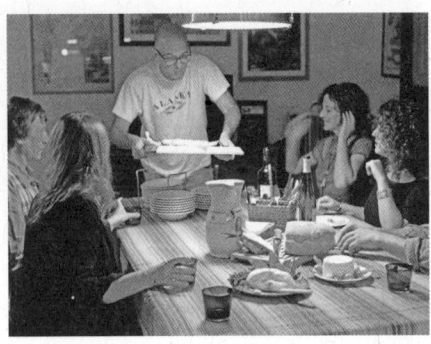

The next day, we were meeting the Petrelli-Peruta family:
Marcia, Marco, their son Michele, their dog Matildei, and
Marcia's brother Paolo.

The family runs *Caffè Letterario* in the city center, a literary café that hosts concerts, readings, and other cultural events.

Four-year-old Michele briefly greeted us and was then taken for a nap, missing a lunch of pasta and salads but strategically waking up just in time for the dessert. ↙ P. 53

Am nächsten Tag trafen wir die Familie Petrelli-Peruta: Marcia, Marco, ihr Sohn Michele, ihr Hund Matildei und Marcias Bruder Paolo.

Die Familie betreibt das *Caffè Letterario* im Stadtzentrum, ein literarisches Café, das Konzerte, Lesungen und andere kulturelle Veranstaltungen organisiert.

Der vierjährige Michele begrüßte uns kurz und wurde dann zum Mittagsschlaf hingelegt, verpasste also das Mittagessen mit Pasta und Salaten, wachte aber strategisch klug genau zum Nachtisch wieder auf. ↙ S. 53

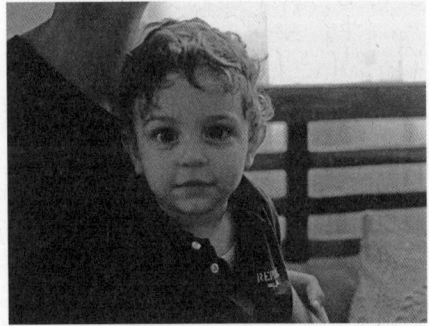

Gabriele's Fava Bean Purée with Chicory

300 grams dried fava beans,
soaked overnight
400 grams chicory
good-quality extra virgin olive oil
salt

The evening before:
Remember to soak the dried fava beans.

The day of:
Drain and rinse the fava beans.
Transfer them into a pan and cover abundantly
with cold water. Add a pinch of salt and bring to the boil.
Then lower the flame and simmer, half–covered, for about
3 hours. Add additional hot water only if necessary, but make
sure that your fava beans are always covered with water.

Meanwhile, clean, wash, and boil the chicory until tender.
Drain it very well and put aside.

After 3 hours switch off the gas and stir the fava beans
continuously with a wooden spoon, adding the olive oil
a little at a time. You will have a smooth and soft purée.
Taste and add additional salt only if necessary.

Plate mashed fava beans next to the boiled chicory,
sprinkle with olive oil. Serve immediately.

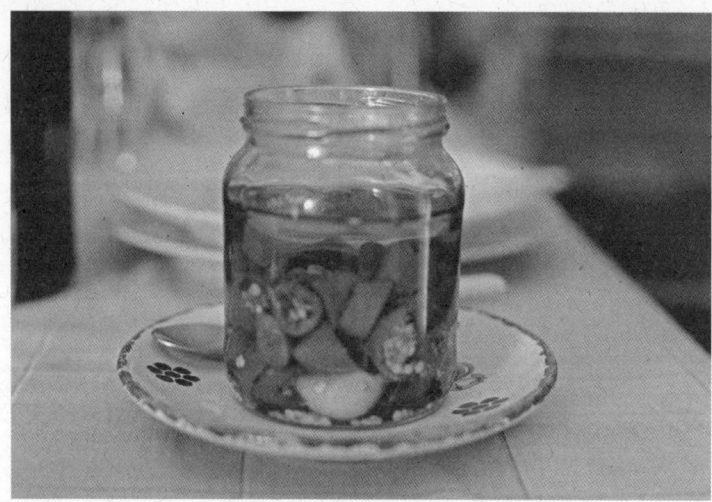

Later that day, we met Francesca Nannini and Alessandro Gravili. They were both born in North Italy and after traveling around the world from Tunisia to England, picked Lecce as their home.

FROM FRANCESCA'S EMAIL: "... Alessandro and I met, and we immediately clicked. There was a book presentation and wine was served. The owner of the place, in order to prevent running out of wine glasses because people were taking more than one, decided to tie labels to the glasses so that one could write their name on it.
Alessandro was one of the few who did that and when I saw his label I couldn't help laughing. The label with the name Ale G. reminded me of those children's parties. :)"
A gift from Francesca and Alessandro was a jar of chili-infused olive oil. ∠ P. 54

Später am Tag trafen wir Francesca Nannini und Alessandro Gravili. Beide wurden in Norditalien geboren und haben nach Reisen rund um die Welt — von Tunesien bis England — Lecce als ihr Zuhause gewählt.

AUS FRANCESCAS E-MAIL: „... Alessandro und ich trafen uns, und es hat sofort gefunkt. Es gab eine Buchvorstellung und es wurde Wein serviert. Um zu verhindern, dass die Weingläser ausgehen, weil die Leute mehr als eines nahmen, band die Ladenbetreiberin Etiketten an die Gläser, auf die man seinen Namen schreiben konnte. Alessandro war einer der wenigen, der das tat, und als ich sein Etikett sah, musste ich einfach lachen. Das Etikett mit dem Namen Ale G. erinnerte mich an Kindergeburtstage. :)"
Ein Geschenk von Francesca und Alessandro war ein Glas mit Chili–Olivenöl. ∠ S. 54

Francesca and Alessandro's Chilli-Infused Olive Oil

200 grams red hot peppers
1 garlic clove
2–3 mint leaves
extra virgin olive oil
nut oil
white wine vinegar
salt

Preparation:
Cover the peppers with cooking salt and
leave them for half a day. Wash them with water to get
rid of the salt and then rinse them with white vinegar.
Put the garlic clove and mint leaves in the jar. Fill ¼ of
the jar with nut oil and ¾ with extra virgin olive oil,
and put the chili peppers into the jar.

Close the jar and keep it in a cool and dry place
(no fridge though). The chili-infused oil is ready to be tasted!

The more time passes, the more the peppers
will give a stronger flavor to the oil :)

The next day, we were visiting Simona Cleopazzo, her husband, and her two kids. She also invited her good friend Melissa Perrone, her husband, and their two kids.

Simona is a writer, and she leads a weekly Orti Di Guerra, gruppo di lettura (Gardens of War reading group) at Ammirato. Each of their meetings has a subject. Here is a sample of the reading list for the subject "The Meat":

MADAME BOVARY
by Gustave Flaubert,
BUTCHER EQUITALIA
by Giuseppe Cristaldi,
RAGAZZI DI VITA
by Pier Paolo Pasolini,
WOMEN WHO RUN WITH
THE WOLVES
by Clarissa Pinkola Estes,
WHY I AM A VEGETARIAN
by Margherita Hack.

She cooked her special vegan chocolate cake that evening and shared her recipe with us. ✓ P. 55

Am nächsten Tag besuchten wir Simona Cleopazzo, ihren Ehemann und ihre zwei Kinder. Sie lud auch ihre gute Freundin Melissa Perrone, deren Ehemann und deren zwei Kinder ein.

Simona ist Autorin und leitet eine wöchentliche Lesegruppe namens „Orti Di Guerra" (Gärten des Krieges) im Ammirato. Jedes ihrer Treffen hat ein Thema. Hier ist eine Auswahl der Leseliste zum Thema „Das Fleisch":

MADAME BOVARY
von Gustave Flaubert,
BUTCHER EQUITALIA
von Giuseppe Cristaldi
RAGAZZI DI VITA
von Pier Paolo Pasolini,
WOMEN WHO RUN WITH THE WOLVES
von Clarissa Pinkola Estes,
WHY I AM A VEGETARIAN
von Margherita Hack.

Sie machte an diesem Abend ihren speziellen veganen Schokoladenkuchen und gab uns das Rezept. ✓ S. 55

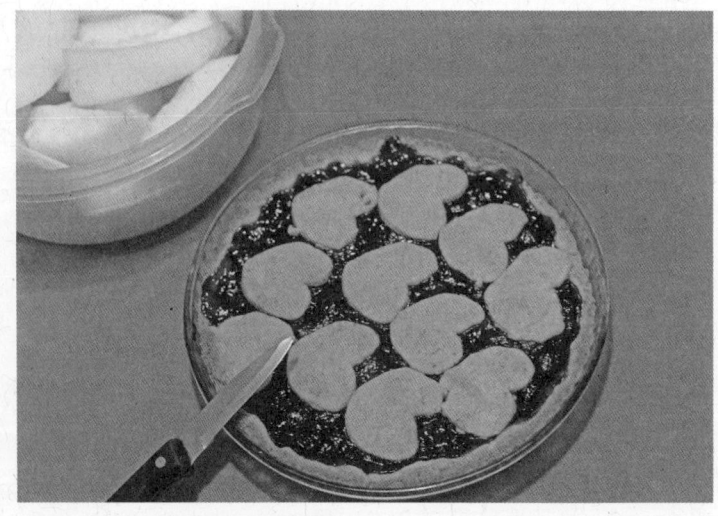

Simona's
Vegan Chocolate Cake

1 glass soy milk
½ glass olive oil
1 glass sugar
2 glasses flour
1 cup cocoa
vanilla or nutmeg
chopped walnuts

Pour soy milk into a bowl and add sugar.
Mix well until the sugar has dissolved completely.
Add cocoa, oil, nutmeg. Stir again and keep
adding flour until the consistency of the dough
resembles creamy yogurt.

Add the walnuts.

Grease the pan with a little oil and add the dough.
Leave in oven 30—40 minutes at a temperature
of 340—355 degrees °F.

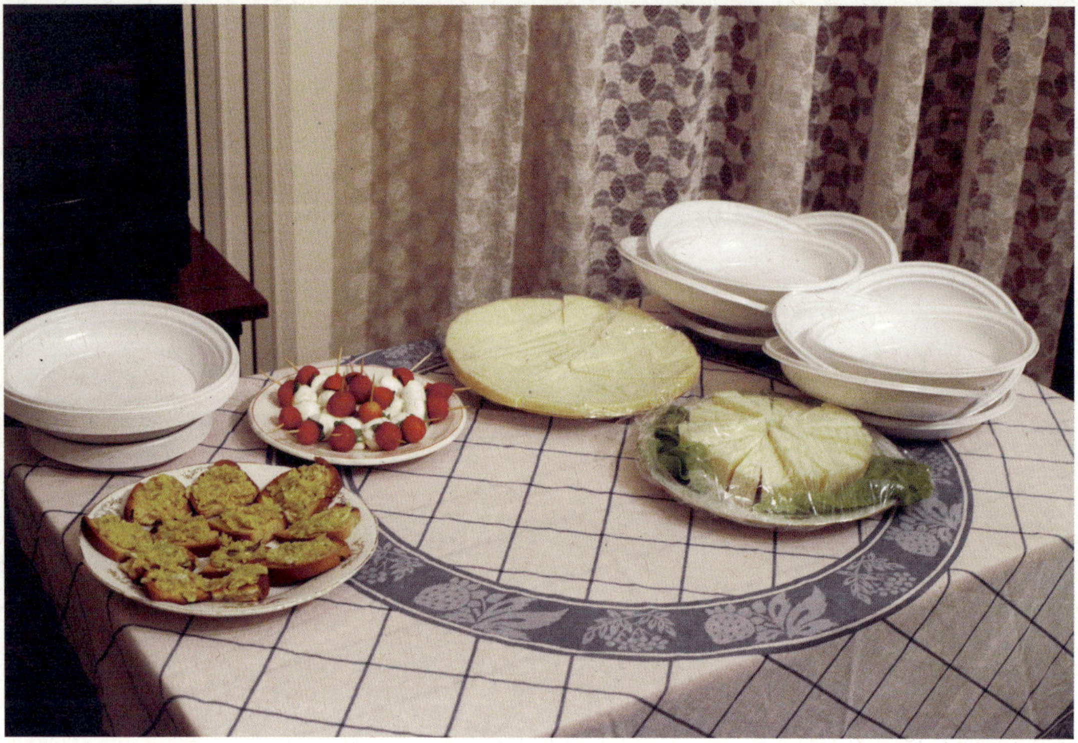

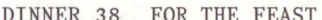

DINNER 38   BE READY ...   SEI BEREIT...

DINNER 38   FOR THE FEAST   FÜR DAS FESTMAHL

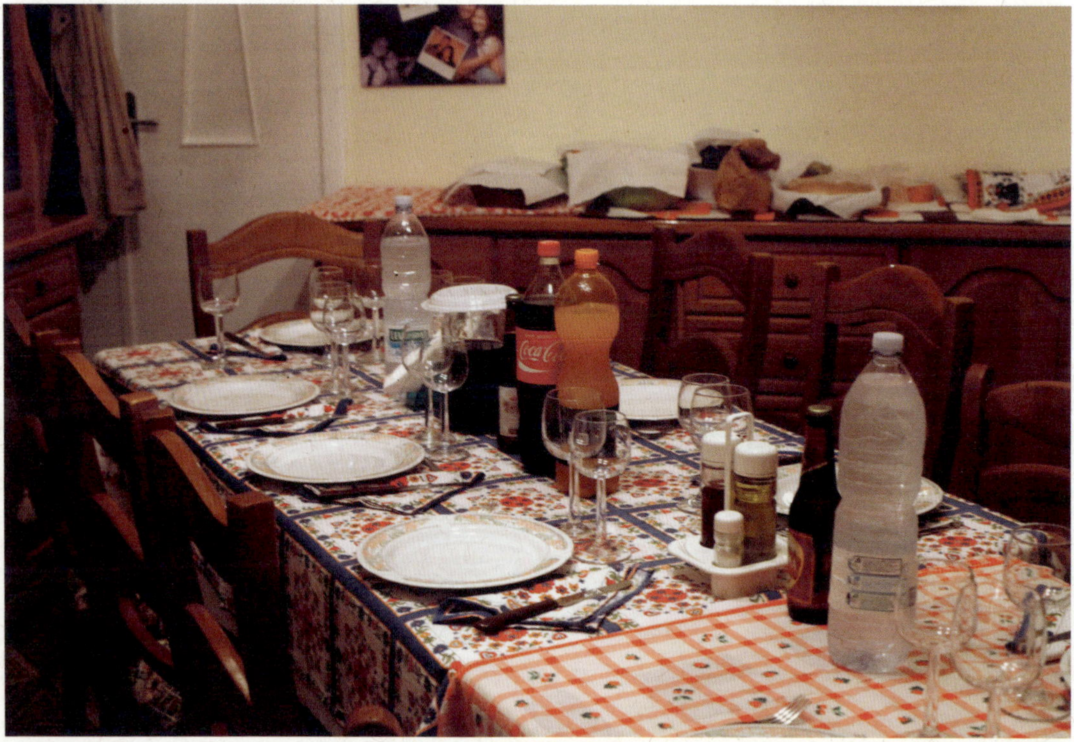

Gianluca Rollo was our translator in Lecce. We were invited to the house of his grandmother "Nonna Tetta" and his parents, Mirella and Giuseppe.
Two of Gianluca's friends, Giulia and Francesco, joined us that evening.
Gianluca told us not to eat anything that day and to be ready for the feast of hand-made pasta, fava beans with chicory, grilled vegetables, arancini, and homemade limoncello, made from garden-grown lemons. All of that was served with grandma's motto "eat or be eaten." Jeff's reply was "I am not done yet."
The homemade food in the Rollo family doesn't start in the kitchen but in the garden and is rooted in the family tradition.

GIANLUCA: "Every July, all our relatives gather in the big garden of my grandmother's house with millions of tomatoes waiting to be transformed into tomato sauce. This is a 'job' we do for about three days. Our relatives stay for a weekend and have dinner in the garden between the tomatoes and all the instruments to prepare the sauce. It is a great family moment." ⬐ P. 56

Gianluca Rollo war unser Dolmetscher in Lecce. Wir wurden ins Haus seiner Großmutter „Nonna Tetta" und seiner Eltern, Mirella und Giuseppe, eingeladen. Zwei von Gianlucas Freund*innen, Giulia und Francesco, gesellten sich an diesem Abend zu uns.
Gianluca riet uns, an diesem Tag nichts zu essen und uns auf ein Festmahl aus handgemachter Pasta, Saubohnen mit Chicorée, gegrilltem Gemüse, Arancini und selbstgemachtem Limoncello, gewonnen aus Zitronen aus dem eigenen Anbau, vorzubereiten. Alles wurde mit der Devise der Großmutter serviert: „Iss oder werde gegessen." Jeffs Antwort war: „Ich bin noch nicht fertig."
Das hausgemachte Essen in der Familie Rollo beginnt nicht in der Küche, sondern im Garten und ist tief in der Familientradition verwurzelt.

GIANLUCA: „Jeden Juli versammeln sich alle unsere Verwandten im großen Garten des Hauses meiner Großmutter, wo Millionen von Tomaten darauf warten, in Tomatensauce verwandelt zu werden. Diese ‚Arbeit' erledigen wir in etwa drei Tagen. Unsere Verwandten bleiben übers Wochenende und essen im Garten zwischen den Tomaten und all den Utensilien, die zur Zubereitung der Sauce benötigt werden. Es ist ein großartiger Familienmoment." ⬐ S. 56

On our last day in Lecce, we met Mirella Sacquegno, Beppe De Giovanni, and their son. We enjoyed local wine, homemade mozzarella, various antipasti, pasta with tomato sauce, served with many funny stories and laughs. ⬐ P. 57

An unserem letzten Tag in Lecce trafen wir Mirella Sacquegno, Beppe De Giovanni und ihren Sohn. Wir genossen lokalen Wein, hausgemachten Mozzarella, verschiedene Antipasti, Pasta mit Tomatensauce, serviert mit vielen lustigen Geschichten und viel Lachen. ⬐ S. 57

Nonna Tetta's Pasta
with Garbanzo Beans

⅔ cup warm water
1 teaspoon sea salt
1 pound durum wheat flour, divided
1 pound dried chickpeas
1 onion
1 carrot
1 rib celery
1 tomato

Pasta (Tria):
The pasta is made with flour and water,
mixing them by hand. After mixing the pasta,
roll it very thin with a rolling pin.
Check if it's ready by blowing under the pasta;
if the pasta rises, it's ready. After this, cut the
pasta in lines, and cook it.

Ciciri:
Put the garbanzo beans in a pot of water
the night before cooking them. Then, the following day,
cook them with tomato, onion, and a bit of celery.
When both are ready, mix pasta and garbanzo beans
together in a pan with onion and oil.

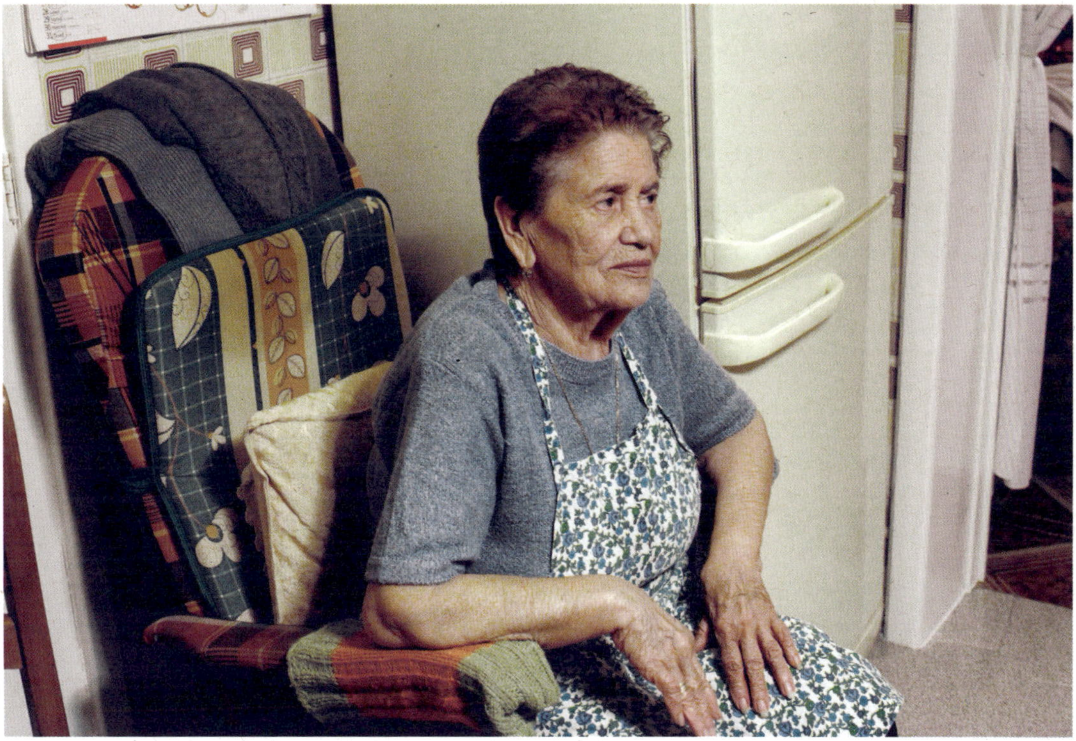

DINNER 38 NONNA TETTA

DINNER 39 EAT OR BE EATEN

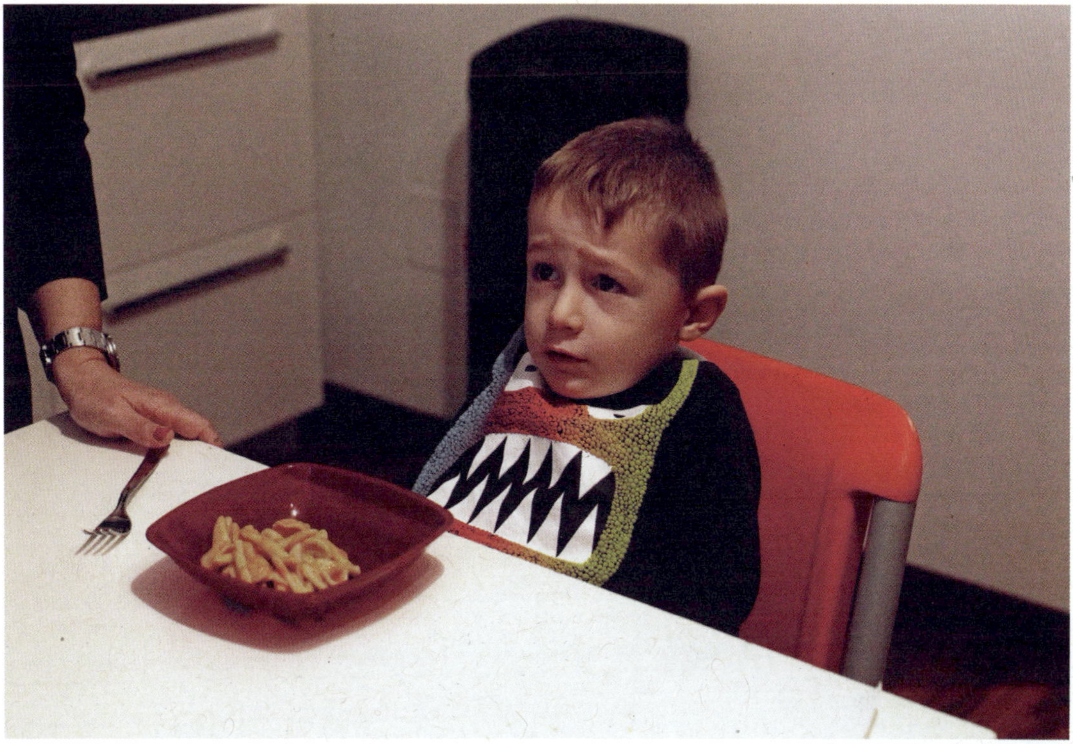

If someone were to ask us to describe our project in two words, it would be *Social Dive*—the theme of the Tokyo Biennale 2021. We were looking forward to realizing our project in Tokyo. Then the pandemic happened. What is social interaction in times of isolation? Suddenly Zoom wasn't just for the corporate world. Our Tokyo Biennale call for participation read:

Wenn jemand uns bitten würde, unser Projekt in zwei Worten zu beschreiben, wären diese Social Dive — das Thema der Tokyo Biennale 2021. Wir freuten uns darauf, unser Projekt in Tokyo zu verwirklichen. Dann kam die Pandemie. Was ist soziale Interaktion in Zeiten der Isolation? Plötzlich war Zoom nicht nur für die Geschäftswelt da. Unser Tokyo-Biennale-Aufruf lautete:

夫婦でもある2人組のアーティストが、家族の晩ご飯への招待と引き換えに絵画をプレゼントします。詳細はメールか電話でお問い合わせください。

"Husband and wife artist team is offering a painting in exchange for an invitation to a family dinner. However, because of the pandemic, the artists will meet with participants for dinner remotely via Zoom."
Between July 3 and 18, 2021, we met with twelve Tokyo families via Zoom from our NY home. Because of the time difference, dinner for Tokyo was breakfast for us, and lunch in Tokyo was a late snack. We were concerned about the interaction with the families over Zoom, would it work? Because of the pandemic, we asked the families to choose where their family portraits would be taken, inside or outside.

„Künstler*innenteam-Ehepaar bietet ein Gemälde im Austausch für eine Einladung zum Familienabendessen. Aufgrund der Pandemie treffen die Künstler*innen die Teilnehmenden jedoch per Zoom zum Essen."
Zwischen dem 3. und 18. Juli 2021 trafen wir uns per Zoom von unserem Zuhause in New York aus mit zwölf Familien in Tokyo. Aufgrund der Zeitverschiebung war das Abendessen in Tokyo für uns Frühstück, und das Mittagessen in Tokyo war ein später Snack für uns. Wir waren besorgt, ob die Interaktion mit den Familien über Zoom funktionieren würde. Aufgrund der Pandemie baten wir die Familien, den Ort für ihre Familienporträts selbst zu wählen, ob drinnen oder draußen.

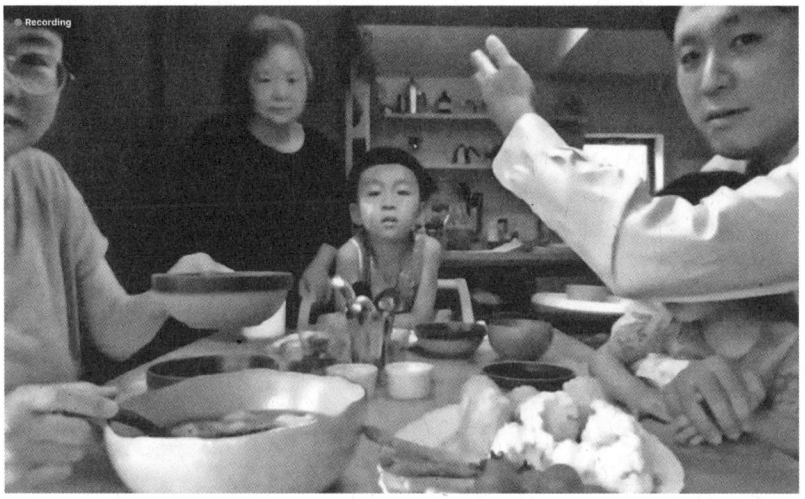

The first Zoom dinner, dinner for us—breakfast for the family. We are meeting Mr. Miyazaki's family. His wife and mother-in-law are just finishing serving the table.

Everyone is at the table now, and Mr. Miyazaki is introducing his family. We share the dishes that we have in front of each screen. We are having roasted chicken with salad, the family is having a soup with tofu, mushrooms, and combinations of vegetables, scallions, tomatoes, and corn. Mr. Miyazaki's mother-in-law is Chinese. His family enjoys combining Chinese and Japanese cuisines. ↙ P. 58

Das erste Zoom–Abendessen, Abendessen für uns — Frühstück für die Familie. Wir treffen die Familie von Herrn Miyazaki. Seine Frau und seine Schwiegermutter sind gerade dabei, den Tisch zu decken.

Jetzt sind alle am Tisch, und Herr Miyazaki stellt seine Familie vor. Wir teilen Gerichte, die wir jeweils vor den Bildschirmen haben. Wir essen Brathühnchen mit Salat, die Familie isst eine Suppe mit Tofu, Pilzen und einer Kombination aus Gemüse, Frühlingszwiebeln, Tomaten und Mais. Die Schwiegermutter von Herrn Miyazaki ist Chinesin. Seine Familie genießt es, chinesische und japanische Küche zu kombinieren. ↙ S. 58

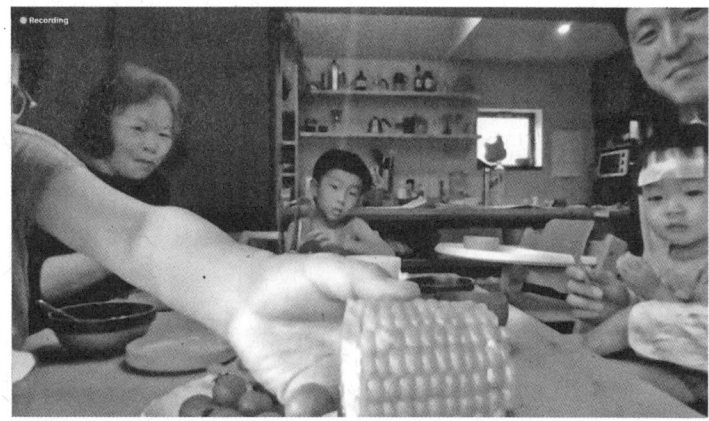

Dinner for us, roasted salmon with kale salad, and breakfast for the family, various steamed and fresh vegetables, eggs, and toast.
We are meeting Naosuke, Ayako, Anne, Kiko, Tomo. The family is sitting at a big table in a bright room. Every dish was presented and described by the family, and we learned about a new dish: natto, fermented soybeans. ↙ P. 59

Abendessen für uns, gebratener Lachs mit Grünkohlsalat, und Frühstück für die Familie: verschiedenes gedämpftes und frisches Gemüse, Eier und Toast.
Wir treffen Naosuke, Ayako, Anne, Kiko und Tomo. Die Familie sitzt an einem großen Tisch in einem hellen Raum. Jedes Gericht wurde von der Familie präsentiert und beschrieben, und wir lernten ein neues Gericht kennen: Natto, fermentierte Sojabohnen. ↙ S. 59

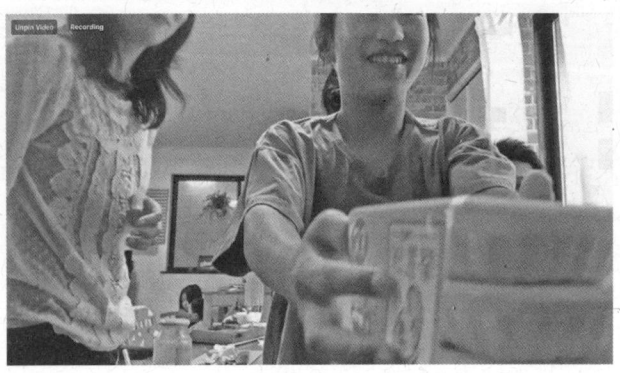

Now it's late in NY. We are having a light dinner of smoked trout with potatoes and arugula salad, while Ms. Hayashi's family is sitting for lunch.
The family has four kids. They were showing their dishes to us: noodle soup, satay vegetables, corn, tofu, and fried rice. Later on the oldest son played the flute for us while the youngest fell asleep. ↙ P. 60

Jetzt ist es spät in New York. Wir essen ein leichtes Abendessen mit geräucherter Forelle, Kartoffeln und Rucolasalat, während die Familie von Frau Hayashi zu Mittag isst.
Die Familie hat vier Kinder. Sie zeigten uns ihre Gerichte: Nudelsuppe, Satay-Gemüse, Mais, Tofu und gebratener Reis. Später spielte der älteste Sohn für uns Flöte, während der Jüngste einschlief. ↙ S. 60

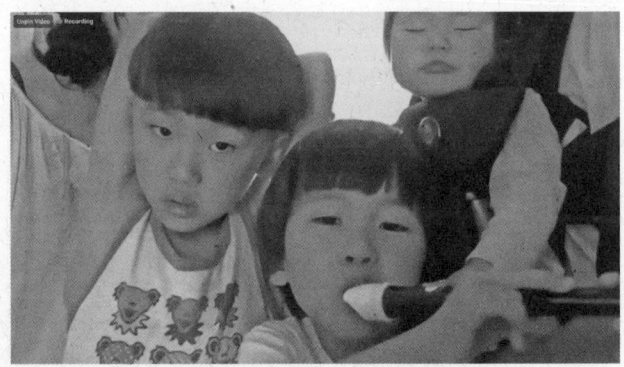

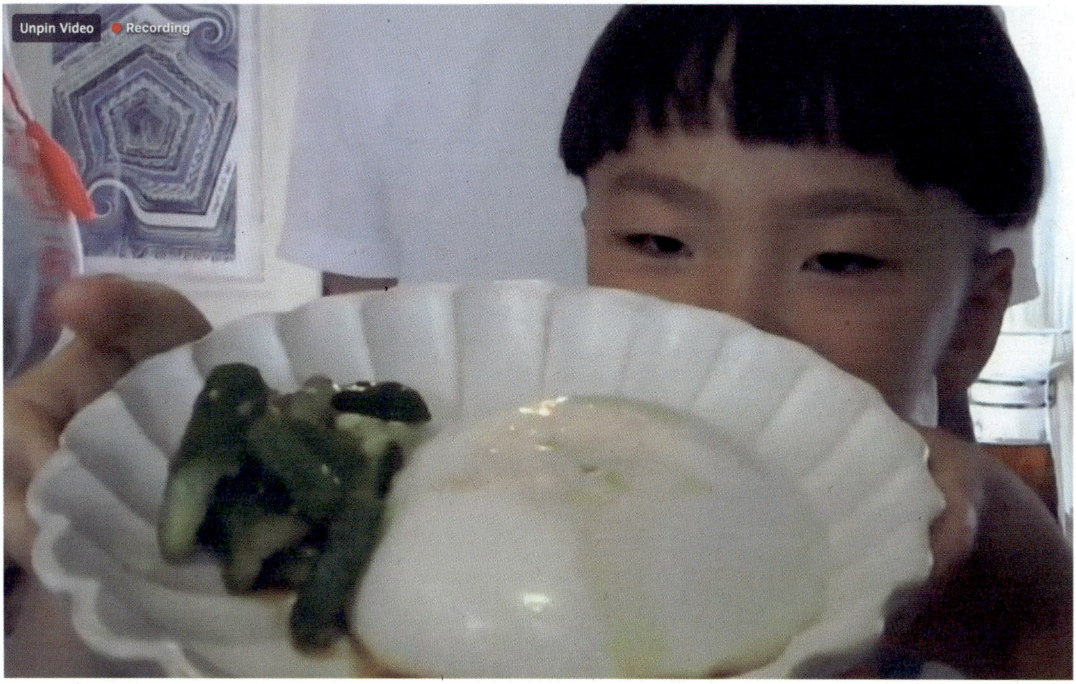

DINNER 42   SHOWING THEIR DISHES TO US   SIE ZEIGEN UNS IHRE GERICHTE

DINNER 42   ... WHILE THE YOUNGEST FELL ASLEEP   ... WÄHREND DER JÜNGSTE EINSCHLIEF

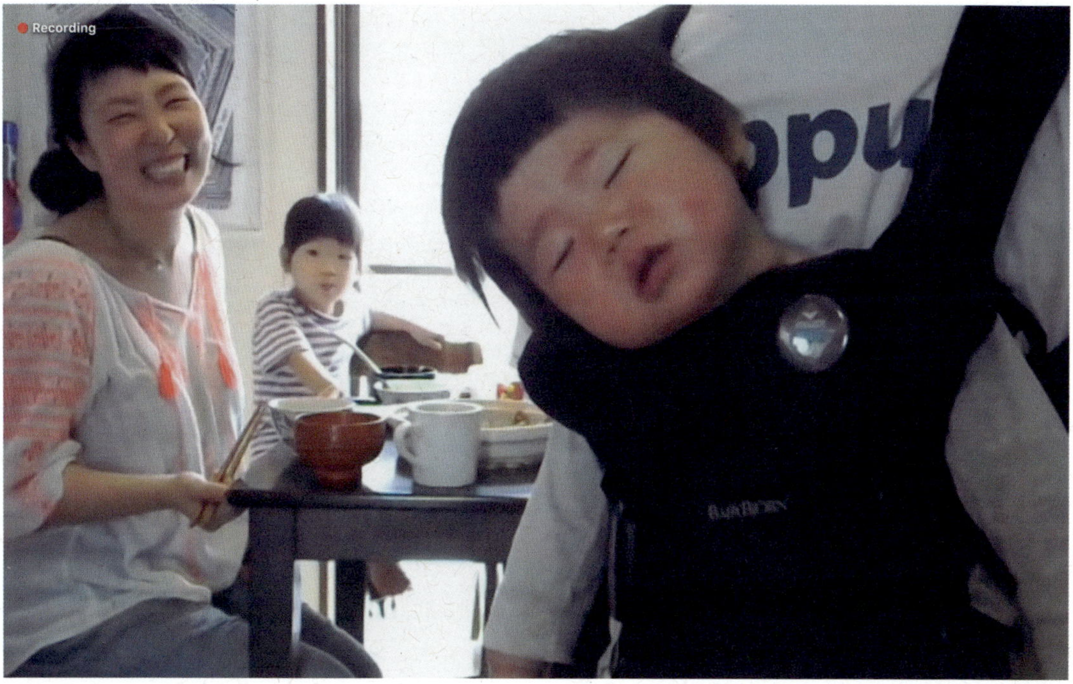

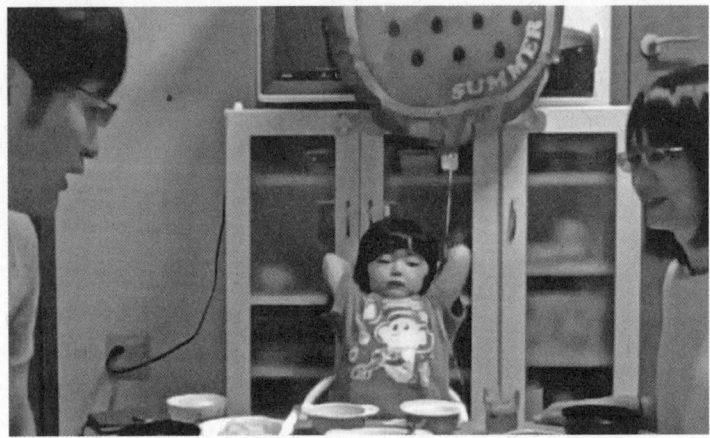

Dinner for us, lamb with arugula tomato salad, and breakfast for the family—vegetables and tamagoyaki, Japanese rolled omelette.
As with every meal with Japanese families, this one started with us putting both hands together in front of our chests and saying: itadakimasu (to humbly receive).
The Sakura family is sitting at the table, the daughter in the middle, with a big watermelon balloon tied to her high chair.
We described our dishes to each other, compared recipes and ingredients, sharing our mutual love for miso on both sides of the screen.

During our conversation, we learned that eating out is not so common for Japanese families during the week, it is more for special occasions and weekends. That evening we learned about a new dish: omurice, a popular Japanese comfort dish of fried rice covered with a soft omelet and topped with ketchup. ↙ P. 61

Abendessen für uns, Lamm mit Rucola-Tomatensalat, und Frühstück für die Familie — Gemüse und Tamagoyaki, japanisches Omelett.
Wie bei jedem Essen mit japanischen Familien begann auch dieses damit, dass wir beide Hände vor der Brust zusammenlegten und sagten: itadakimasu (um demütig zu empfangen).
Die Familie Sakura sitzt am Tisch, die Tochter in der Mitte, mit einem großen Wassermelonenballon, der an ihren Hochstuhl gebunden ist.
Wir beschrieben uns gegenseitig unsere Gerichte, verglichen Rezepte und Zutaten und teilten unsere gemeinsame Liebe zu Miso auf beiden Seiten des Bildschirms.
Während unseres Gesprächs erfuhren wir, dass es für japanische Familien unter der Woche nicht üblich ist, auswärts zu essen. Das ist eher etwas für besondere Anlässe und Wochenenden. An diesem Abend lernten wir ein neues Gericht kennen: Omurice, ein beliebtes japanisches Comfort Food aus gebratenem Reis, bedeckt mit einem weichen Omelett und Ketchup.
↙ S. 61

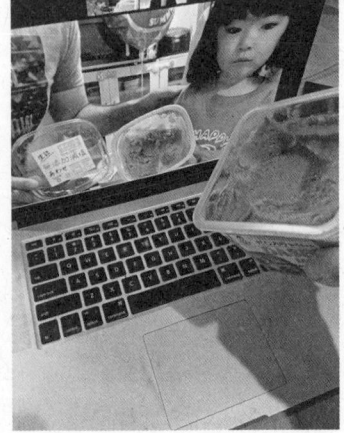

Sakura's Omurice

eggs
rice
ketchup
soy sauce
oil

Cook and fry the rice.
Cook the eggs until thickened and nearly set.
Drape the eggs over the rice.
Top with sauce.

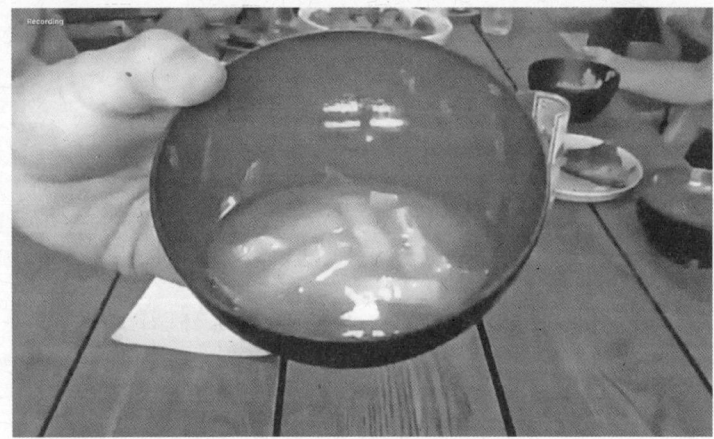

We are having after-dinner tea with pastries, cheese, and fruit plates, while Ms. Abe's family is sitting for lunch: miso soup with tofu, chicken with steamed vegetables, green salad, and shumai.

We started by putting our hands together and then reached our hands to the screen for a virtual handshake.

From our experience so far, we noticed that the family members don't like to talk about their jobs. Hobbies, kids, travel, food, and family traditions were more common subjects. This family was an exception. We talked about their jobs and hobbies. We raised glasses hoping to meet one day in the future.

↙ P. 62

Nach dem Abendessen gibt es bei uns Tee mit Gebäck, Käse und einen Obstteller, während die Familie von Frau Abe zu Mittag isst: Misosuppe mit Tofu, Hühnchen mit gedämpftem Gemüse, grüner Salat und Shumai–Teigtaschen.

Wir begannen, indem wir unsere Hände zusammenlegten und dann unsere Hände zum Bildschirm ausstreckten, um ein virtuelles Händeschütteln zu vollziehen.

Unsere bisherigen Erfahrungen haben gezeigt, dass die Familienmitglieder nicht gerne über ihre Arbeit sprechen. Stattdessen waren häufige Themen Hobbys, Kinder, Reisen, Essen und Familientraditionen. Diese Familie war eine Ausnahme. Wir sprachen über ihre Jobs und Hobbys. Wir stießen auf die Hoffnung an, uns eines Tages persönlich treffen zu können.

↙ S. 62

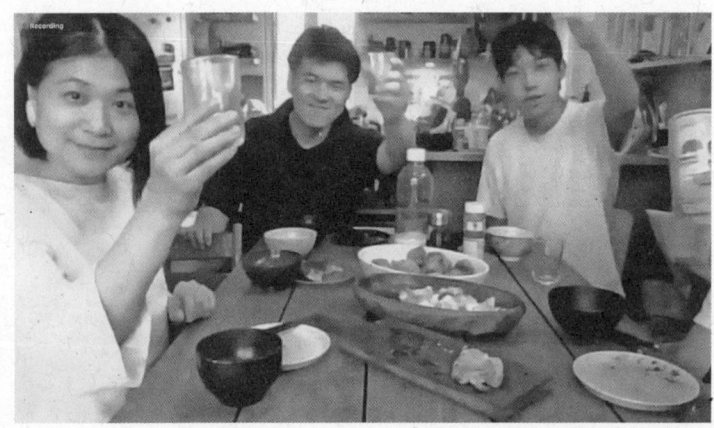

We are having a dinner of steak with asparagus and sliced tomatoes, while the Kaneyoa family is sitting for lunch: chicken with vegetables and green salad. We started by talking about our neighborhoods, sharing pictures and the dishes via the screen, then talked about a range of things from pandas to baseball. ↙ P. 63

Wir essen Steak mit Spargel und Tomatenspalten, während die Familie Kaneoya zu Mittag isst: Hühnchen mit Gemüse und grünem Salat. Wir begannen mit einem Gespräch über unsere Wohnviertel, teilten Bilder und die Gerichte über den Bildschirm und sprachen dann über verschiedene Themen: von Pandas bis Baseball. ↙ S. 63

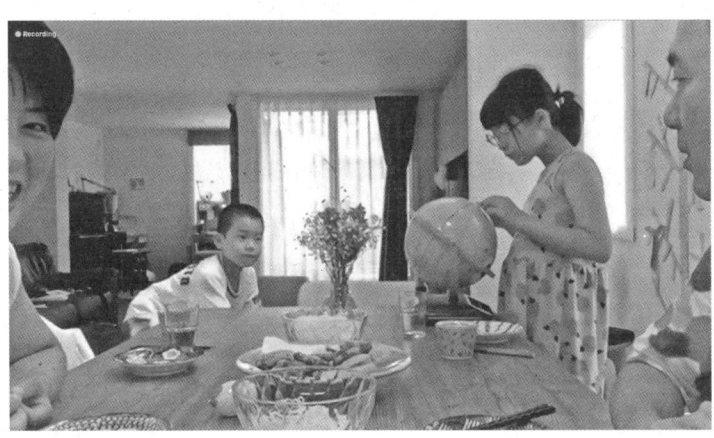

Now we're having breakfast yogurt with berries, and it is dinner time for the family: a large sushi plate, soup, and a range of vegetable dishes, ice cream for dessert.
We are meeting Shimpei, Yumi, Fukumi and Ayami, starting with itadakimasu and meeting family pets, a fluffy white dog (Wito) and a yellow parakeet. After the meal, the girls shared their dance routine with us. ↙ P. 64

Jetzt essen wir Frühstücksjoghurt mit Beeren und für die Familie ist es Abendessenzeit: eine große Sushi-Platte, Suppe und eine Auswahl an Gemüsegerichten, zum Nachtisch Eis.
Wir treffen Shimpei, Yumi, Fukumi und Ayami, beginnen mit itadakimasu und lernen die Haustiere der Familie kennen, einen fluffigen weißen Hund (Wito) und einen gelben Wellensittich. Nach dem Essen zeigten uns die Mädchen ihre Tanz-Choreographie. ↙ S. 64

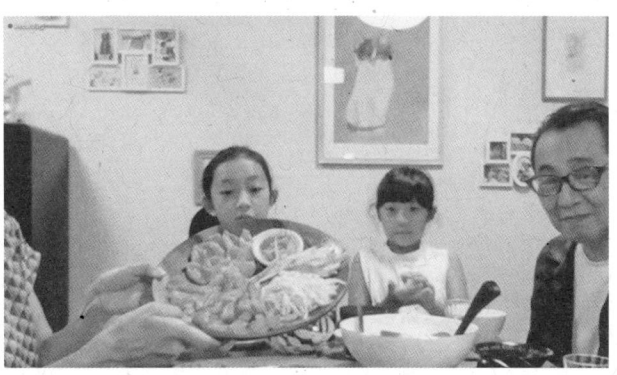

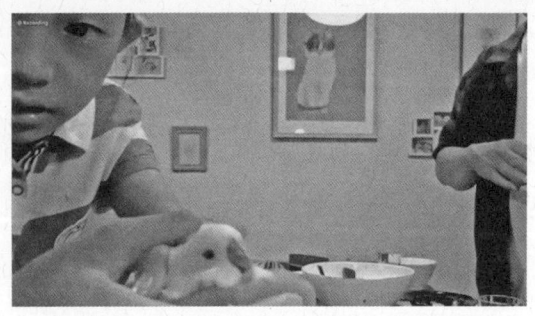
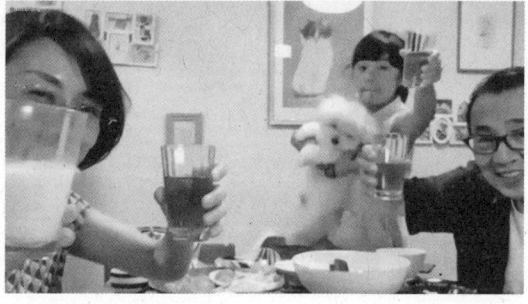

DINNER 47 JULY 10, 2021

It is dinner time for the family, itadakimasu. We meet the Suzuki family, mother and daughter, and their friend is joining us via Zoom.

Their tables were full of small bowls with various fresh, steamed, and fermented vegetables, shumai, and tofu. We talked about Japanese people mostly keeping a very traditional family lifestyle, as many women choose to stay at home to raise kids and care for the family. ↙ P. 65

Für die Familie ist es Zeit fürs Abendessen, itadakimasu. Wir treffen die Familie Suzuki, Mutter und Tochter, und ihre Freundin schaltet sich per Zoom dazu. Ihre Tische waren voller kleiner Schüsseln mit verschiedenen frischen, gedämpften und fermentierten Gemüsesorten, Shumai-Teigtaschen und Tofu. Wir sprachen darüber, dass viele Japaner*innen einen sehr traditionellen Familienlebensstil pflegen, da viele Frauen sich entscheiden, zu Hause zu bleiben, um Kinder zu erziehen und sich um die Familie zu kümmern. ↙ S. 65

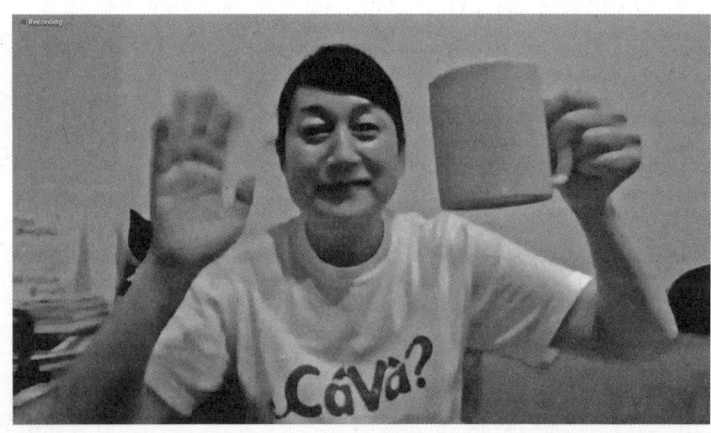

DINNER 48 JULY 11, 2021

The Horibe family is a young family with three boys. The family is having breakfast: shumai, steamed vegetables, tofu, and tamagoyaki. As with many Tokyo families, the kids are the center of attention and conversations often revolve around them. We were entertained by the eldest son, who shared his origami skills, drawings, and his interest in chess. Jeff played chess with him online that summer. ↙ P. 66

Die Familie Horibe ist eine junge Familie mit drei Jungen. Die Familie frühstückt: Shumai, gedämpftes Gemüse, Tofu und Tamagoyaki. Wie bei vielen Familien aus Tokyo stehen die Kinder im Mittelpunkt und die Gespräche drehen sich oft um sie. Wir wurden vom ältesten Sohn unterhalten, der seine Origami-Fähigkeiten, Zeichnungen und sein Interesse an Schach teilte. Jeff spielte diesen Sommer online Schach mit ihm. ↙ S. 66

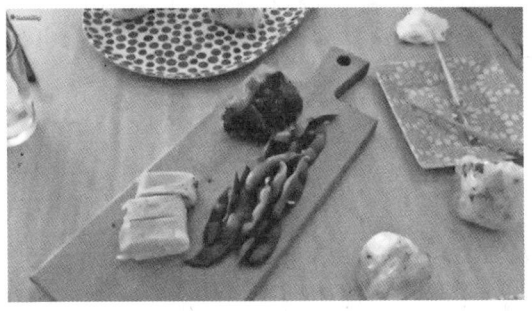
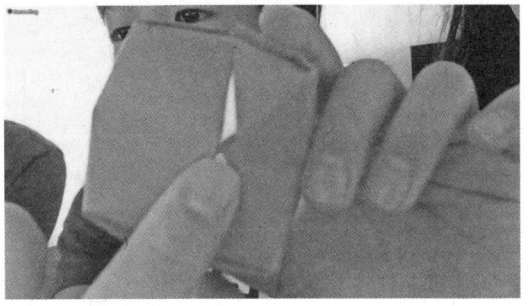

DINNER 49

We are meeting the Koyama family. First we meet Asako and her son. It is lunchtime for them.

A few minutes later, her husband entered the room, holding a pan of pasta and serving his family. This is the only multicultural family we met during our project in Tokyo: the wife is Japanese and the husband is European. It was the only family of the twelve we met where the husband served the meal. Cheers—Kanpai. ↙ P. 67

Wir treffen die Familie Koyama. Zuerst treffen wir Asako und ihren Sohn. Für sie ist es Mittagszeit.

Ein paar Minuten später betrat ihr Mann den Raum, er trug eine Pfanne mit Pasta und servierte seiner Familie. Dies ist die einzige multikulturelle Familie, die wir während unseres Projekts in Tokyo trafen: Die Frau ist Japanerin und der Mann ist Europäer. Es war die einzige Familie der zwölf, bei der der Mann das Essen servierte. Prost — Kanpai. ↙ S. 67

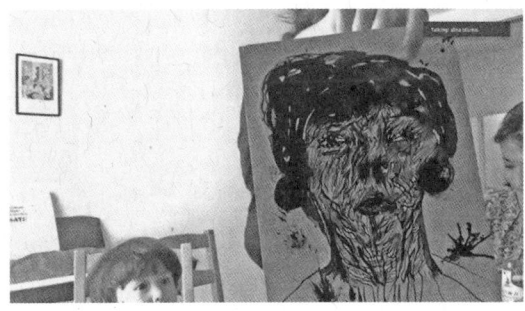

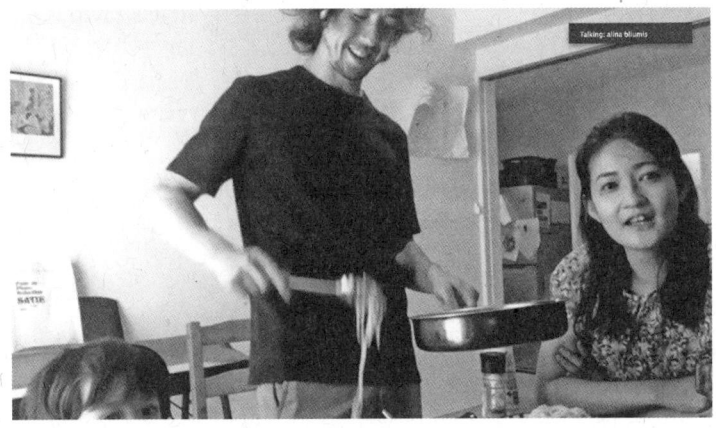

Lunch for the Kawasaki family. The wife shares the dishes she cooked and served: meat with broccoli, mushrooms, and tomatoes.
The family told us about the difficulties of traveling abroad with children, and many families prefer to travel around Japan, camping or visiting their relatives. ↙ P. 68

Mittagessen für die Familie Kawasaki. Die Frau teilt die Gerichte, die sie gekocht und serviert hat: Fleisch mit Brokkoli, Pilzen und Tomaten.
Die Familie erzählte uns erzählte uns, wie schwierig es ist, mit Kindern ins Ausland zu reisen, und dass viele Familien lieber innerhalb von Japan reisen, campen oder Verwandte besuchen. ↙ S. 68

Dinner time for the family. We are meeting Tomomi, Numakura, Mima, Mayuko. The family is sitting at the coffee table in the living room. Parents took turns holding their newborn daughter.
We talked about parenthood, and they told us that it is customary in Japan for women to stay at their maternal home for up to eight weeks after the baby is born, so the new mothers can rest, recuperate, and learn how to take care of their kids.

The table was full of dishes: fresh vegetables, steamed broccoli and dumplings, meat with potatoes and carrots, salmon, and a bowl of fried rice. ↙ P. 69

Abendessen für die Familie. Wir treffen Tomomi, Numakura, Mima und Mayuko. Die Familie sitzt am Couchtisch im Wohnzimmer. Die Eltern hielten abwechselnd ihre neugeborene Tochter.
Wir sprachen über Elternschaft und sie erzählten uns, dass es in Japan üblich ist, dass Frauen bis zu acht Wochen nach der Geburt des Babys im Haus ihrer Mutter bleiben, damit sie sich ausruhen, erholen und lernen können, wie sie sich um ihre Kinder kümmern.
Der Tisch war voller Gerichte: frisches Gemüse, gedämpfter Brokkoli und Dumplings, Fleisch mit Kartoffeln und Karotten, Lachs und eine Schüssel gebratener Reis. ↙ S. 69

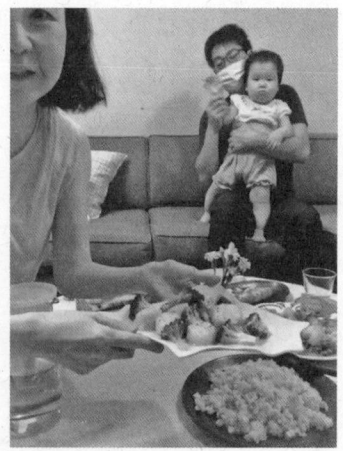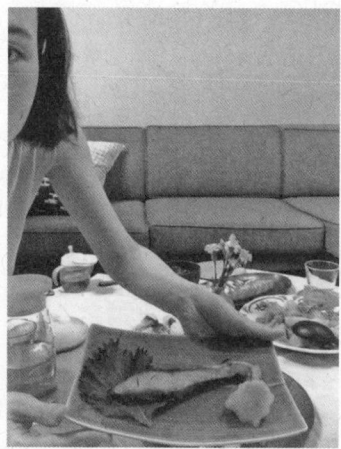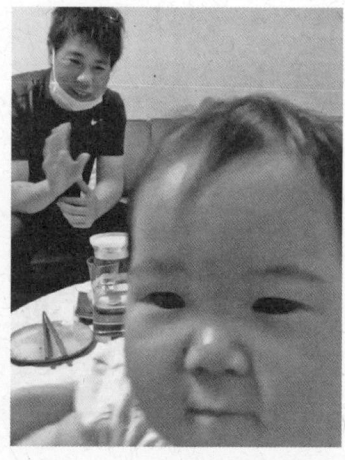

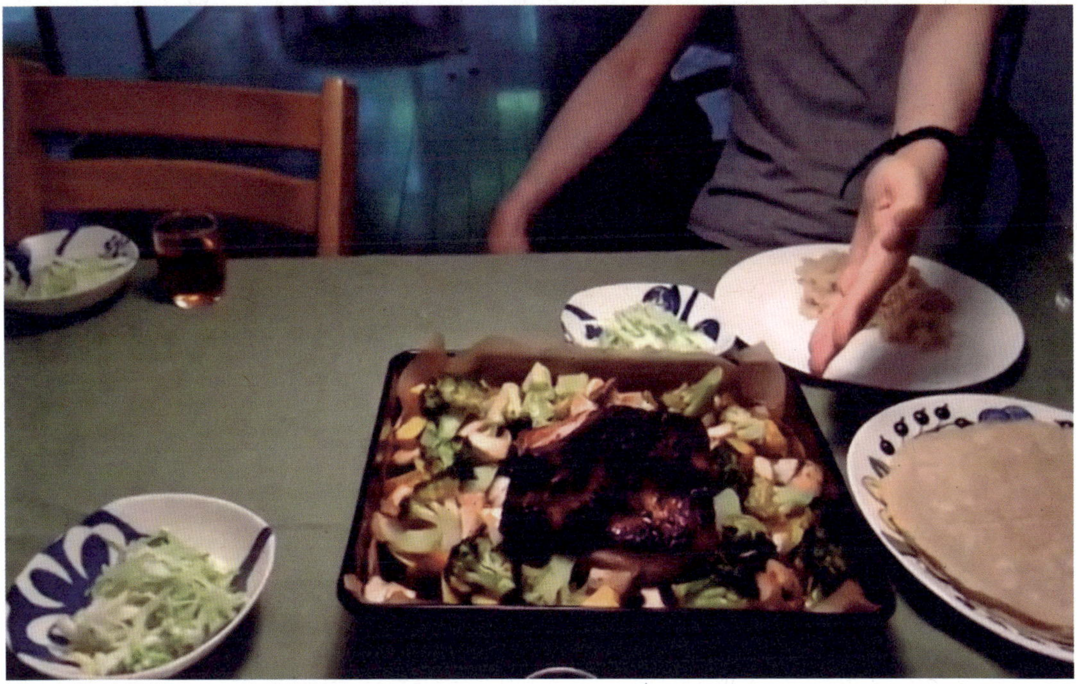

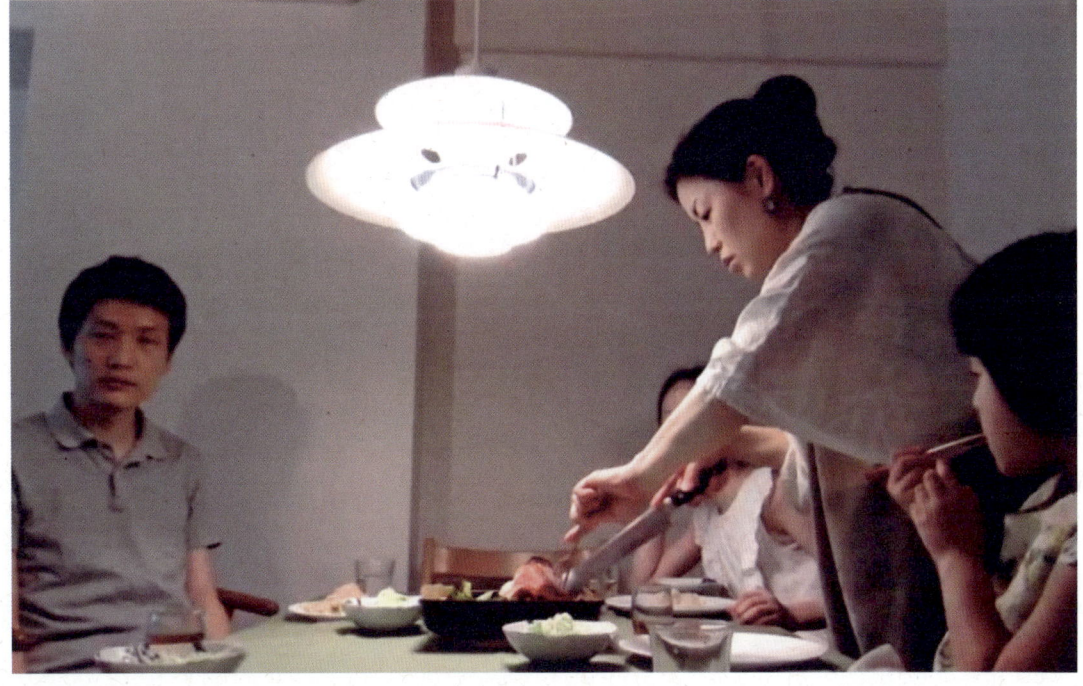

DINNER 50   SHARING THE DISHES SHE COOKED   TEILEN DER GERICHTE, DIE SIE GEKOCHT HAT

DINNER 50   ... AND SERVED   ... UND ES IST ANGERICHTET

In early December 2024, we placed the following call for participation in a local Dortmund newspaper and distributed postcards in local businesses:

(Dortmund, 2025)

Künstler*innen–Ehepaar aus New York bietet Gemälde für Einladung zu gemeinsamem Abendessen bei Ihnen zuhause an. Für weitere Informationen bitte telefonisch oder per E–Mail melden.

"Married artist couple from New York is offering a painting in exchange for an invitation to a dinner at your home. Please e-mail or call for more information."
Between February 2 and 14, 2025, we had dinners with eleven families in Dortmund and nearby towns.

Anfang Dezember 2024 veröffentlichten wir folgenden Aufruf zur Teilnahme in einer lokalen Dortmunder Zeitung und verteilten Postkarten in örtlichen Geschäften:
„Künstler*innen–Ehepaar aus New York bietet Gemälde für Einladung zu gemeinsamem Abendessen bei Ihnen zuhause an. Für weitere Informationen bitte telefonisch oder per E-Mail melden."
Zwischen dem 2. und 14. Februar 2025 aßen wir gemeinsam mit elf Familien in Dortmund und nahegelegenen Städten.

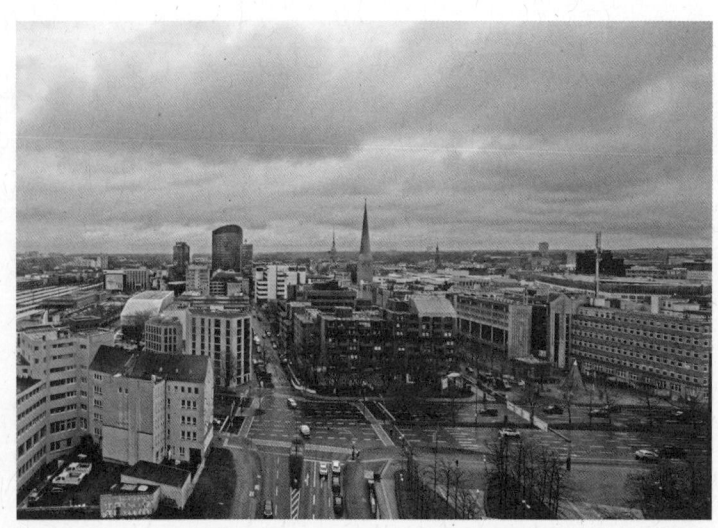

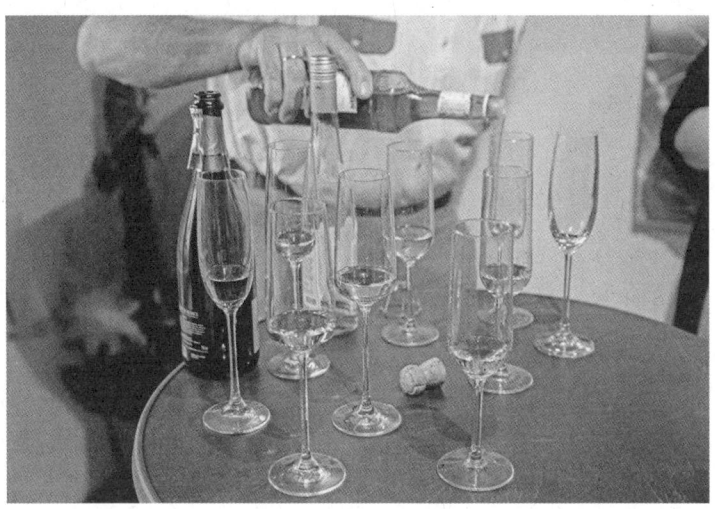

Our early dinner is in the house of Hans and Heike in Selm, a small town near Dortmund. All their four kids gathered from far and near for this occasion.

We started with sparkling wine with peach liquor served by Hans.

Hans and Heike met at the Red Cross and have been married for forty years. One of their family traditions over the years is to gather for the Swiss dish raclette, based on melting cheese over vegetables, cold cuts, and fish, which they serve with boiled potatoes. In their words, it's an "easy way to entertain."

We ended the evening with homemade crème brûlée, "burnt" with a torch by Marc.

↙ P. 70

Unser frühes Abendessen findet im Haus von Hans und Heike in Selm, einer kleinen Stadt in der Nähe von Dortmund, statt. Alle ihre vier Kinder kamen von nah und fern für diesen Anlass zusammen.

Zum Auftakt gab es Sekt mit Pfirsichlikör, serviert von Hans.

Hans und Heike trafen sich beim Roten Kreuz und sind seit vierzig Jahren verheiratet. Eine ihrer Familientraditionen, die sich über die Jahre entwickelt hat, ist es, sich zum Raclette-Essen zu treffen, bei dem Käse über Gemüse, Aufschnitt und Fisch geschmolzen wird, serviert mit gekochten Kartoffeln. In ihren Worten ist es eine „einfache Art, die Gäste zu unterhalten."

Wir beendeten den Abend mit einer hausgemachten Crème brûlée, die Marc mit einem Brenner „anbrannte".

↙ S. 70

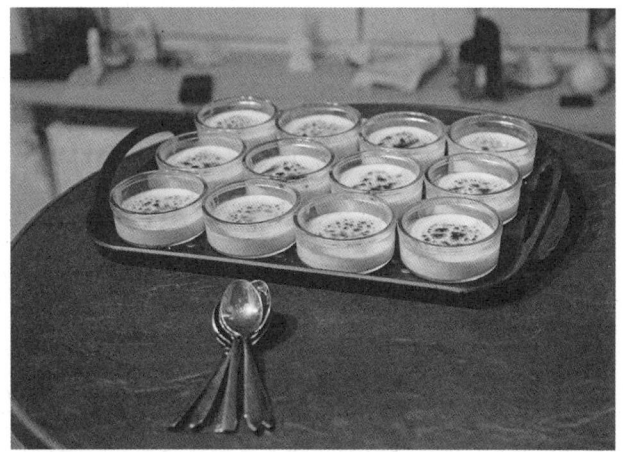

Heikes Spätzle

300 g Mehl
3 Eier
½ TL Salz
150 ml Wasser

Alle Zutaten mit dem Kochlöffel vermischen und gut abschlagen, der Teig soll „Blasen werfen". Den Teig portionsweise mit einer Spätzlepresse oder einem Spätzlehobel in das kochende Salzwasser drücken, Spätzle im offenen Topf rasch aufkochen lassen, bis sie an der Oberfläche schwimmen, Garzeit 2—3 Min., mit einem Sieblöffel herausnehmen, warmstellen oder auf eine breite Platte legen und kurz vor dem Servieren nochmals in heißem Wasser erwärmen.

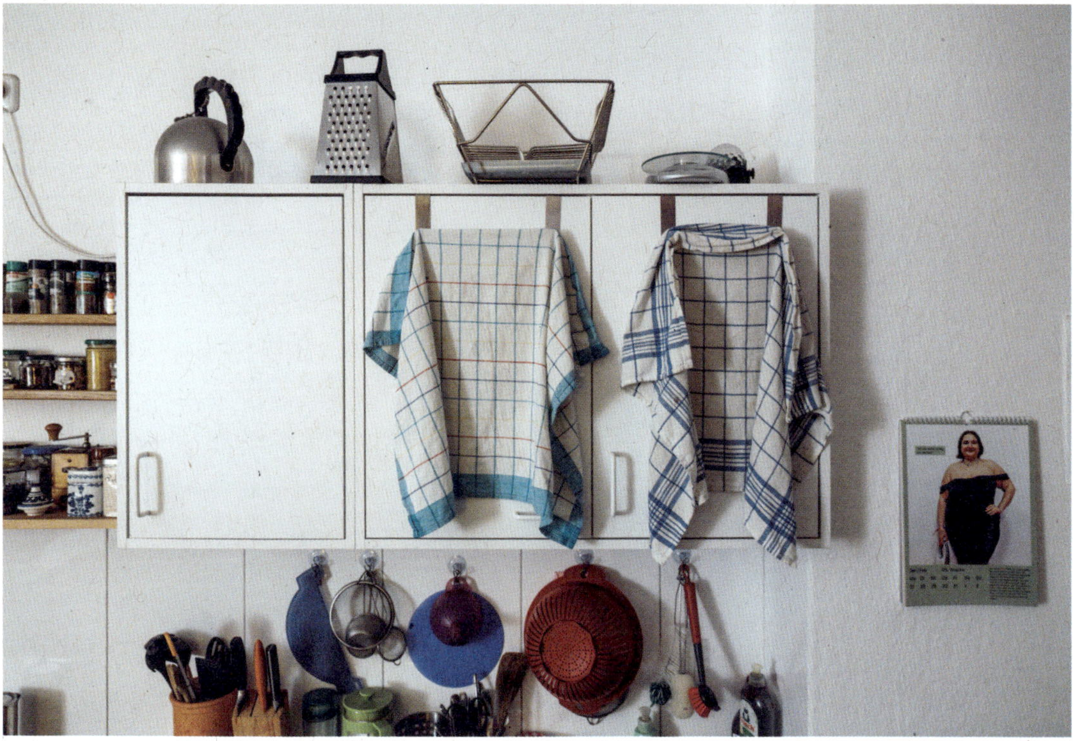

DINNER 53   COLORFUL APARTMENT   FARBENFROHE WOHNUNG

DINNER 54   WE ALL PLAYED DRESS UP   WIR VERKLEIDETEN UNS

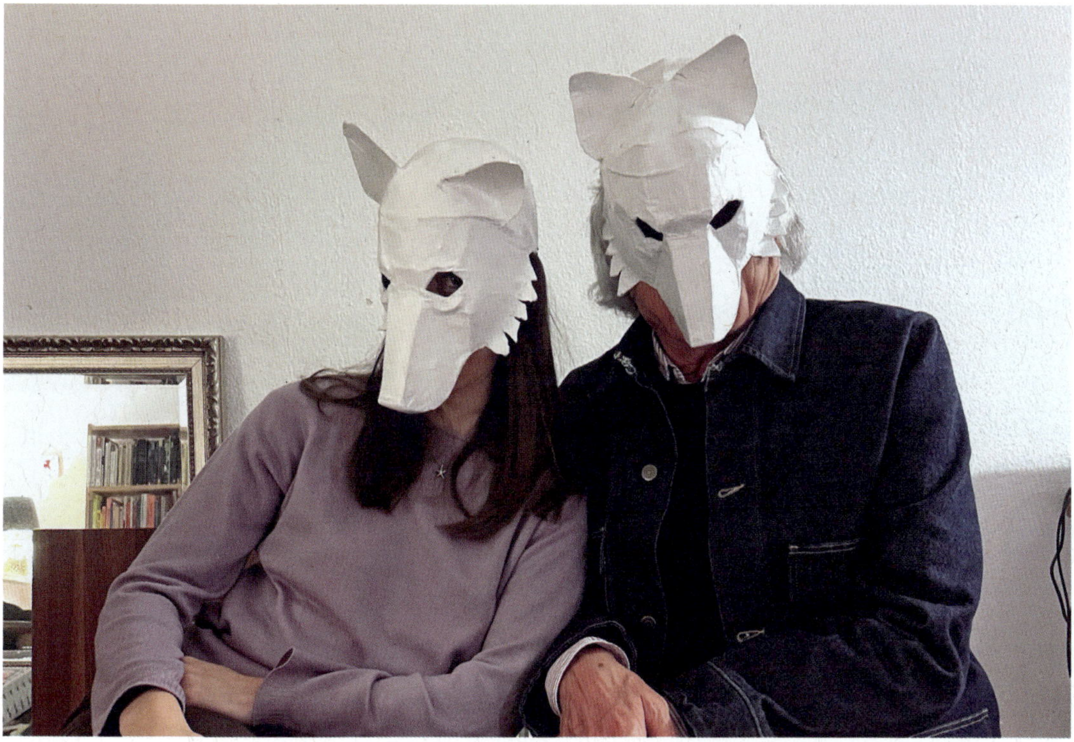

Later that day we are invited by Alexis and Torben to their
colorful apartment in the nearby town of Bochum. Their
friend Aakash is staying with them for few days.

The hosts love to meet new people, from their neighbors to organizing meeting spaces for local youth. They were also active members of the CouchSurfing community and hosted about 200 people.

Spicy tofu, green salad with apples, and a rice-lentil dish was served in a kitchen decorated with New Year's party tinsel. ↙ P. 71

Später wurden wir von Alexis und Torben in ihre farbenfrohe Wohnung in Bochum eingeladen, einer nahegelegenen Stadt. Ihr Freund Aakash wohnt für ein paar Tage bei ihnen.

Sie lieben es, neue Menschen kennenzulernen, von ihren Nachbar*innen bis hin zur Organisation von lokalen Jugendtreffs. Sie waren auch aktive Mitglieder der CouchSurfing-Community und haben etwa 200 Menschen beherbergt.

Scharf gewürzter Tofu, grüner Salat mit Äpfeln und ein Reis-Linsen-Gericht wurden in einer Küche serviert, die mit Lametta von einer Neujahrsparty geschmückt war. ↙ S. 71

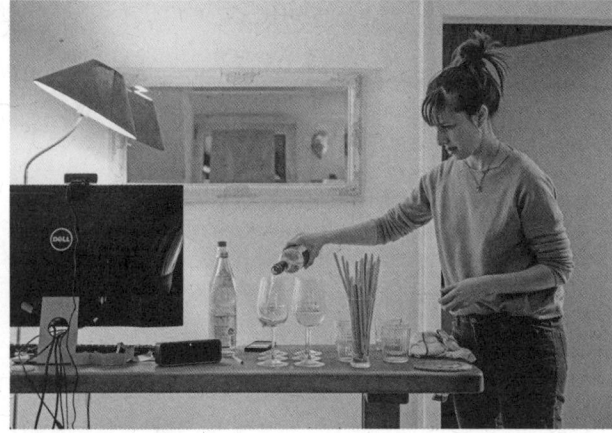

We are visiting Elena in an apartment near the
famous Dortmund Stadium. Her friends Florencia
and Charles are joining us.

Elena was born in Italy, Florencia in Argentina, and Charles in Ghana. After years of traveling and studying, they chose the Dortmund area as their home, at least for now.

Elena served cheese, bread sticks, garlic pasta with shrimps and herbs, green salad with olive oil dressing—oil that she brings back from Italy in big metal containers. In her words, "she can't live without it."

After dinner, we all played dress up by trying on her hand-made papier-mâché fox and pig masks. ↙ P. 72

Wir besuchen Elena in einer Wohnung in der Nähe des berühmten Dortmunder Stadions. Ihre Freund*innen Florencia und Charles sind dabei.

Elena wurde in Italien geboren, Florencia in Argentinien und Charles in Ghana. Nach Jahren des Reisens und Studierens haben sie Dortmund als ihr Zuhause gewählt, zumindest vorerst.

Elena servierte Käse, Brotstangen, Knoblauchnudeln mit Garnelen und Kräutern, grünen Salat mit Olivenöldressing — Öl, das sie in großen Metallbehältern aus Italien mitbringt. In ihren Worten: „Ohne kann sie nicht leben."

Nach dem Abendessen spielten wir alle Verkleiden, indem wir ihre handgemachten Pappmaché-Fuchs- und Schweinemasken anprobierten. ↙ S. 72

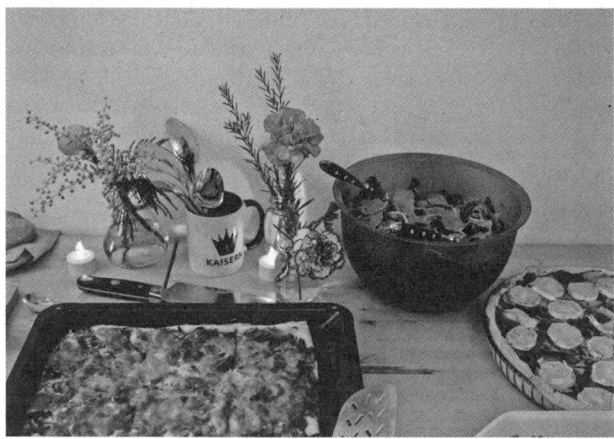

We were invited by KA!SERN Started ten years ago by a group of neighbors, this creative initiative runs a range of programs for anyone to join, from film and book clubs to something called "running dinner."

Running dinner: a three-course dinner where every course is cooked and served by a different host at their own apartment. A group of guests travels from one household to another to complete the dinner, then everyone meets up at the bar afterward for a nightcap. ↙ P. 73

Wir wurden von KA!SERN eingeladen. Vor zehn Jahren von einer Gruppe von Nachbar*innen gegründet, bietet diese kreative Initiative eine Reihe von Programmen für alle an, von Film– und Buchclubs bis hin zu etwas, das „laufendes Abendessen" genannt wird.

Laufendes Abendessen: Ein dreigängiges Menü, bei dem jeder Gang von einer anderen gastgebenden Person in der eigenen Wohnung gekocht und serviert wird. Eine Gruppe von Gästen reist von einem Haushalt zum anderen, um das Abendessen zu vervollständigen, und im Anschluss trifft man sich noch in einer Bar für einen Schlummertrunk. ↙ S. 73

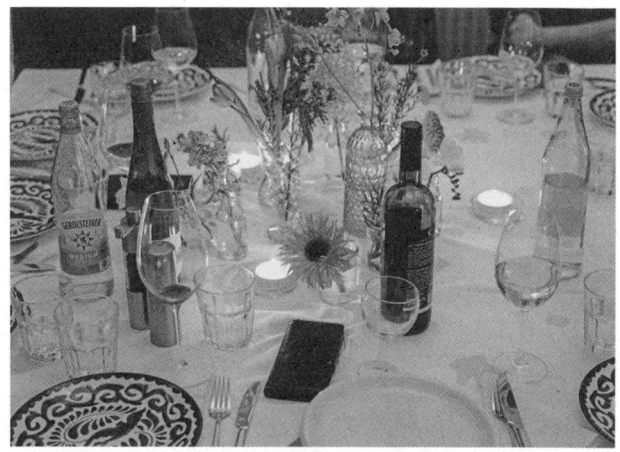

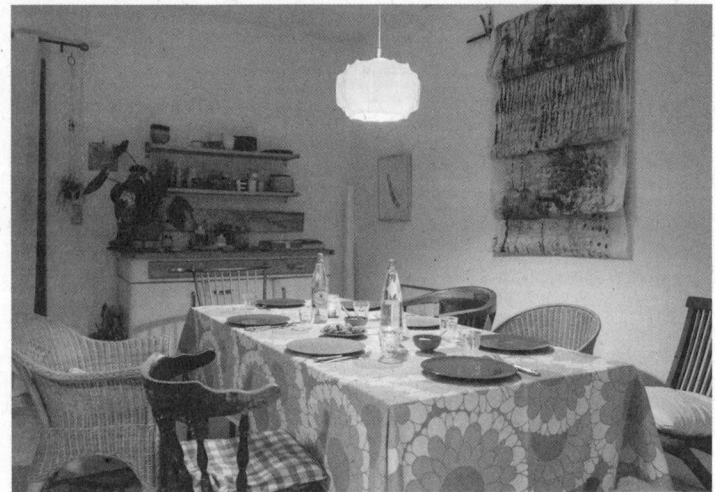

We are visiting Susanne and Hans-Peter in a large old schoolhouse. Three families came together to buy the building about thirty years ago, slowly renovating it.

Their daughter Judith and her roommate Cleo are joining us that evening. The kitchen is spacious with a wall of windows. All the family members were putting finishing touches on their dishes. Susanne prepared homemade bread and a dessert of pumpernickel bread with quark and cherries. Hans-Peter and Judith were plating salmon with roasted celery, rice with feta and pomegranate seeds, broccolini with peanuts and soy sauce, roasted carrots with harissa marinade. Cleo was helping to set up a big table with a bright orange tablecloth and blue plates.

The family brings their creativity into the kitchen. The mother is an art and math teacher. The father is an actor, playwright, and musician. Judith is a theater major. One of her classes is art and food—from Flemish still-lifes to Fluxus and feminist performance art. ↙ P. 74

Wir besuchen Susanne und Hans-Peter in einem großen alten Schulhaus. Drei Familien kauften das Gebäude vor etwa dreißig Jahren gemeinsam und renovierten es nach und nach.

Ihre Tochter Judith und ihre Mitbewohnerin Cleo sind an diesem Abend dabei. Die Küche ist geräumig, mit einer langen Fensterwand. Alle Familienmitglieder gaben den Gerichten den letzten Schliff. Susanne backte selbstgemachtes Brot und bereitete ein Dessert aus Pumpernickel mit Quark und Kirschen zu. Hans-Peter und Judith richteten Lachs mit geröstetem Sellerie an, dazu Reis mit Feta und Granatapfelkernen, Broccolini mit Erdnüssen und Sojasauce sowie geröstete Karotten mit Harissa-Marinade. Cleo half dabei, einen großen Tisch mit einer leuchtend orangefarbenen Tischdecke und blauen Tellern zu decken.

Die Familie bringt ihre Kreativität in die Küche ein. Die Mutter ist Kunst- und Mathematiklehrerin. Der Vater ist Schauspieler, Dramatiker und Musiker. Judith studiert im Hauptfach Theater. Einer ihrer Kurse handelt von Kunst und Essen — von flämischen Stillleben bis hin zu Fluxus und feministischer Performancekunst. ↙ S. 74

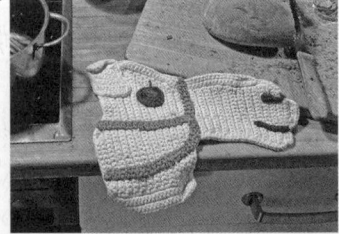

Susannes Nachtisch mit Pumpernickel

1 Glas Sauerkirschen
(720 ml; Abtropfgewicht: 370 g)
150 g Pumpernickel
125 g brauner Zucker
2–3 EL Kirschwasser
100 g Zartbitterschokolade
500 g Sahnequark
125 ml Kuhmilch

Kirschen abtropfen lassen. Pumpernickel mit den Händen zerbröseln, mit 25 g Zucker mischen und mit Kirschwasser beträufeln. Schokolade fein hacken und untermischen. Zur Garnierung etwas Schokolade beiseitestellen. Quark, 100 g Zucker und Milch glattrühren. In 4 Gläser (200–250 ml Inhalt) nacheinander Pumpernickel, Kirschen und Creme einschichten. Fortfahren, bis alles verbraucht ist. 1–2 Stunden kaltstellen.

Christian is our host, and in the kitchen we met the other guests: his friend Tim, a musician who is also cooking for us this evening, and Barbara, a journalist for WDR radio doing a story about our project (she joined us that evening with Christian's permission).

The table is set in his living room. We slowly discovered his family's history through the classical table setting: the white linen tablecloth has been in the family for years and passed down over generations; all the silverware has the family name engraved on it, trays and glass coasters as well. His family tree goes back to the fourteenth century and used to own a beer brewery called Brand, the restaurant Krone on the main town square, and other businesses in the area.

Tim prepared a six-course meal, bringing each one with a bell (literally). In order of serving: rye bread with duck pâté, tomato soup with a pinch of crème fraîche, fish on a bed of roasted fennel and olives, green salad, chicken with roasted peppers, a cheese plate, cookies with tea and coffee. The red wine was a cuvée produced by Tim's family winery in France.

We left with gifts: a Krone restaurant plate and an old glass horse Christmas tree decoration. ↙ P. 75

Christian ist unser Gastgeber, und in der Küche trafen wir die anderen Gäste: seinen Freund Tim, einen Musiker, der auch heute Abend für uns kocht, und Barbara, eine Journalistin vom WDR, die einen Beitrag über unser Projekt macht (sie kam mit Christians Erlaubnis an diesem Abend dazu).

Der Tisch ist in seinem Wohnzimmer gedeckt. Wir entdeckten langsam die Geschichte seiner Familie durch das klassische Tischgedeck: Das weiße Leinentischtuch ist seit Jahren in der Familie und wurde über Generationen weitergegeben; in alle Teile des Bestecks ist der Familienname eingraviert, ebenso wie in die Tabletts und Glasuntersetzer. Sein Stammbaum reicht bis ins 14. Jahrhundert zurück, und seine Familie besaß früher eine Brauerei namens Brand, das Restaurant Krone am Markt und andere Geschäfte in der Gegend.

Tim bereitete ein sechsgängiges Menü zu und läutete jeden Gang mit einer (echten) Glocke ein. In der Reihenfolge des Servierens: Roggenbrot mit Entenpastete, Tomatensuppe mit einem Hauch Crème fraîche, Fisch auf einem Bett aus geröstetem Fenchel und Oliven, grüner Salat, Hühnchen mit gerösteten Paprika, eine Käseplatte, Kekse mit Tee und Kaffee. Der Rotwein war ein Cuvée aus dem Familienweingut von Tim in Frankreich.

Wir gingen mit Geschenken: einem Teller aus dem Restaurant Krone und einem alten gläsernen Christbaumschmuck–Pferd. ↙ S. 75

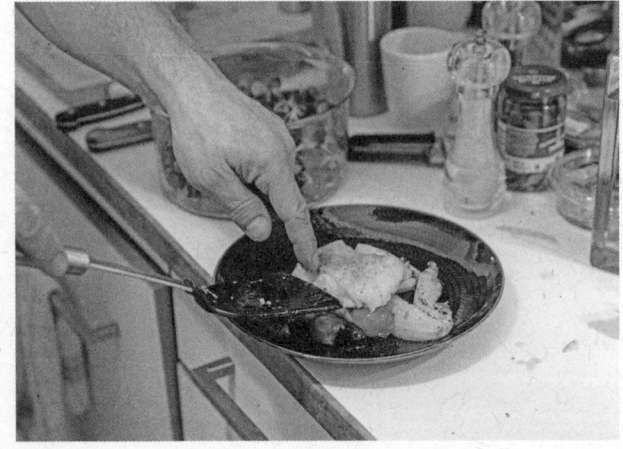

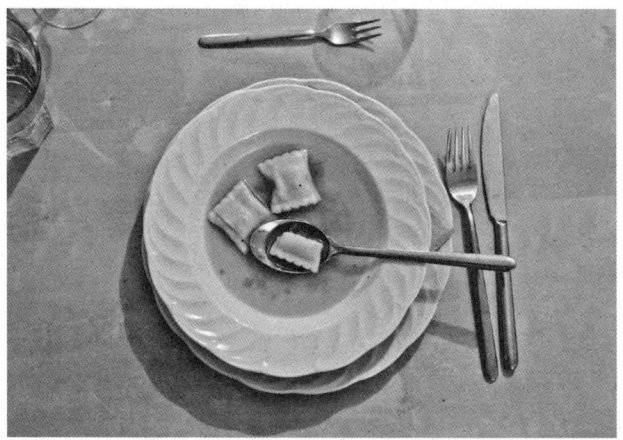

Britta is our host, and her daughter Lena, her son Tom, and her two longtime friends joined us. Britta decorated a table with flowers and candles in the living room. Menus were printed and placed near the plates: a menu inspired by her family recipes.

APPETIZER
SUPPE MIT MAULTASCHEN
A flavorful broth with traditional Swabian dumplings filled with seasoned meat and spinach.

MAIN COURSE
LEBERKÄS MIT SPÄTZLE UND KARTOFFELSALAT
A hearty Bavarian-style meatloaf, served with handmade soft egg noodles (Spätzle) and a classic South German potato salad with a dressing made of broth.
Despite its name, Leberkäs contains neither liver nor cheese—it's made from finely ground pork and beef.

DESSERT
OFENSCHLUPFER MIT VANILLESOSSE
A warm baked dessert made of layered apples, bread, and raisins, topped with a rich vanilla sauce.

Britta gifted us a wool angel doll that she made herself. ↙ P. 76

Britta ist unsere Gastgeberin, ihre Tochter Lena, ihr Sohn Tom und zwei langjährige Freund*innen sind auch dabei. Britta deckte einen Tisch mit Blumen und Kerzen im Wohnzimmer. Menüs wurden gedruckt und neben die Teller gelegt. Das Menü war inspiriert von ihren Familienrezepten.

VORSPEISE
SUPPE MIT MAULTASCHEN
Eine würzige Brühe mit traditionellen schwäbischen Teigtaschen, gefüllt mit gewürztem Fleisch und Spinat.

HAUPTGERICHT
LEBERKÄS MIT SPÄTZLE UND KARTOFFELSALAT
Ein herzhafter Fleischkäse im bayerischen Stil, serviert mit selbstgemachten Spätzle und einem klassischen süddeutschen Kartoffelsalat mit Brühe-Dressing.
Trotz des Namens enthält Leberkäs weder Leber noch Käse — er wird aus feinem Schweine- und Rinderhack hergestellt.

DESSERT
OFENSCHLUPFER MIT VANILLESOSSE
Ein warmes Dessert aus geschichteten Äpfeln, Brot und Rosinen, übergossen mit einer reichhaltigen Vanillesoße.

Britta schenkte uns eine selbstgemachte Engelpuppe aus Wolle. ↙ S. 76

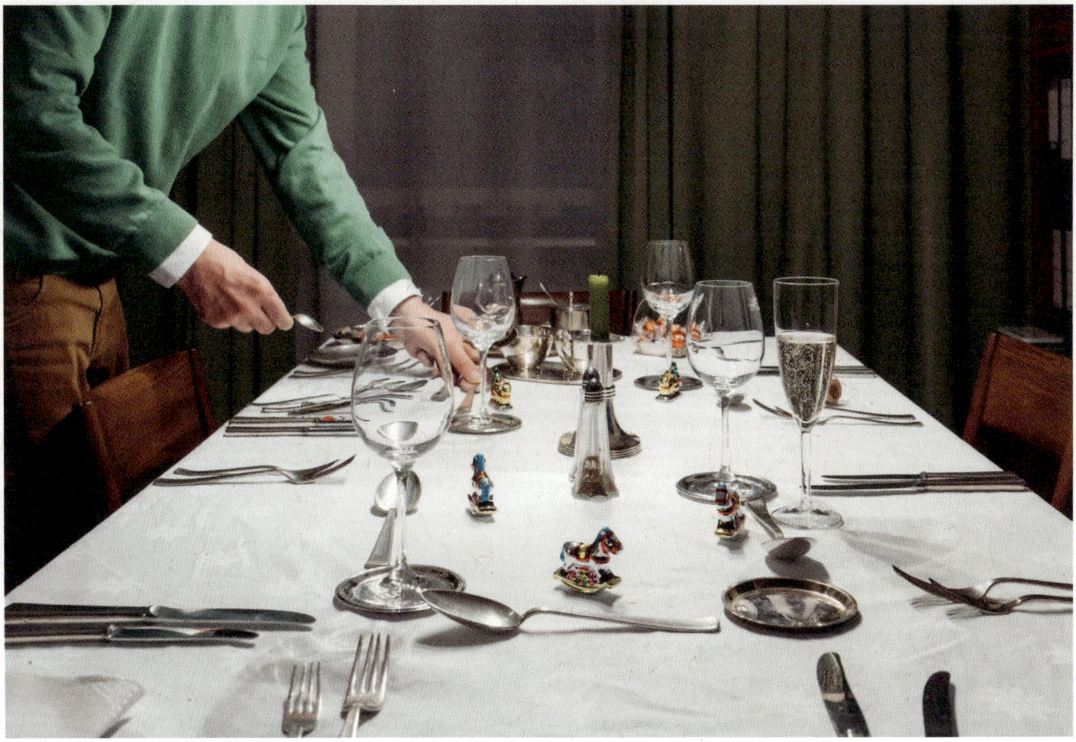

DINNER 57   FAMILY HISTORY·THROUGH THE CLASSICAL TABLE SETTING
DIE FAMILIENGESCHICHTE ALS KLASSISCHES TISCHGEDECK

DINNER 58   DESPITE ITS NAME, LEBERKÄS CONTAINS NEITHER LIVER NOR CHEESE
TROTZ SEINES NAMENS ENTHÄLT LEBERKÄS WEDER LEBER NOCH KÄSE

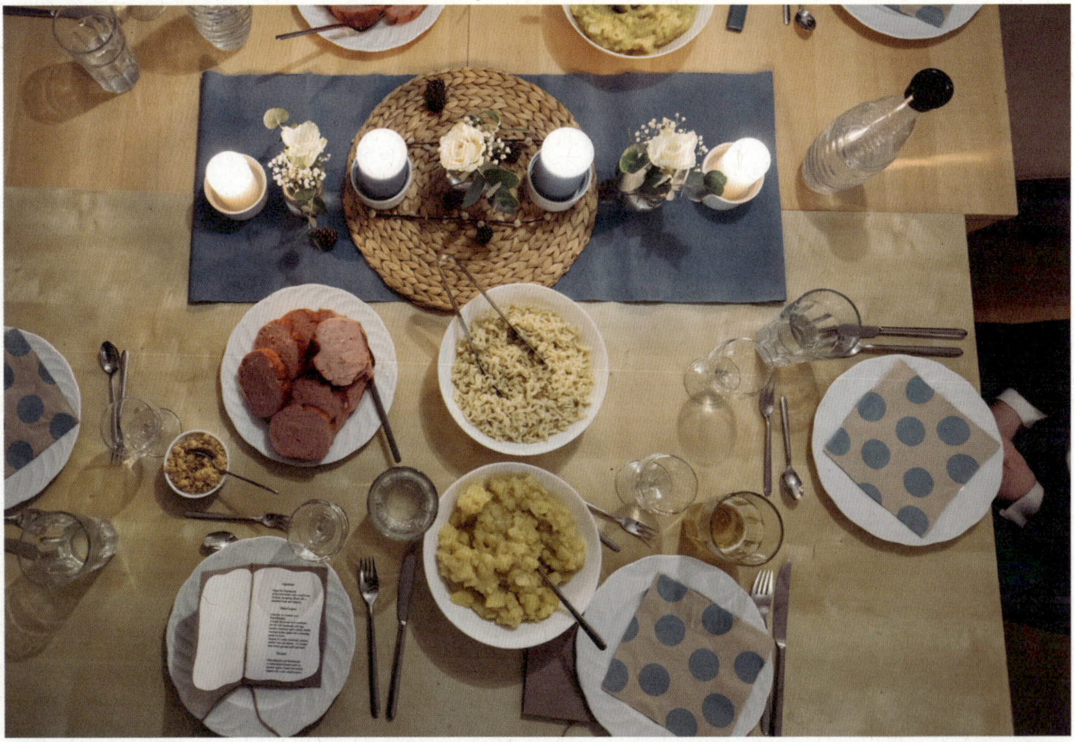

Arianne and Laurens are our hosts. Upon entering, we briefly met three of their five kids and the family dog Socke. Our hosts are both priests. They met during their religious studies, while they were both teenagers.

They both travel a lot. Arianne just came back from Bangladesh and cooked a tropical-themed dinner inspired by her travels. We started with a mango lassi with a pinch of cardamom. Each glass was decorated with a slice of mango. The plates were full of colors: endive with green salad and pomegranate seeds, salmon cucumber skewers, filo pastry tartlets with green salad, followed by tomato soup, then eggplant, oranges, and orange zest with tahini.

During the dinner, we couldn't find Socke but eventually found her hiding under the couch just in time for the family portrait. ⬐ P. 77

Arianne und Laurens sind unsere Gastgeber*innen. Beim Eintreffen trafen wir kurz drei ihrer fünf Kinder und den Familienhund Socke. Arianne und Laurens sind Pfarrerin und Pfarrer. Sie trafen sich im Religionsunterricht, als sie beide Teenager waren.

Sie reisen viel. Arianne war gerade aus Bangladesch zurückgekommen und kochte ein tropisch angehauchtes Abendessen, das von ihren Reisen inspiriert war. Wir begannen mit einem Mango-Lassi mit einer Prise Kardamom. Jedes Glas war mit einer Mangoscheibe verziert. Die Teller waren voller Farben: Endivie mit grünem Salat und Granatapfelkernen, Lachs-Gurken-Spieße, Filo-Pastetchen mit grünem Salat, gefolgt von Tomatensuppe, dann Auberginen, Orangen und Orangenschale mit Tahini.

Während des Abendessens konnten wir Socke nicht finden, entdeckten sie aber schließlich unter dem Sofa, gerade rechtzeitig für das Familienporträt. ⬐ S. 77

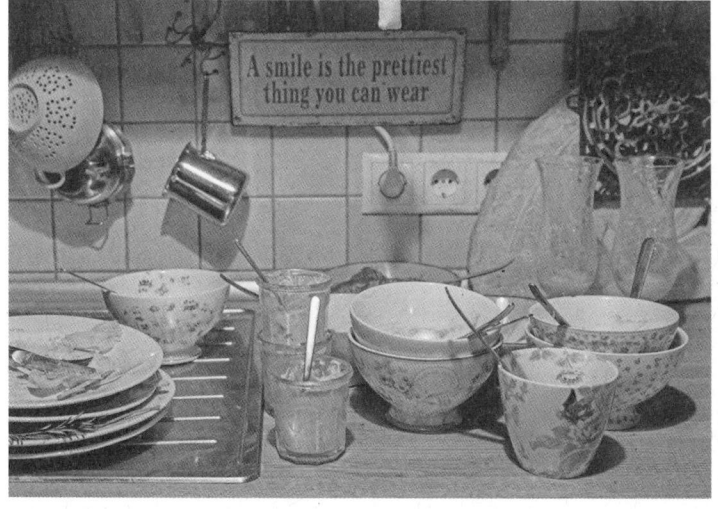

We meet our hosts Lioba and Lisa, cat Ouzo, and dog
Fiona in their elegantly designed apartment, filled
with plants, multiple Fiona daybeds, and Ouzo cat
houses. Lioba and Lisa met in 2018, and their first
date was eating fries. In memory of that, they got
matching fork tattoos.
They served a plate of cheeses, bread with butter,
olives, cream cheese stuffed piquant peppers, and a
stew of leeks and beans with burrata served in a pan.
We discussed feminist art and manifestos.
The meal was accompanied by Lioba's curated playlist "Year of Growth":

> GARDEN SONG
> by Phoebe Bridgers,
> IF YOU COULD READ MY MIND
> by Gordon Lightfoot,
> EVERYTHING I WANT TO DO
> by Albert Hammond,
> WHEN THE MORNING COMES
> by Daryl Hall & John Oates,
> THIS WORLD TODAY IS A MESS
> by Donna Hightower.

The titles of her playlist could form
a manifesto too :) We left with gifts:
a hand-knitted wool scarf and Polaroids. ↙ P. 78

Wir treffen unsere Gastgeberinnen Lioba und Lisa,
die Katze Ouzo und den Hund Fiona in ihrer elegant
eingerichteten Wohnung, die voller Pflanzen, mehrerer
Fiona-Liegeplätze und Ouzo-Katzenhäuser ist. Lioba
und Lisa trafen sich 2018, und ihr erstes Date bestand
darin, Pommes zu essen. Zur Erinnerung daran haben
sie sich passende Gabel-Tattoos stechen lassen.
Sie servierten eine Käseplatte, Brot mit Butter, Oliven, mit Frischkäse gefüllte Paprika und einen Eintopf
aus Lauch und Bohnen mit Burrata, serviert in einer
Pfanne. Wir unterhielten uns über feministische Kunst
und Manifeste.
Das Essen wurde von Liobas kuratierter Playlist „Year
of Growth" begleitet:

> GARDEN SONG
> von Phoebe Bridgers,
> IF YOU COULD READ MY MIND
> von Gordon Lightfoot,
> EVERYTHING I WANT TO DO
> von Albert Hammond,
> WHEN THE MORNING COMES
> von Daryl Hall & John Oates,
> THIS WORLD TODAY IS A MESS
> von Donna Hightower.

Die Titel ihrer Playlist könnten auch ein Manifest dar-
stellen :). Wir gingen mit Geschenken: einem hand-
gestrickten Wollschal und Polaroids. ↙ S. 78

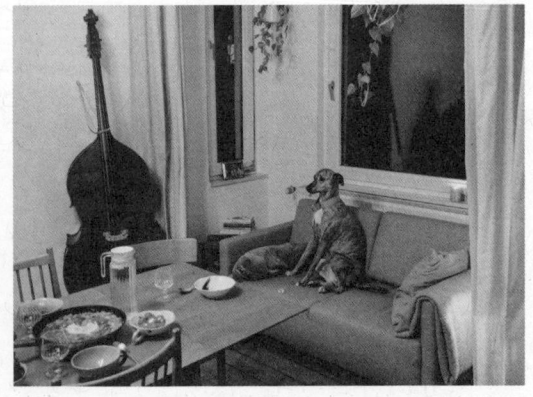

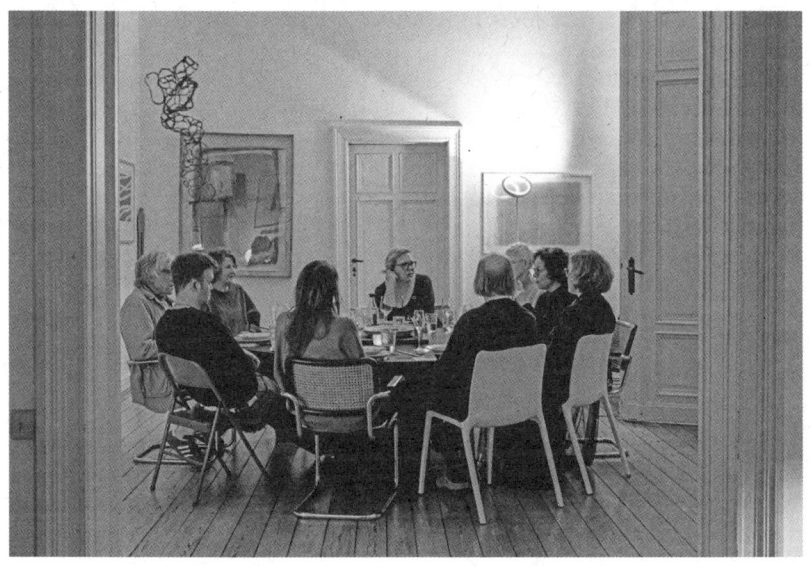

We visit Dagmar and Manfred at an eighteenth-century villa with a picturesque garden in the town of Witten. Their daughter Maika, her boyfriend Jonas, and family friends Ruth, Susanne, and Cornelia are joining us. We gather around a large octagonal table in the living room.

Wine and conversation flowed freely all night, with a German and Italian language teacher, a Professor Dr. Virologist, an art educator, a firefighter, a physiologist, a photographer, and four artists—there was certainly no shortage of things to talk about.

MENU: bruschetta, arugula with beets and goat cheese, cheese and bread plate, cannelloni with spinach and ricotta, and Dagmar's famous panna cotta with raspberry sauce.

By midnight it was time to go. ↙ P. 79

Wir besuchen Dagmar und Manfred in der Stadt Witten, in einer Villa aus dem 18. Jahrhundert mit einem malerischen Garten. Ihre Tochter Maika, ihr Freund Jonas und die Familienfreundinnen Ruth, Susanne und Cornelia sind dabei. Wir versammeln uns um einen großen achteckigen Tisch im Wohnzimmer.

Wein und Gespräche flossen den ganzen Abend, mit einer Deutsch- und Italienischlehrerin, einem Professor Dr. Virologen, einer Kunstpädagogin, einem Feuerwehrmann, einer Physiologin, einer Fotografin und vier Künstler*innen — da gab es definitiv keine Gesprächspausen.

MENÜ: Bruschetta, Rucola mit Rote Bete und Ziegenkäse, Käse- und Brotplatte, Cannelloni mit Spinat und Ricotta sowie Dagmars berühmte Panna cotta mit Himbeersauce.

Um Mitternacht war es an der Zeit zu gehen. ↙ S. 79

Our hosts are Alina and Melina, both theater majors, their friends, and the performance collective Lover Girls. As a collective, they record couples' love stories and ask them what their definition of love is, with the goal of publishing it one day. It is our last *A Painting For A Family Dinner* in Dortmund. The menu had a Valentine's Day theme: raspberry lemonade, red peppers with melted feta, lasagna pomodoro, and chocolate mousse with pink heart-shaped sprinkles. From the kitchen window we could enjoy the nighttime view of Dortmund with the neon U of Dortmunder U towering over the city. ↙ P. 80

Unsere Gastgeberinnen sind Alina und Melina, beide Theaterstudentinnen, ihre Freund*innen und das Performancekollektiv Lover Girls. Als Kollektiv zeichnen sie Liebesgeschichten von Paaren auf und fragen sie, was ihre Definition von Liebe ist, mit dem Ziel, dies eines Tages zu veröffentlichen. Es ist unser letztes *Ein Gemälde für ein Familienessen* in Dortmund. Das Menü hatte ein Valentinstags-Thema: Himbeerlimonade, rote Paprika mit geschmolzenem Feta, Lasagne Pomodoro und Schokoladenmousse mit pinken herzförmigen Streuseln. Vom Küchenfenster aus konnten wir den nächtlichen Blick auf Dortmund genießen, wo das Neon-U des Dortmunder U über der Stadt thront. ↙ S. 80

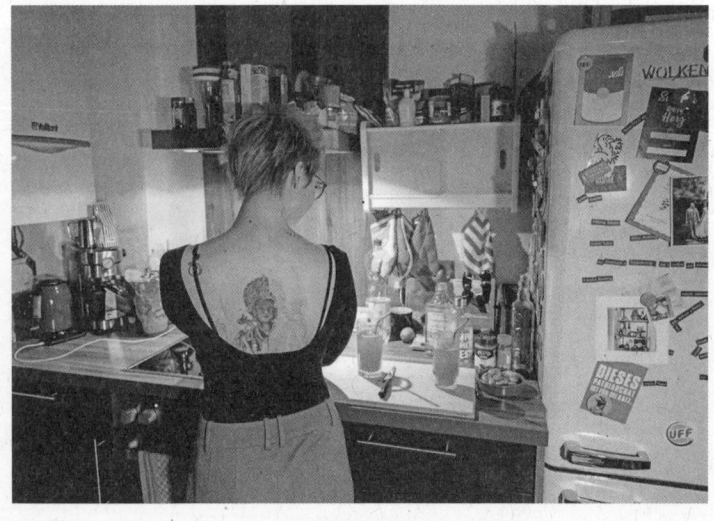

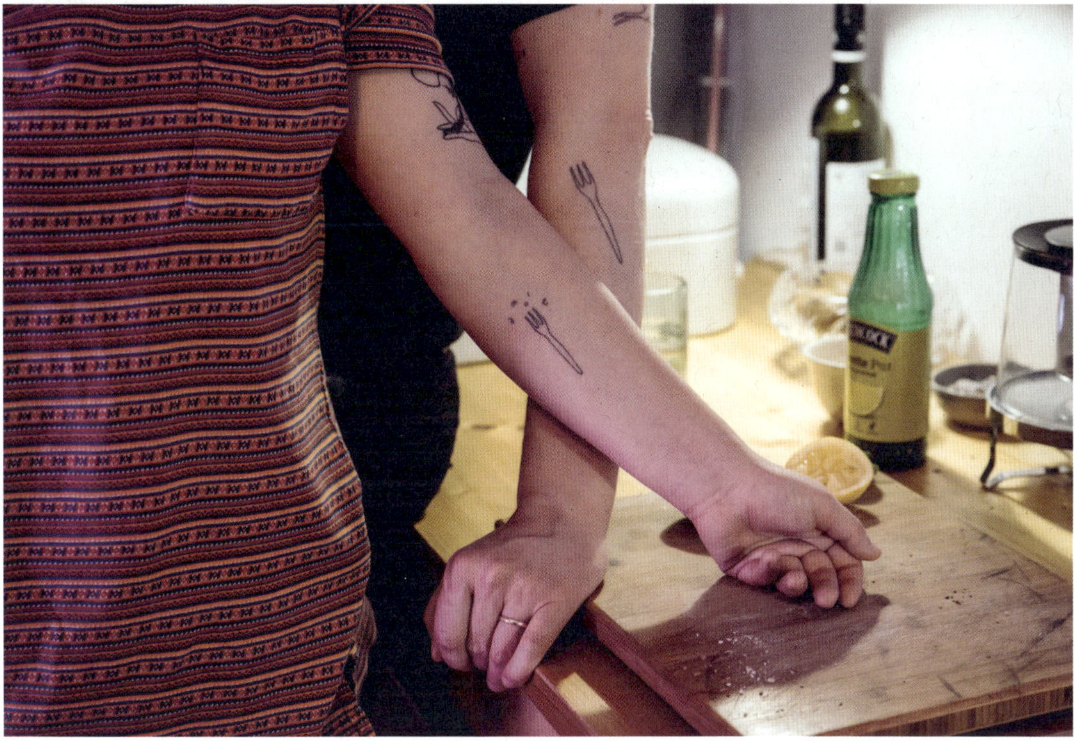

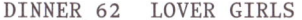

DINNER 60   IN MEMORY OF THAT, THEY GOT MATCHING FORK TATTOOS
          ALS ERINNERUNG HABEN SIE SICH POMMESGABEL-TATTOOS STECHEN LASSEN

DINNER 62   LOVER GIRLS

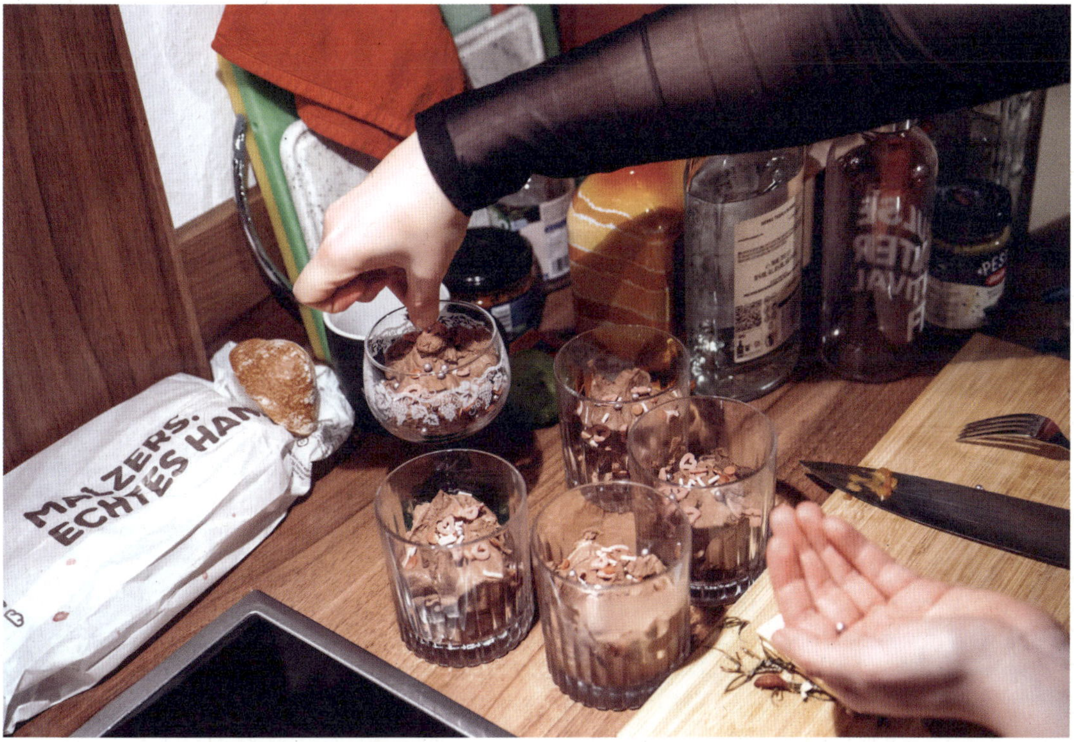

Thank you for your dinner!
Danke für das Abendessen!

BAT YAM

PHOTOGRAPHER / FOTOGRAFIN Dana Gazit
Dafna Gazit was born in Israel and lives
and works in Tel Aviv. She is co-founder
and a member of the Alfred Contemporary Art organization.
    Dafna Gazit wurde in Israel geboren,
sie lebt und arbeitet in Tel Aviv. Sie ist Mit-
begründerin und Mitglied der Alfred Contemporary Art Organization.

A Painting For A Family Dinner, Bat Yam,
Israel was produced by Museums of
Bat Yam (MOBY), Israel and part of the
exhibition *Hosting* curated by Milana
Gitzin-Adiram and Leah Abir, 2008.
    A Painting For A Family Dinner, Bat Yam,
Israel wurde von den Museums of Bat Yam
(MOBY), Israel produziert und war Teil der
Ausstellung *Hosting*, kuratiert von Milana
Gitzin–Adiram und Leah Abir, 2008.

SPECIAL THANKS / MIT BESONDEREM DANK AN
Milana Gitzin-Adiram, Leah Abir,
Museums of Bat Yam (MOBY).

Toda raba to all the families.
Toda raba an alle Familien.

BRONX

PHOTOGRAPHER / FOTOGRAF Anton Trofymov
Anton Trofymov was born in Kiev,
Ukraine and now lives in New York. He
studied at the Kiev National University
of Theatre, Film and Television.
Anton Trofymov wurde in Kyjiw geboren und
lebt heute in New York. Er studierte an der
Kyjiwer Nationaluniversität für Theater, Film
und Fernsehen.

A Painting For A Family Dinner, Bronx,
NY, US was part of the exhibition *This Side
of Paradise* curated by the organization
NoLongerEmpty at the Bronx Museum of
the Arts NY, 2012.
    A Painting For A Family Dinner, Bronx,
NY, US war Teil der Ausstellung *This Side of
the Paradise* kuratiert von der Organisation
NoLongerEmpty am Bronx Museum of the
Arts NY, 2012.

SPECIAL THANKS / MIT BESONDEREM DANK AN
Manon Slome, Naomi Hersson-Ringskog,
Jodie Dinapoli, NoLongerEmpty,
Holly Block, Sergio Bessa, Lia Zaaloff,
Susan Chevlowe, Dasha Zibrova, Rachel
Corbett (Artnet), Shazia T. Khan (NY1),
Tanyanika Samuels (the Daily News),
Bronx Channel 12.

Thank you to all the families.
Thank you an alle Familien.

BEIJING

PHOTOGRAPHER / FOTOGRAFIN Du Yang
Du Yang is a photographer based in
Beijing. She graduated from Beijing Film
Academy.
    Du Yang lebt und arbeitet als Fotografin
in Beijing. Sie absolvierte die Filmhochschule
in Beijing.

A Painting For A Family Dinner, Beijing,
China was produced with assistance
from the Inside-Out Art Museum (IOAM)
Artist Residency, Beijing, China, 2013.
    A Painting For A Family Dinner, Beijing,
China wurde mit der Unterstützung der
Künstlerresidenz des Inside–Out Art Museum
(IOAM) in Beijing, China im Jahr 2013
realisiert.

SPECIAL THANKS / MIT BESONDEREM DANK AN
Yaya Hu, Cici Zeng, Richard Hsu, Mr Chen,
Harry Qiu, Serena Qiu, David J. Petersen,
Darina Karpov, Maya Benton, Christopher
Phillip, Ying-Ying Lu, Teri Chan-Herner,
Anna Moschovakis, Stanislas Bourgain,
Philip Hammerle, Di Di Lin.

Xie xie to all the families.
Xie xie an alle Familien.

LECCE

PHOTOGRAPHER / FOTOGRAFIN Alessia Rollo
Alessia Rollo was born and lives in Lecce.
She studied conceptual photography
in Madrid.
    Alessia Rollo wurde in Lecce geboren und
lebt dort auch. Sie studierte konzeptionelle
Fotografie in Madrid.
A Painting For A Family Dinner, Lecce,
Italy was produced by Ammirato Culture
House (ACH), Lecce, Italy, 2013.

A Painting For A Family Dinner, Lecce, Italien wurde vom Ammirato Culture House (ACH) in Lecce, Italien, im Jahr 2013 durchgeführt.

SPECIAL THANKS / MIT BESONDEREM DANK AN
Alessandra Pomarico, Marcella Buttazzo, Gianluca Rollo, Musagetes Foundation.

Grazie mille to all the families.
Grazie Mille an alle Familien.

TOKYO

PHOTOGRAPHER / FOTOGRAFIN Aya Morimoto
Born in Chiba in 1989, Aya Morimoto is a freelance based in Tokyo since 2022.
Geboren in Chiba, 1989. Freiberufliche Fotografin mit Sitz in Tokyo seit 2022.

A Painting For A Family Dinner, Tokyo, Japan was produced by Tokyo Biennale 2021 and part of *Social Dive. Tokyo Biennale 2021*.
A Painting For A Family Dinner, Tokyo, Japan, wurde von der Tokyo Biennale 2021 als Teil von *Social Dive. Tokyo Biennale 2021* durchgeführt.

SPECIAL THANKS / MIT BESONDEREM DANK AN
the Tokyo Biennale 2021 team, Hitomi Akuzawa, Yumiko Arakaki, y. nishizawa.

Arigato to all the families.
Arigato an alle Familien.

DORTMUND

PHOTOGRAPHER / FOTOGRAF Daniel Sadrowski
Daniel Sadrowski studied photography at Dortmund University of Applied Sciences and Arts. He lives in Bochum and works mainly in the Ruhr region.
Daniel Sadrowski studierte Fotografie an der Fachhochschule Dortmund. Er lebt in Bochum und arbeitet hauptsächlich im Ruhrgebiet.

A Painting For A Family Dinner, Dortmund, Germany was produced by Museum Ostwall at the Dortmunder U (MO) as part of the exhibition *At the Table. Eating and Drinking in Contemporary Art*, curated by Christina Danick and Michael Griff.
The project was kindly supported by Nikon Germany.

A Painting For A Family Dinner, Dortmund, Germany wurde vom Museum Ostwall im Dortmunder U (MO) als Teil der Ausstellung *Am Tisch. Essen und Trinken in der zeitgenössischen Kunst*, kuratiert von Christina Danick und Michael Griff.
Das Projekt wurde unterstützt von Nikon Deutschland.

SPECIAL THANKS / MIT BESONDEREM DANK AN
Christina Danick, Michael Griff, Regina Selter and the team of Museum Ostwall and Dortmunder U, Lea Szramek / Verlag Kettler, Deutsches Kochbuchmuseum (German Cookbook Museum), Silke Hempel, Olivia Strzoda, Heike Wulf, Barbara Geschwinde, Maria Isserlis, Alex Wiederin, Boris Groys, Irena Popiashvili.

Danke to all the families.
Danke an alle Familien.

Imprint / Impressum

PUBLISHED BY
HERAUSGEGEBEN VOM
Museum Ostwall im Dortmunder U

HEAD OF / LEITUNG
DORTMUNDER U
Stefan Heitkemper

DIRECTOR / DIREKTORIN
MUSEUM OSTWALL IM DORTMUNDER U
Regina Selter

AUTHORS
AUTOR*INNEN
**Alina Bliumis, Jeff Bliumis, Christina
Danick, Michael Griff, Regina Selter**

CONCEPT AND EDITING
KONZEPT, TEXT- UND BILDREDAKTION
**Alina Bliumis, Jeff Bliumis,
Michael Griff, Christina Danick**

EDITORIAL ASSISTANCE
ASSISTENZ BUCHREDAKTION
Olivia Strzoda

PUBLISHING HOUSE
ERSCHIENEN IM
**Verlag Kettler
Robert-Bosch-Str. 14
59199 Bönen
www.verlag-kettler.de
info@verlag-kettler.de**

1st edition / 1. Auflage
ISBN 978-3-98741-185-4
© Verlag Kettler, 2025

PROOFREADING
LEKTORAT
Good & Cheap Translators GbR

TRANSLATION
ÜBERSETZUNG
Good & Cheap Translators GbR

DESIGN
GESTALTUNG
Lea Szramek, Verlag Kettler

PRODUCTION
GESAMTHERSTELLUNG
Druckerei Kettler, Bönen

COPYRIGHTS
BILDNACHWEISE
Bat Yam © Alina Bliumis, Jeff Bliumis,
PHOTOGRAPHER / FOTOGRAFIN **Dafna Gazit**
Bronx © Alina Bliumis, Jeff Bliumis,
PHOTOGRAPHER / FOTOGRAF **Anton Trofymov**
Beijing © Alina Bliumis, Jeff Bliumis,
PHOTOGRAPHER / FOTOGRAF **Du Yang**
Lecce © Alina Bliumis, Jeff Bliumis,
PHOTOGRAPHER / FOTOGRAFIN **Alessia Rollo**
Tokyo © Alina Bliumis, Jeff Bliumis,
PHOTOGRAPHER / FOTOGRAFIN **Aya Morimoto**
Dortmund © Alina Bliumis, Jeff Bliumis,
PHOTOGRAPHER / FOTOGRAF **Daniel Sadrowski**

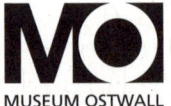

MUSEUM OSTWALL

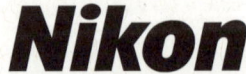

A PAINTING FOR A FAMILY DINNER, DORTMUND WAS
SUPPORTED BY / WURDE UNTERSTÜTZT DURCH
NIKON DEUTSCHLAND

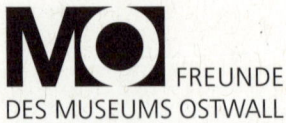

FUNDED BY / GEFÖRDERT DURCH

MO FREUNDE
DES MUSEUMS OSTWALL

**Ministerium für
Kultur und Wissenschaft
des Landes Nordrhein-Westfalen**

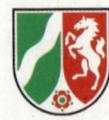